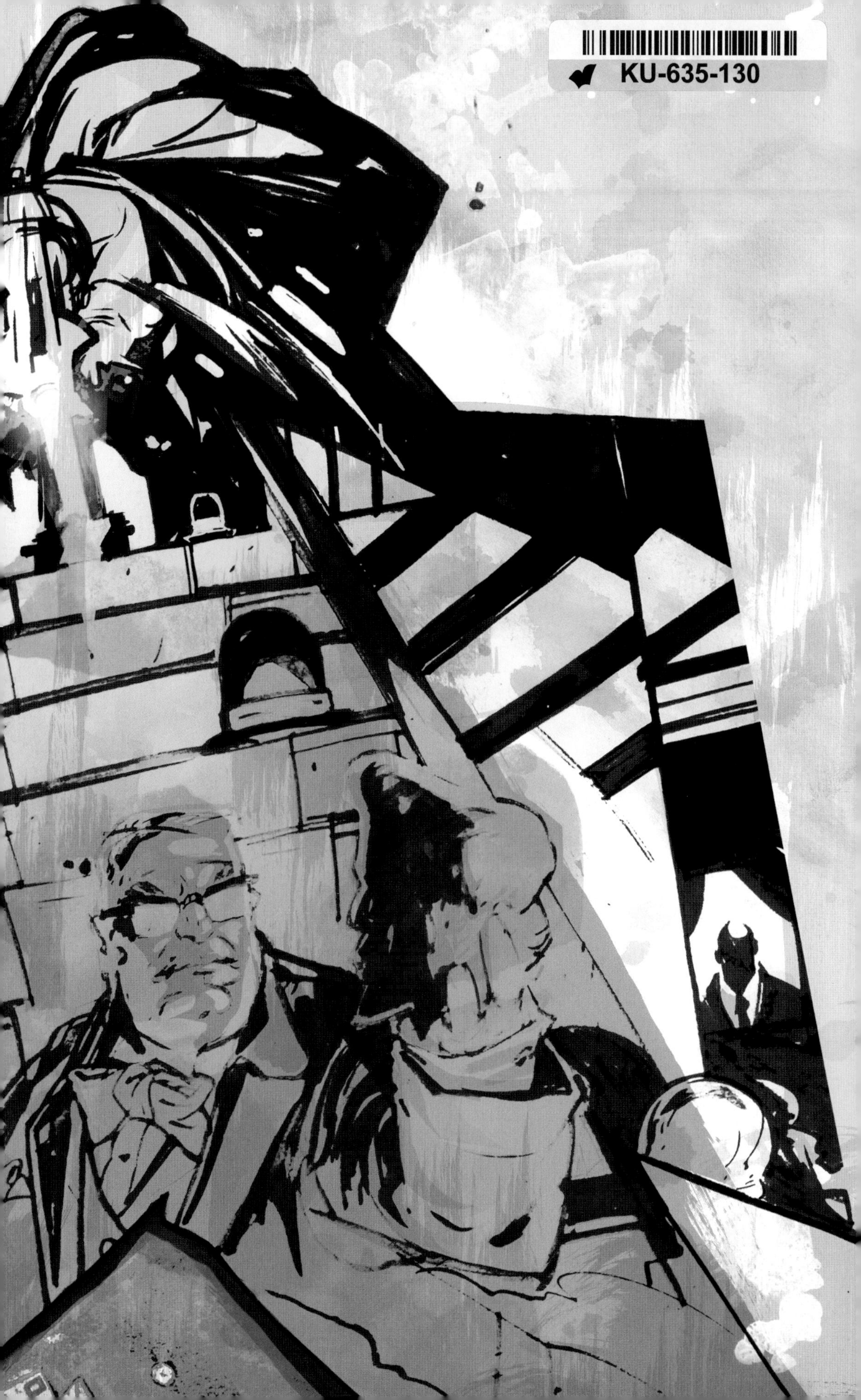

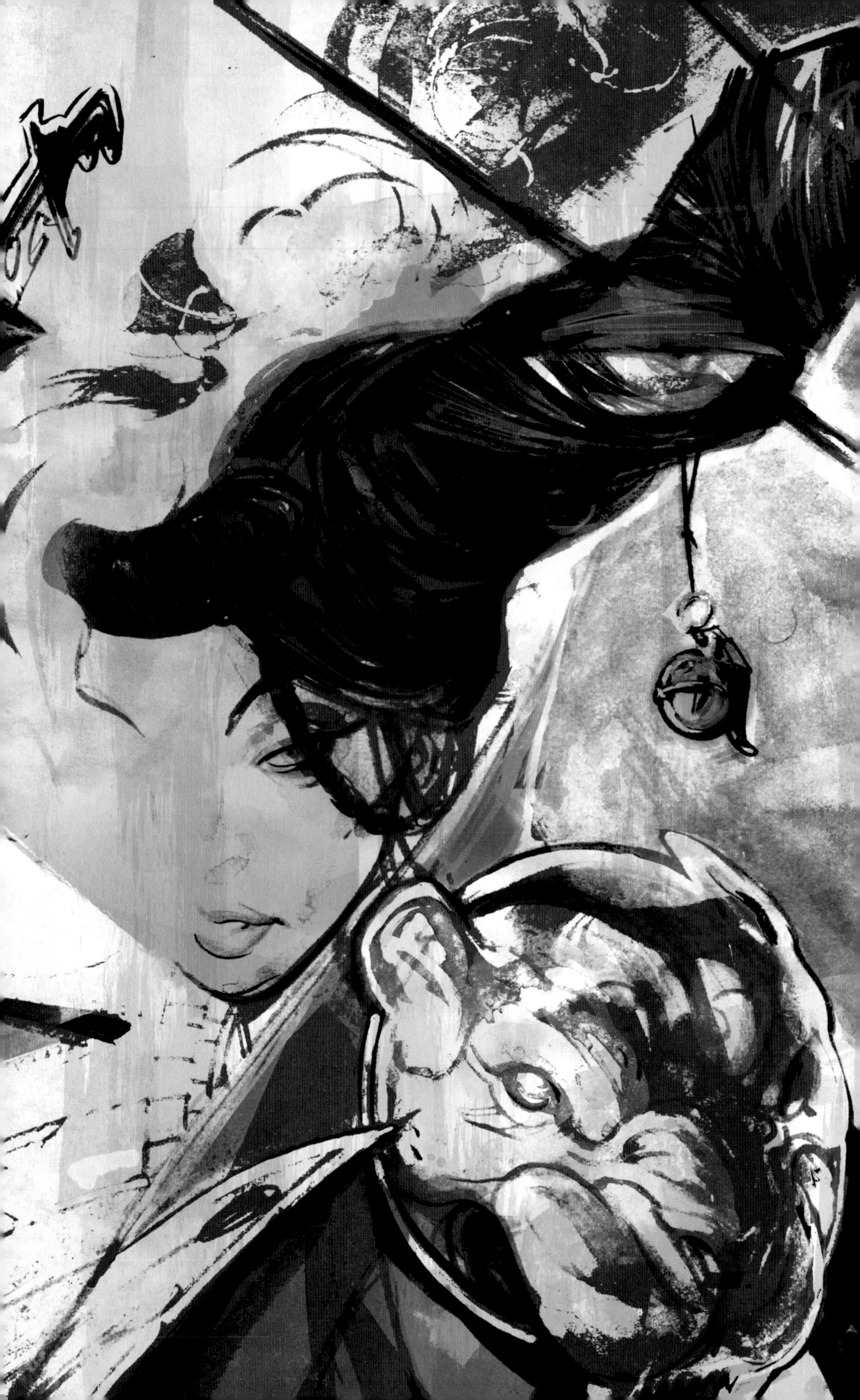

WRITTEN BY
CHRISTOPHER SEBELA

ILLUSTRATED BY
CHRIS VISIONS

COLORS BY
RUTH REDMOND &
MATT BATTAGLIA

LETTERS BY
STEVE WANDS

COVER BY
CHRIS VISIONS

DESIGN
KELSEY DIETERICH

ASSISTANT EDITOR
CHRIS ROSA

EDITOR
ERIC HARBURN

DEAD LETTERS CREATED BY
CHRISTOPHER SEBELA &
CHRIS VISIONS

EPISODE ONE

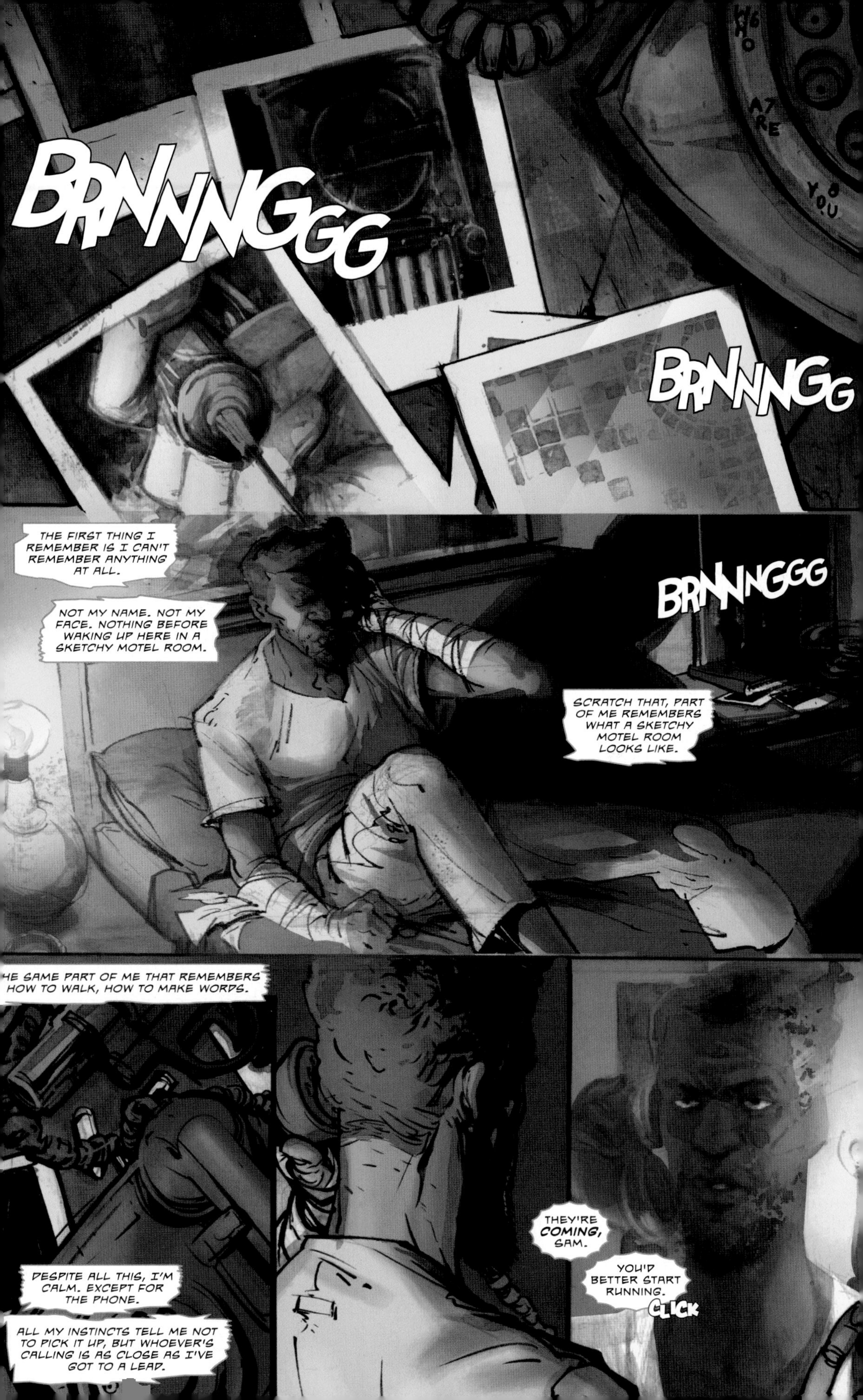
BRNNNGGG
BRNNNGG
THE FIRST THING I REMEMBER IS I CAN'T REMEMBER ANYTHING AT ALL.
NOT MY NAME. NOT MY FACE. NOTHING BEFORE WAKING UP HERE IN A SKETCHY MOTEL ROOM.
BRNNNGGG
SCRATCH THAT, PART OF ME REMEMBERS WHAT A SKETCHY MOTEL ROOM LOOKS LIKE.
HE SAME PART OF ME THAT REMEMBERS HOW TO WALK, HOW TO MAKE WORDS.
DESPITE ALL THIS, I'M CALM. EXCEPT FOR THE PHONE.
ALL MY INSTINCTS TELL ME NOT TO PICK IT UP, BUT WHOEVER'S CALLING IS AS CLOSE AS I'VE GOT TO A LEAD.
THEY'RE COMING, SAM.
YOU'D BETTER START RUNNING.
CLICK

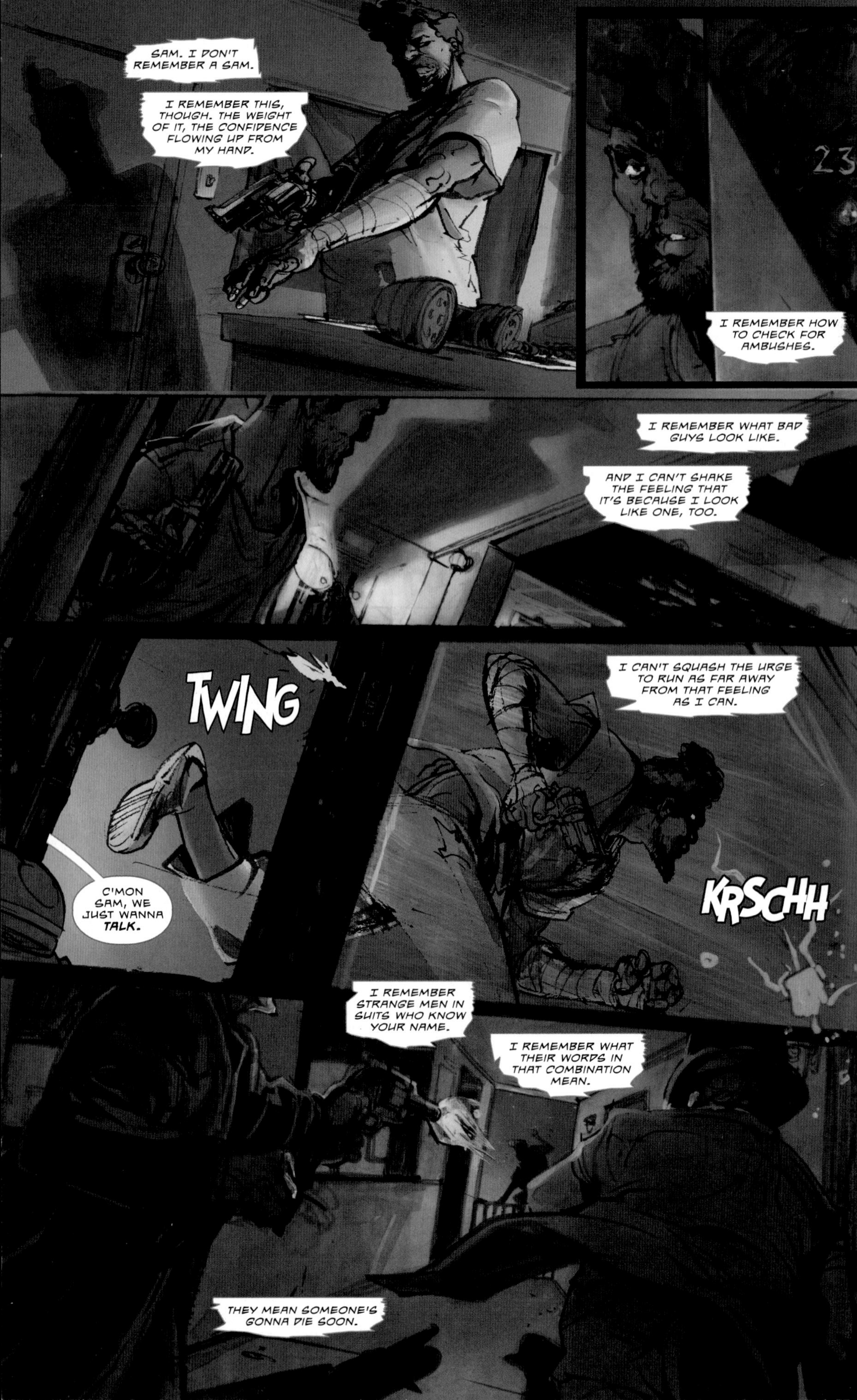
SAM. I DON'T REMEMBER A SAM.
I REMEMBER THIS, THOUGH. THE WEIGHT OF IT, THE CONFIDENCE FLOWING UP FROM MY HAND.
23
I REMEMBER HOW TO CHECK FOR AMBUSHES.
I REMEMBER WHAT BAD GUYS LOOK LIKE.
AND I CAN'T SHAKE THE FEELING THAT IT'S BECAUSE I LOOK LIKE ONE, TOO.
TWING
C'MON SAM, WE JUST WANNA **TALK**.
I CAN'T SQUASH THE URGE TO RUN AS FAR AWAY FROM THAT FEELING AS I CAN.
KRSCHH
I REMEMBER STRANGE MEN IN SUITS WHO KNOW YOUR NAME.
I REMEMBER WHAT THEIR WORDS IN THAT COMBINATION MEAN.
THEY MEAN SOMEONE'S GONNA DIE SOON.

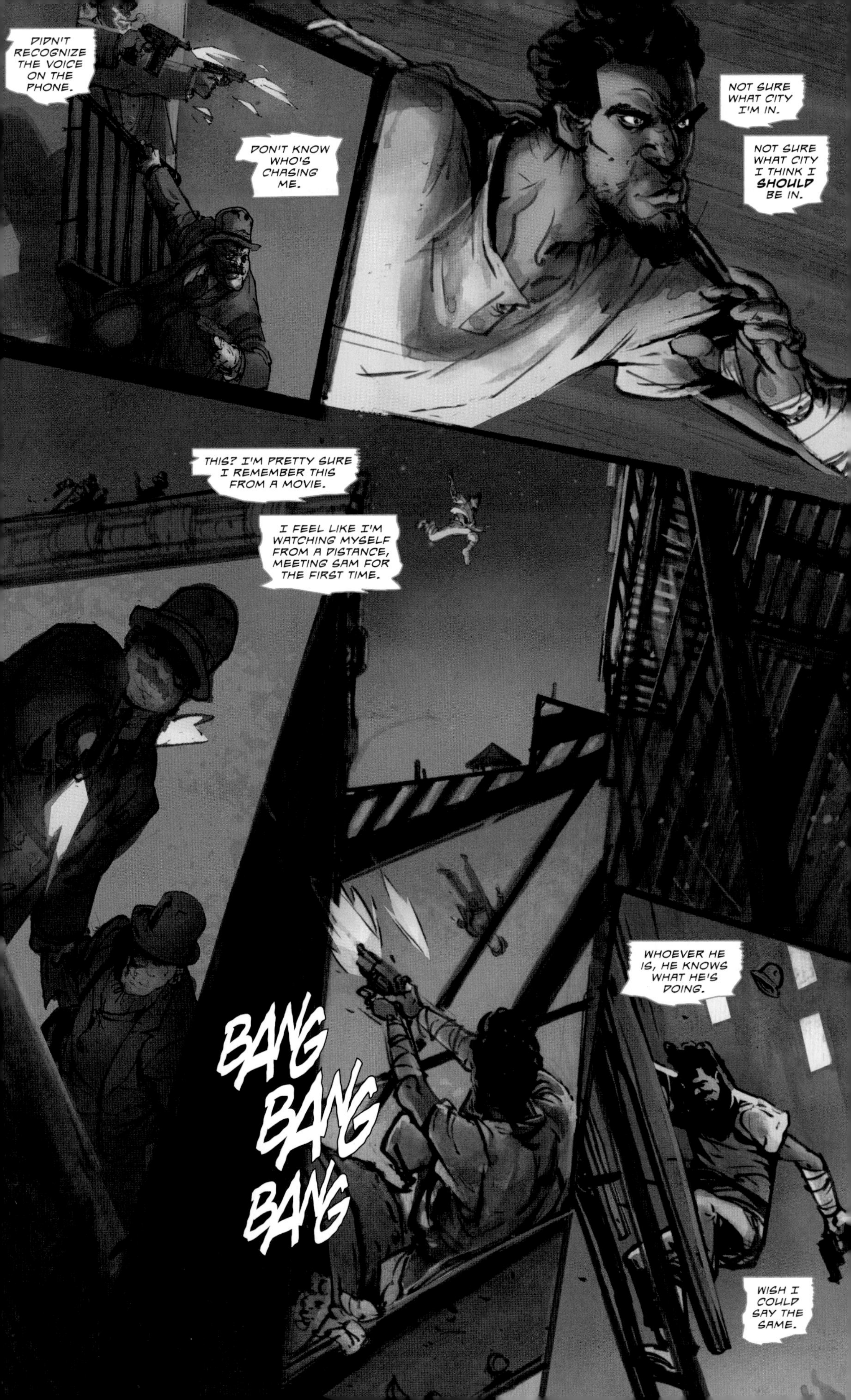
DIDN'T RECOGNIZE THE VOICE ON THE PHONE.
DON'T KNOW WHO'S CHASING ME.
NOT SURE WHAT CITY I'M IN.
NOT SURE WHAT CITY I THINK I **SHOULD** BE IN.
THIS? I'M PRETTY SURE I REMEMBER THIS FROM A MOVIE.
I FEEL LIKE I'M WATCHING MYSELF FROM A DISTANCE, MEETING SAM FOR THE FIRST TIME.
BANG BANG BANG
WHOEVER HE IS, HE KNOWS WHAT HE'S DOING.
WISH I COULD SAY THE SAME.

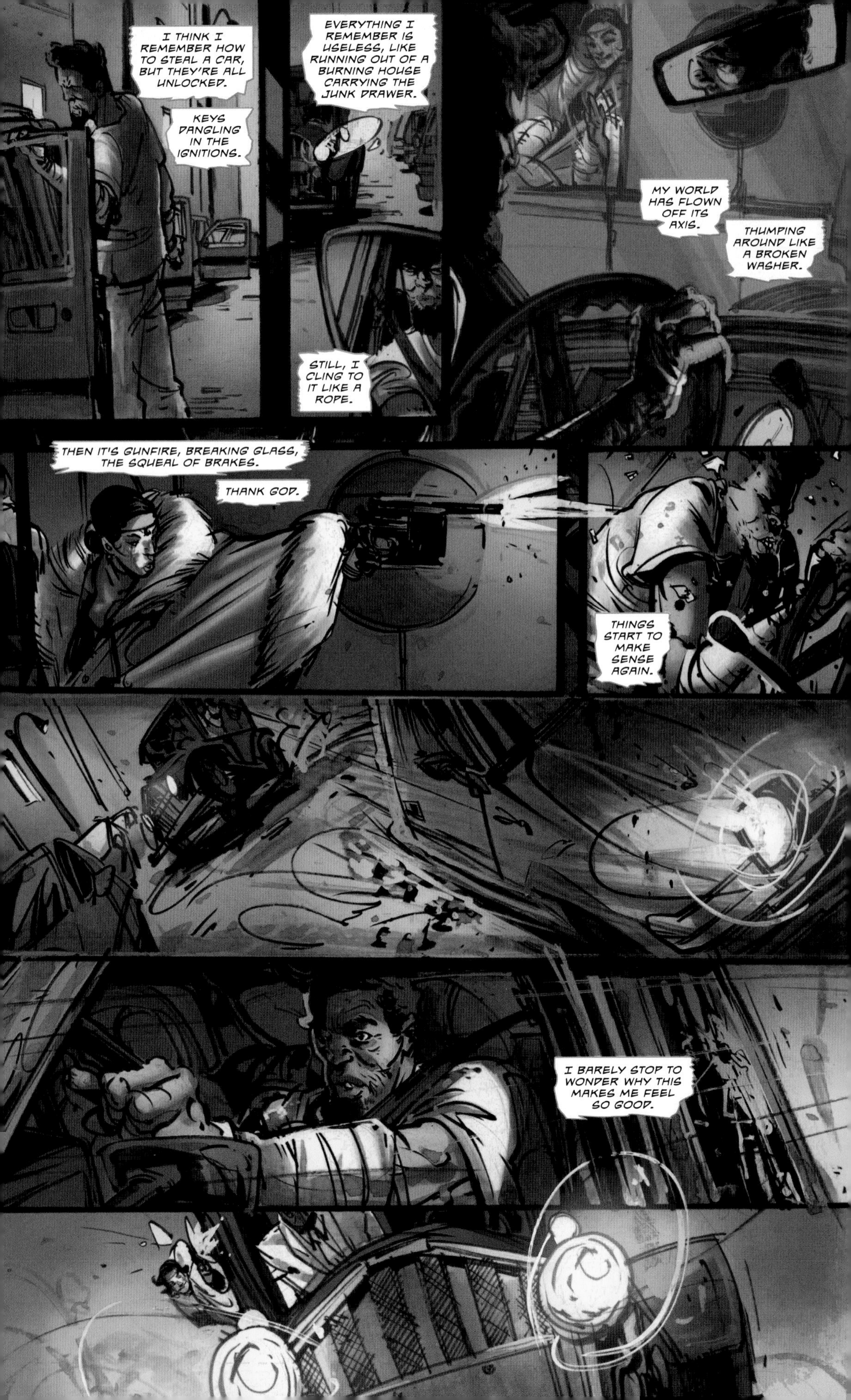
I THINK I REMEMBER HOW TO STEAL A CAR, BUT THEY'RE ALL UNLOCKED.
KEYS DANGLING IN THE IGNITIONS.
EVERYTHING I REMEMBER IS USELESS, LIKE RUNNING OUT OF A BURNING HOUSE CARRYING THE JUNK DRAWER.
STILL, I CLING TO IT LIKE A ROPE.
MY WORLD HAS FLOWN OFF ITS AXIS.
THUMPING AROUND LIKE A BROKEN WASHER.
THEN IT'S GUNFIRE, BREAKING GLASS, THE SQUEAL OF BRAKES.
THANK GOD.
THINGS START TO MAKE SENSE AGAIN.
I BARELY STOP TO WONDER WHY THIS MAKES ME FEEL SO GOOD.

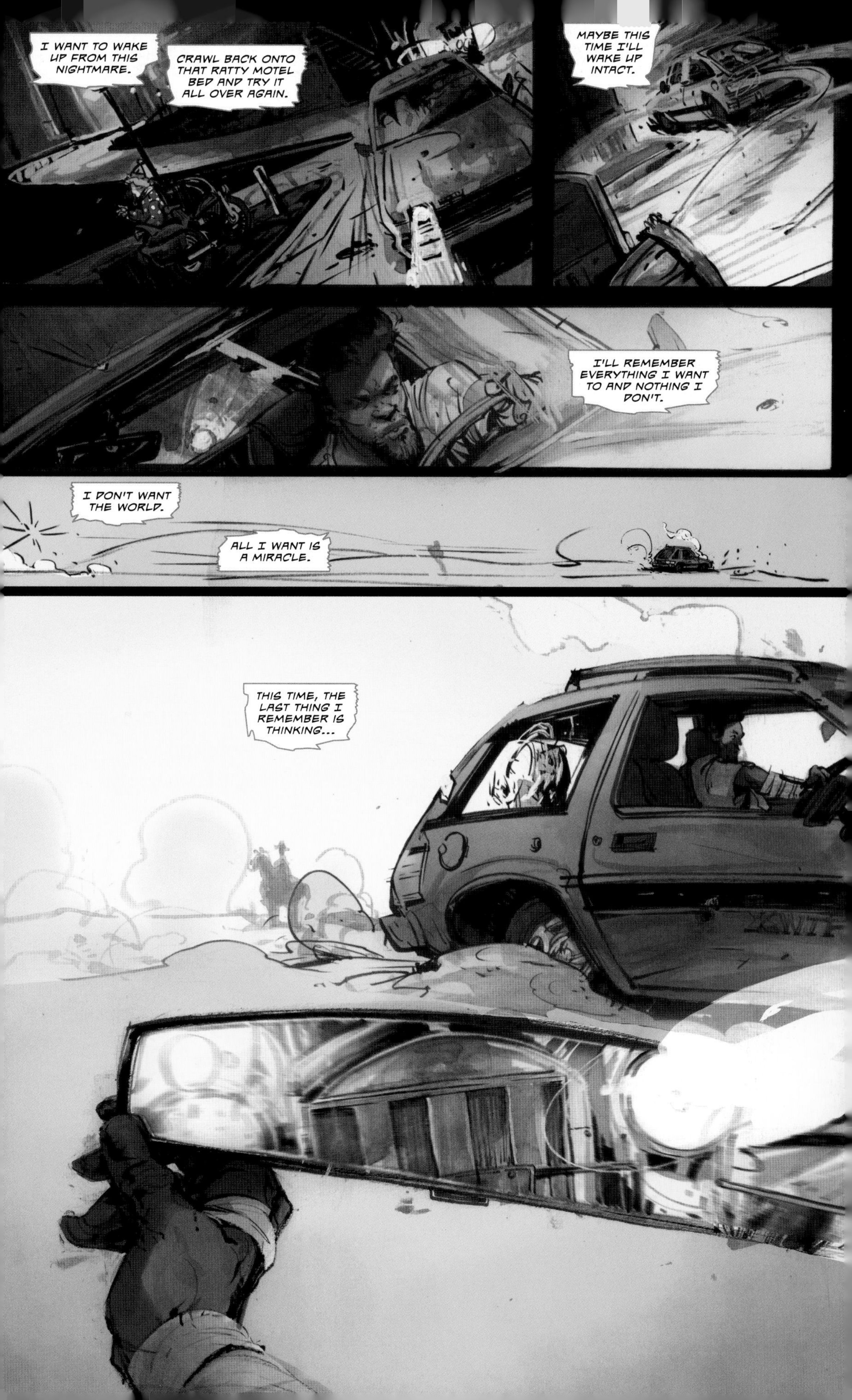
I WANT TO WAKE UP FROM THIS NIGHTMARE.
CRAWL BACK ONTO THAT RATTY MOTEL BED AND TRY IT ALL OVER AGAIN.
MAYBE THIS TIME I'LL WAKE UP INTACT.
I'LL REMEMBER EVERYTHING I WANT TO AND NOTHING I DON'T.
I DON'T WANT THE WORLD.
ALL I WANT IS A MIRACLE.
THIS TIME, THE LAST THING I REMEMBER IS THINKING...

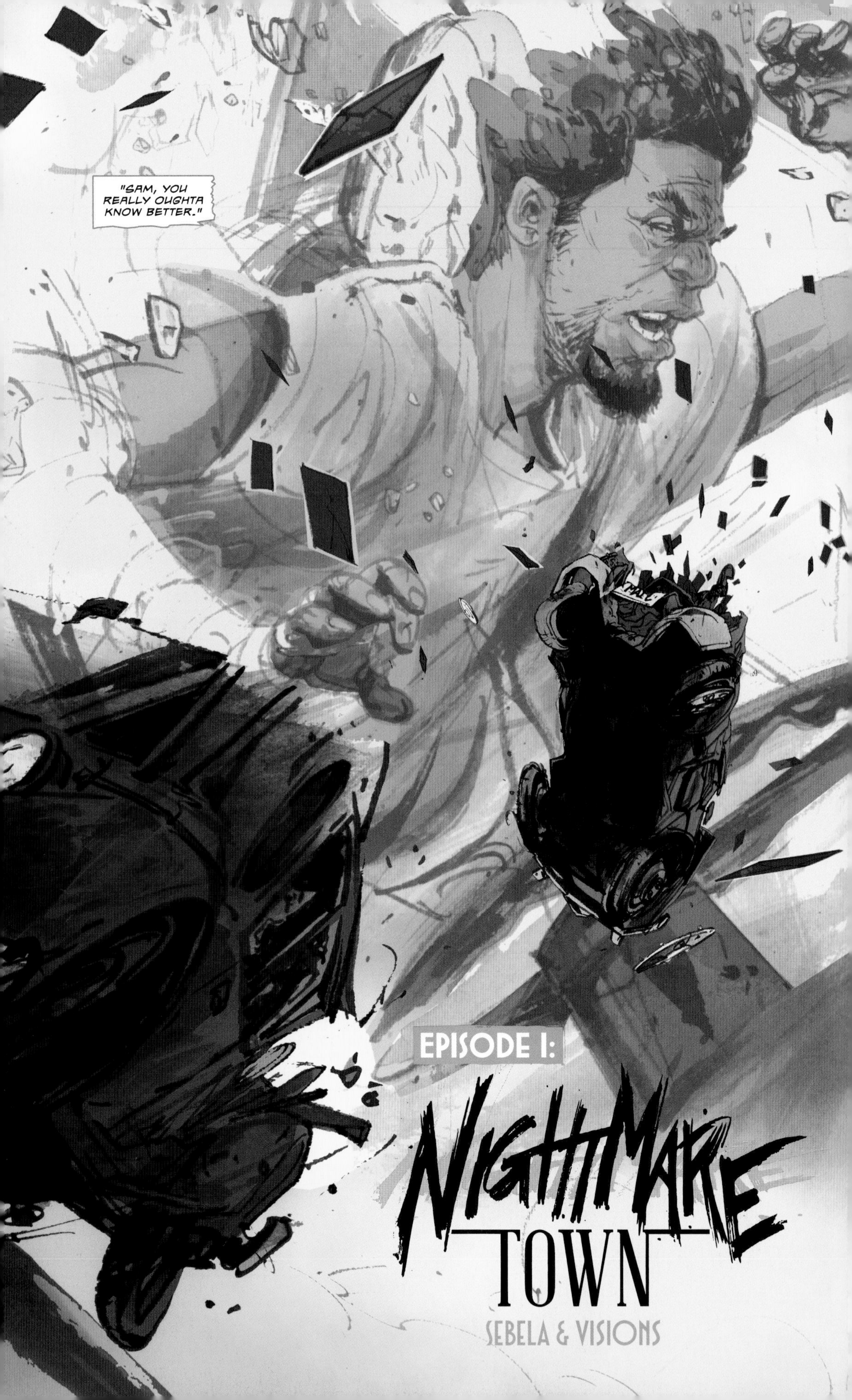
"SAM, YOU REALLY OUGHTA KNOW BETTER."
EPISODE 1:
NIGHTMARE TOWN
SEBELA & VISIONS

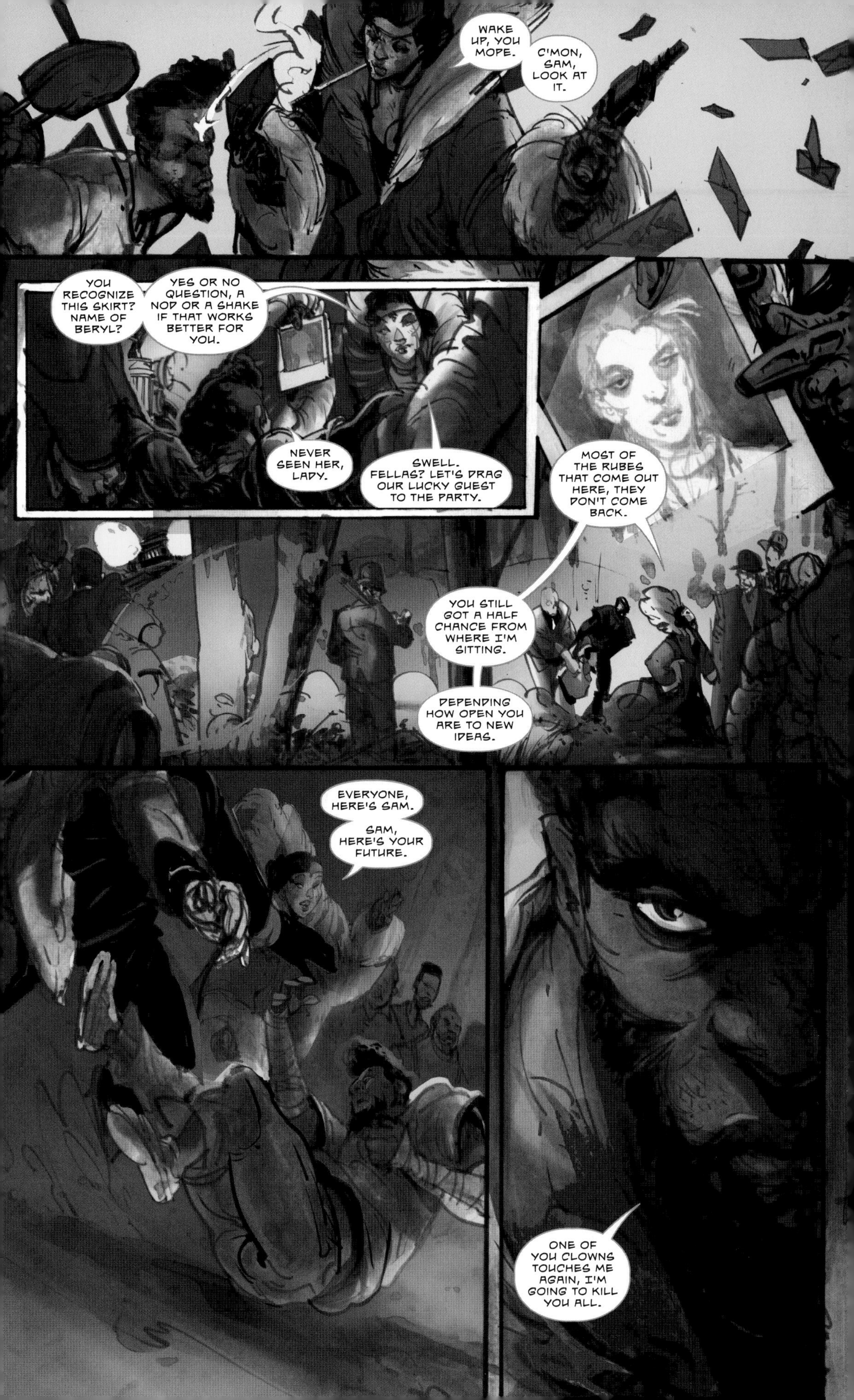
WAKE UP, YOU MOPE.
C'MON, SAM, LOOK AT IT.
YOU RECOGNIZE THIS SKIRT? NAME OF BERYL?
YES OR NO QUESTION, A NOD OR A SHAKE IF THAT WORKS BETTER FOR YOU.
NEVER SEEN HER, LADY.
SWELL. FELLAS? LET'S DRAG OUR LUCKY GUEST TO THE PARTY.
MOST OF THE RUBES THAT COME OUT HERE, THEY DON'T COME BACK.
YOU STILL GOT A HALF CHANCE FROM WHERE I'M SITTING.
DEPENDING HOW OPEN YOU ARE TO NEW IDEAS.
EVERYONE, HERE'S SAM.
SAM, HERE'S YOUR FUTURE.
ONE OF YOU CLOWNS TOUCHES ME AGAIN, I'M GOING TO KILL YOU ALL.

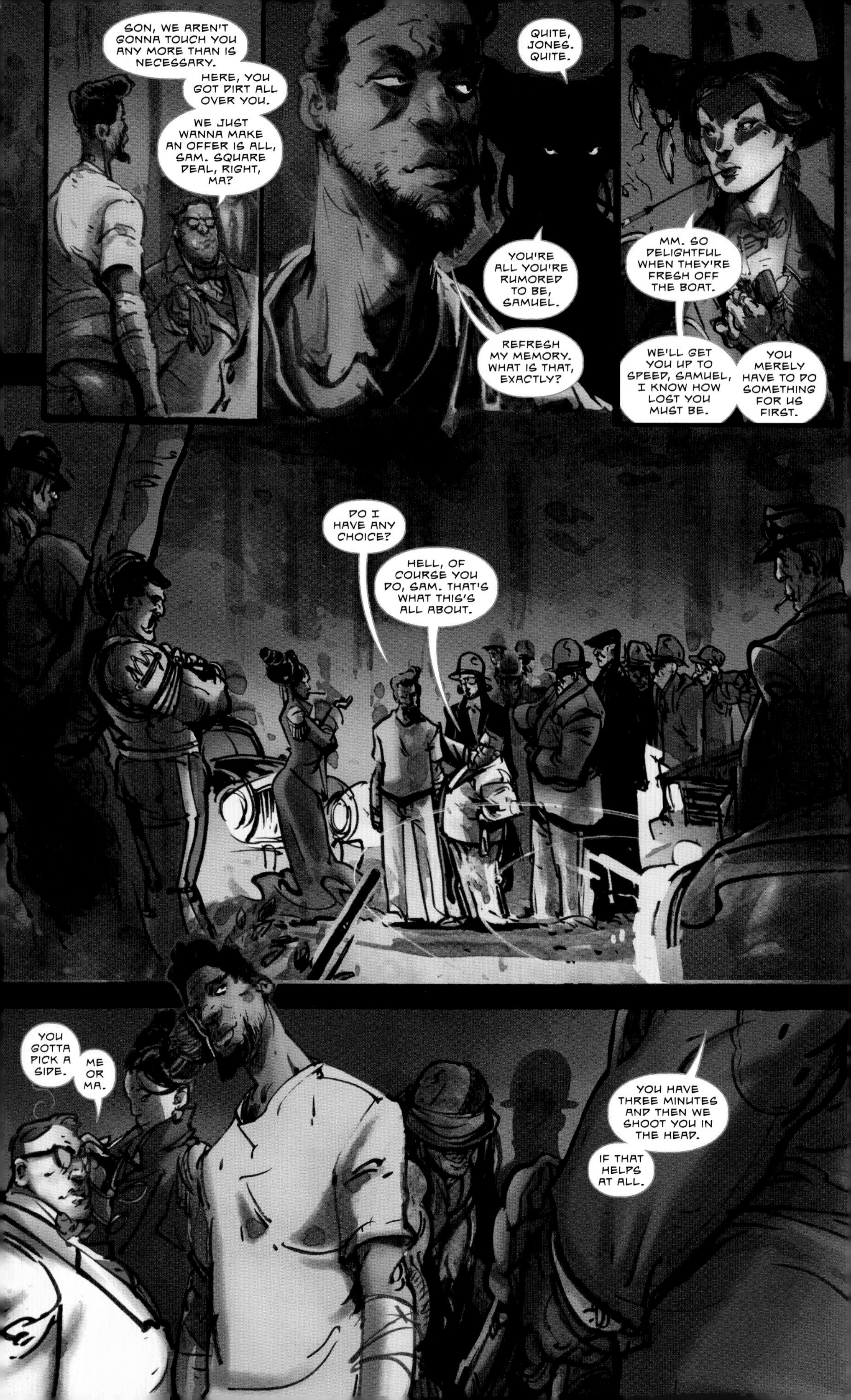
SON, WE AREN'T GONNA TOUCH YOU ANY MORE THAN IS NECESSARY.
HERE, YOU GOT DIRT ALL OVER YOU.
WE JUST WANNA MAKE AN OFFER IS ALL, SAM. SQUARE DEAL, RIGHT, MA?
QUITE, JONES. QUITE.
YOU'RE ALL YOU'RE RUMORED TO BE, SAMUEL.
REFRESH MY MEMORY. WHAT IS THAT, EXACTLY?
MM. SO DELIGHTFUL WHEN THEY'RE FRESH OFF THE BOAT.
WE'LL GET YOU UP TO SPEED, SAMUEL, I KNOW HOW LOST YOU MUST BE.
YOU MERELY HAVE TO DO SOMETHING FOR US FIRST.
DO I HAVE ANY CHOICE?
HELL, OF COURSE YOU DO, SAM. THAT'S WHAT THIS'S ALL ABOUT.
YOU GOTTA PICK A SIDE.
ME OR MA.
YOU HAVE THREE MINUTES AND THEN WE SHOOT YOU IN THE HEAD.
IF THAT HELPS AT ALL.

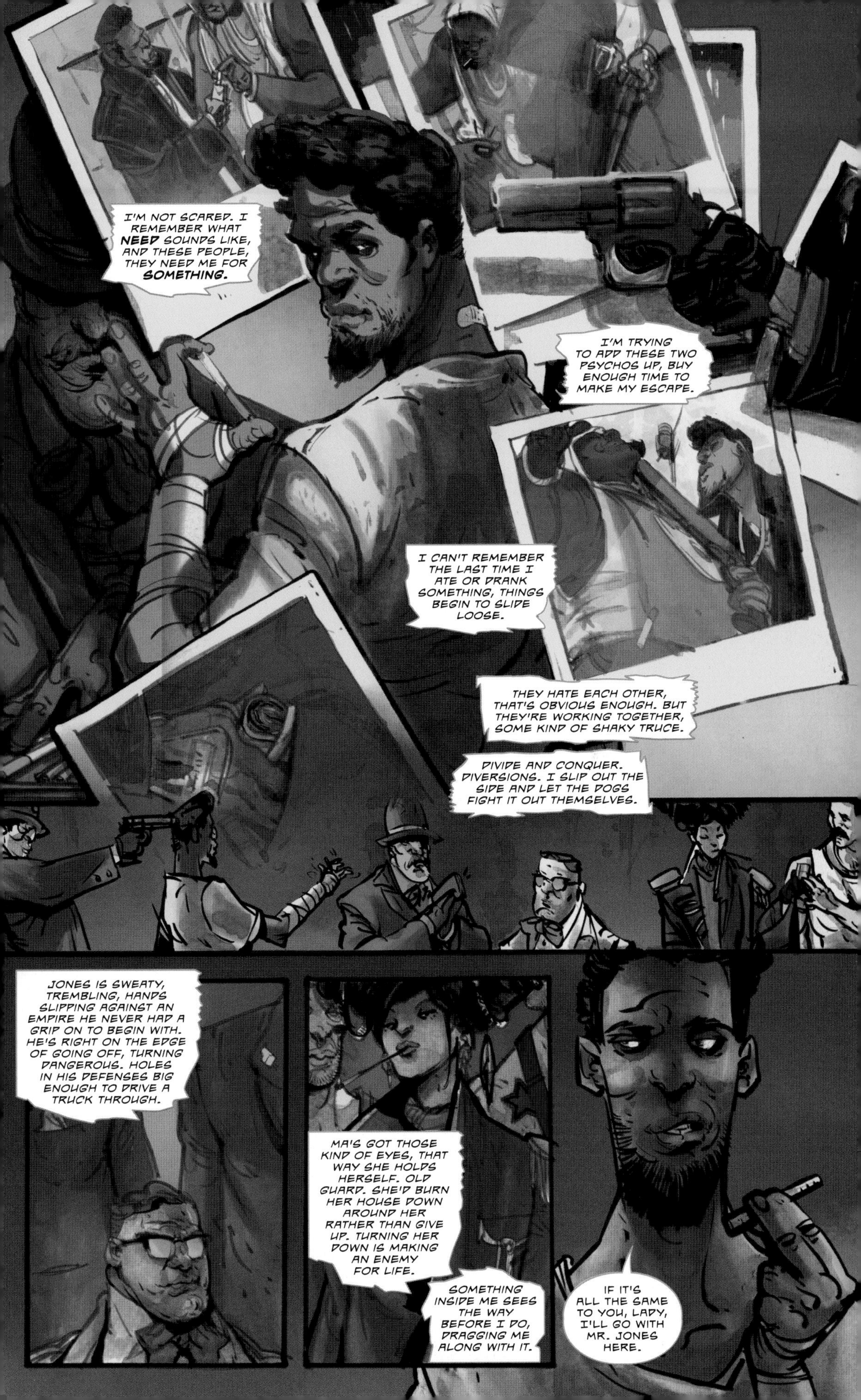
I'M NOT SCARED. I REMEMBER WHAT NEED SOUNDS LIKE, AND THESE PEOPLE, THEY NEED ME FOR SOMETHING.
I'M TRYING TO ADD THESE TWO PSYCHOS UP, BUY ENOUGH TIME TO MAKE MY ESCAPE.
I CAN'T REMEMBER THE LAST TIME I ATE OR DRANK SOMETHING, THINGS BEGIN TO SLIDE LOOSE.
THEY HATE EACH OTHER, THAT'S OBVIOUS ENOUGH. BUT THEY'RE WORKING TOGETHER, SOME KIND OF SHAKY TRUCE.
DIVIDE AND CONQUER. DIVERSIONS. I SLIP OUT THE SIDE AND LET THE DOGS FIGHT IT OUT THEMSELVES.
JONES IS SWEATY, TREMBLING, HANDS SLIPPING AGAINST AN EMPIRE HE NEVER HAD A GRIP ON TO BEGIN WITH. HE'S RIGHT ON THE EDGE OF GOING OFF, TURNING DANGEROUS. HOLES IN HIS DEFENSES BIG ENOUGH TO DRIVE A TRUCK THROUGH.
MA'S GOT THOSE KIND OF EYES, THAT WAY SHE HOLDS HERSELF. OLD GUARD. SHE'D BURN HER HOUSE DOWN AROUND HER RATHER THAN GIVE UP. TURNING HER DOWN IS MAKING AN ENEMY FOR LIFE.
SOMETHING INSIDE ME SEES THE WAY BEFORE I DO, DRAGGING ME ALONG WITH IT.
IF IT'S ALL THE SAME TO YOU, LADY, I'LL GO WITH MR. JONES HERE.

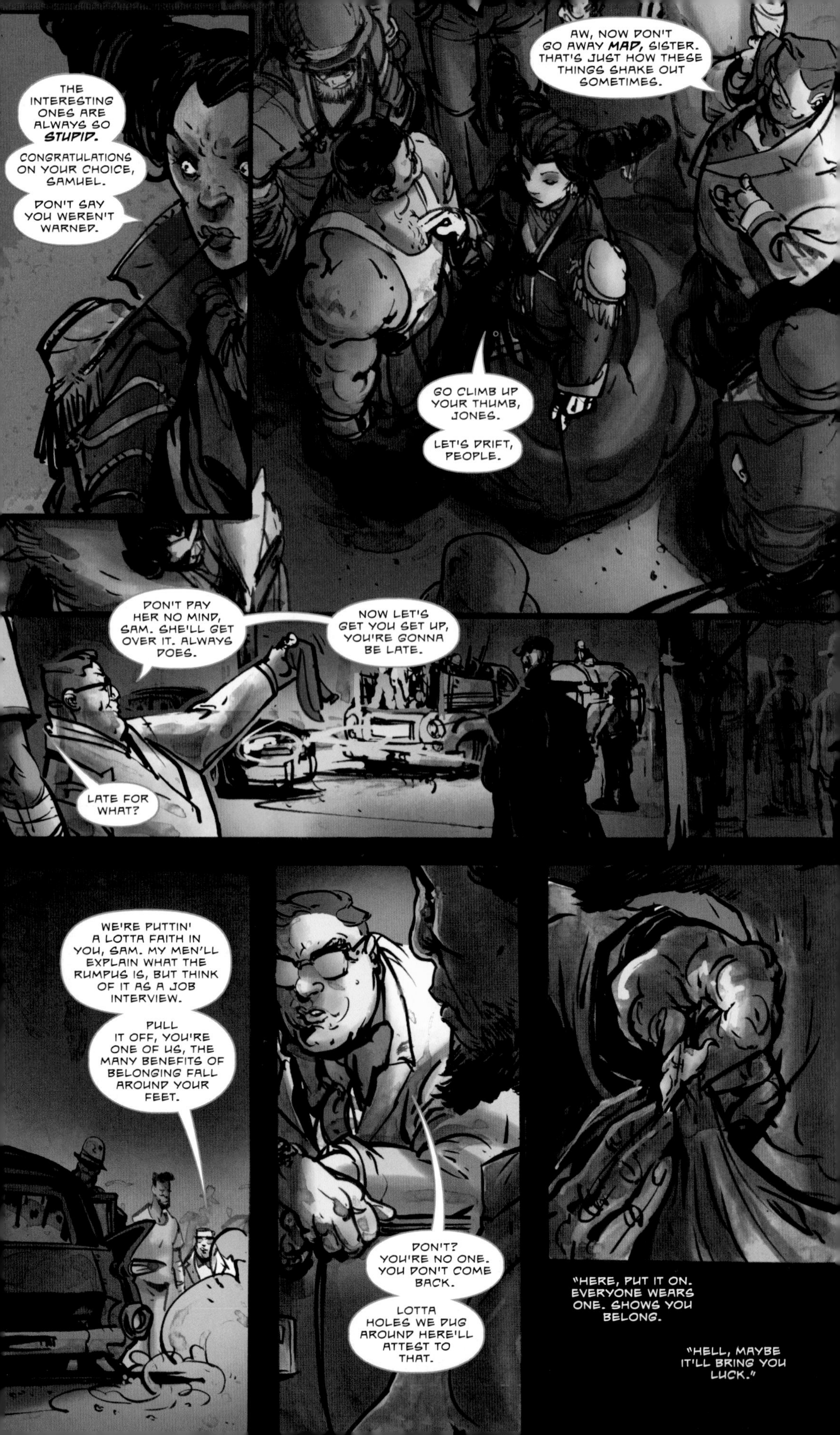
THE INTERESTING ONES ARE ALWAYS SO **STUPID.**
CONGRATULATIONS ON YOUR CHOICE, SAMUEL.
DON'T SAY YOU WEREN'T WARNED.
AW, NOW DON'T GO AWAY **MAD**, SISTER. THAT'S JUST HOW THESE THINGS SHAKE OUT SOMETIMES.
GO CLIMB UP YOUR THUMB, JONES.
LET'S DRIFT, PEOPLE.
DON'T PAY HER NO MIND, SAM. SHE'LL GET OVER IT. ALWAYS DOES.
NOW LET'S GET YOU SET UP, YOU'RE GONNA BE LATE.
LATE FOR WHAT?
WE'RE PUTTIN' A LOTTA FAITH IN YOU, SAM. MY MEN'LL EXPLAIN WHAT THE RUMPUS IS, BUT THINK OF IT AS A JOB INTERVIEW.
PULL IT OFF, YOU'RE ONE OF US, THE MANY BENEFITS OF BELONGING FALL AROUND YOUR FEET.
DON'T? YOU'RE NO ONE. YOU DON'T COME BACK.
LOTTA HOLES WE DUG AROUND HERE'LL ATTEST TO THAT.
"HERE, PUT IT ON. EVERYONE WEARS ONE. SHOWS YOU BELONG.
"HELL, MAYBE IT'LL BRING YOU LUCK."

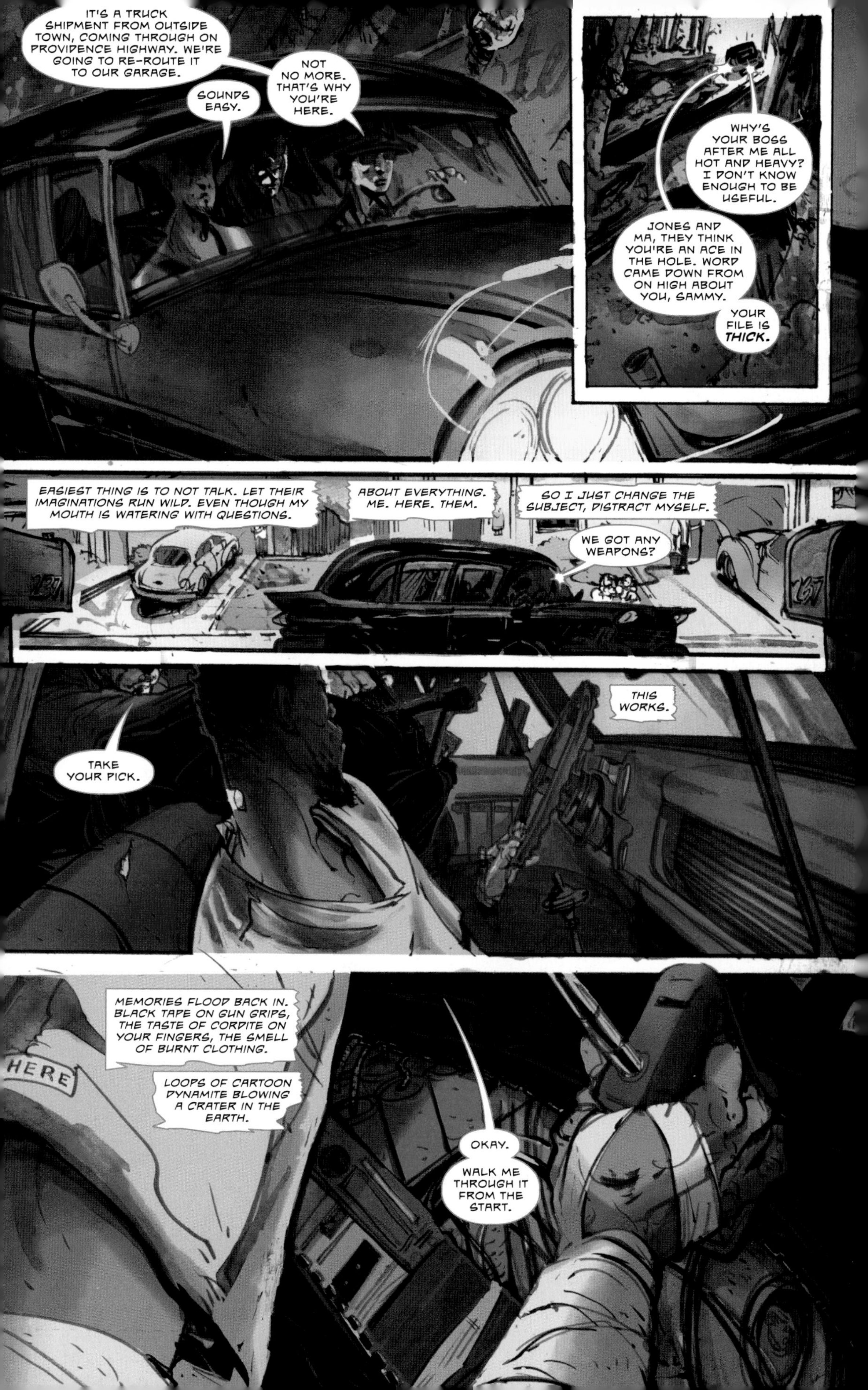
IT'S A TRUCK SHIPMENT FROM OUTSIDE TOWN, COMING THROUGH ON PROVIDENCE HIGHWAY. WE'RE GOING TO RE-ROUTE IT TO OUR GARAGE.
SOUNDS EASY.
NOT NO MORE. THAT'S WHY YOU'RE HERE.
WHY'S YOUR BOSS AFTER ME ALL HOT AND HEAVY? I DON'T KNOW ENOUGH TO BE USEFUL.
JONES AND MA, THEY THINK YOU'RE AN ACE IN THE HOLE. WORD CAME DOWN FROM ON HIGH ABOUT YOU, SAMMY.
YOUR FILE IS THICK.
EASIEST THING IS TO NOT TALK. LET THEIR IMAGINATIONS RUN WILD. EVEN THOUGH MY MOUTH IS WATERING WITH QUESTIONS.
ABOUT EVERYTHING. ME. HERE. THEM.
SO I JUST CHANGE THE SUBJECT, DISTRACT MYSELF.
WE GOT ANY WEAPONS?
TAKE YOUR PICK.
THIS WORKS.
MEMORIES FLOOD BACK IN. BLACK TAPE ON GUN GRIPS, THE TASTE OF CORDITE ON YOUR FINGERS, THE SMELL OF BURNT CLOTHING.
LOOPS OF CARTOON DYNAMITE BLOWING A CRATER IN THE EARTH.
HERE
OKAY.
WALK ME THROUGH IT FROM THE START.

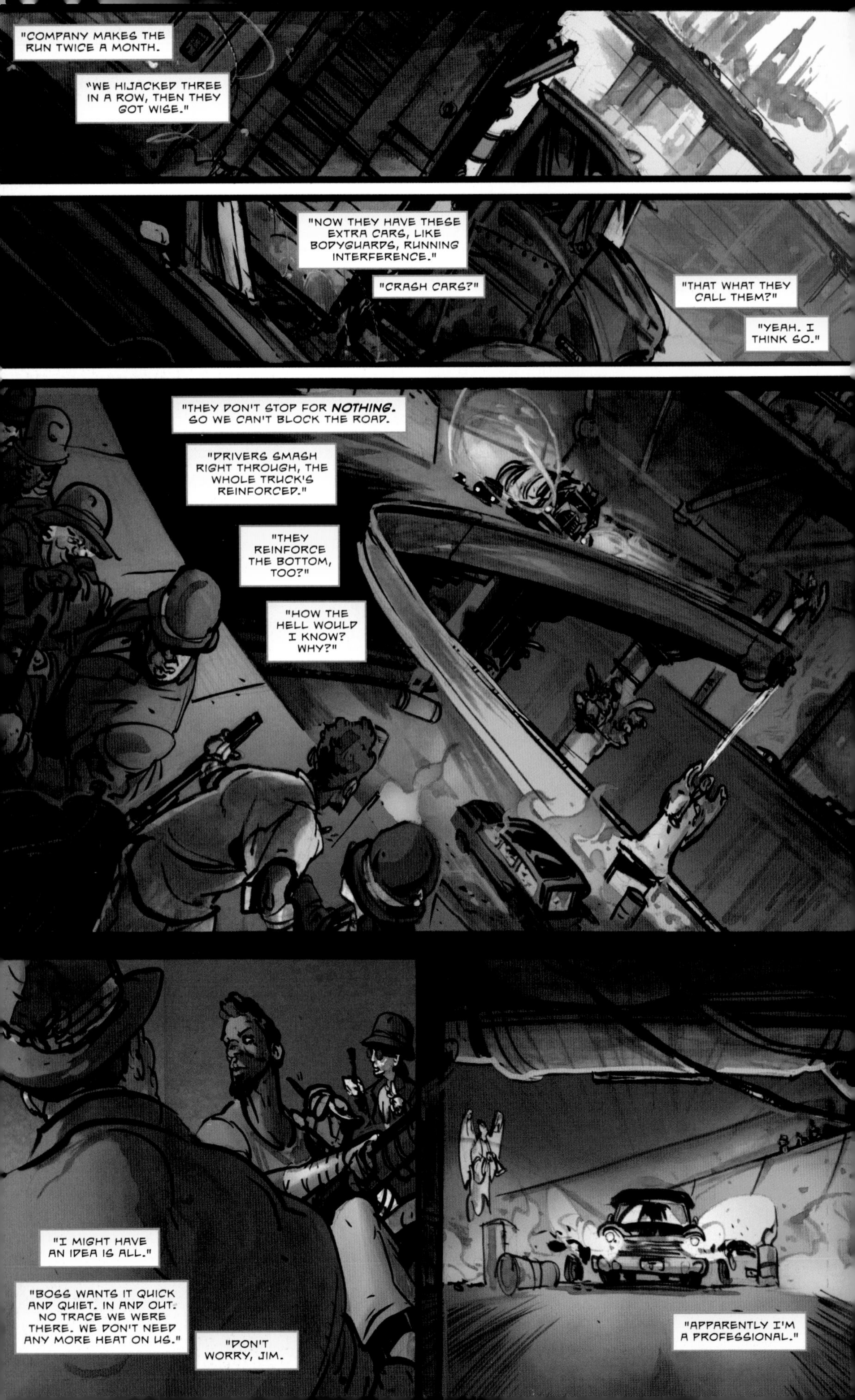
"COMPANY MAKES THE RUN TWICE A MONTH.
"WE HIJACKED THREE IN A ROW, THEN THEY GOT WISE."
"NOW THEY HAVE THESE EXTRA CARS, LIKE BODYGUARDS, RUNNING INTERFERENCE."
"CRASH CARS?"
"THAT WHAT THEY CALL THEM?"
"YEAH. I THINK SO."
"THEY DON'T STOP FOR NOTHING. SO WE CAN'T BLOCK THE ROAD.
"DRIVERS SMASH RIGHT THROUGH, THE WHOLE TRUCK'S REINFORCED."
"THEY REINFORCE THE BOTTOM, TOO?"
"HOW THE HELL WOULD I KNOW? WHY?"
"I MIGHT HAVE AN IDEA IS ALL."
"BOSS WANTS IT QUICK AND QUIET. IN AND OUT. NO TRACE WE WERE THERE. WE DON'T NEED ANY MORE HEAT ON US."
"DON'T WORRY, JIM.
"APPARENTLY I'M A PROFESSIONAL."

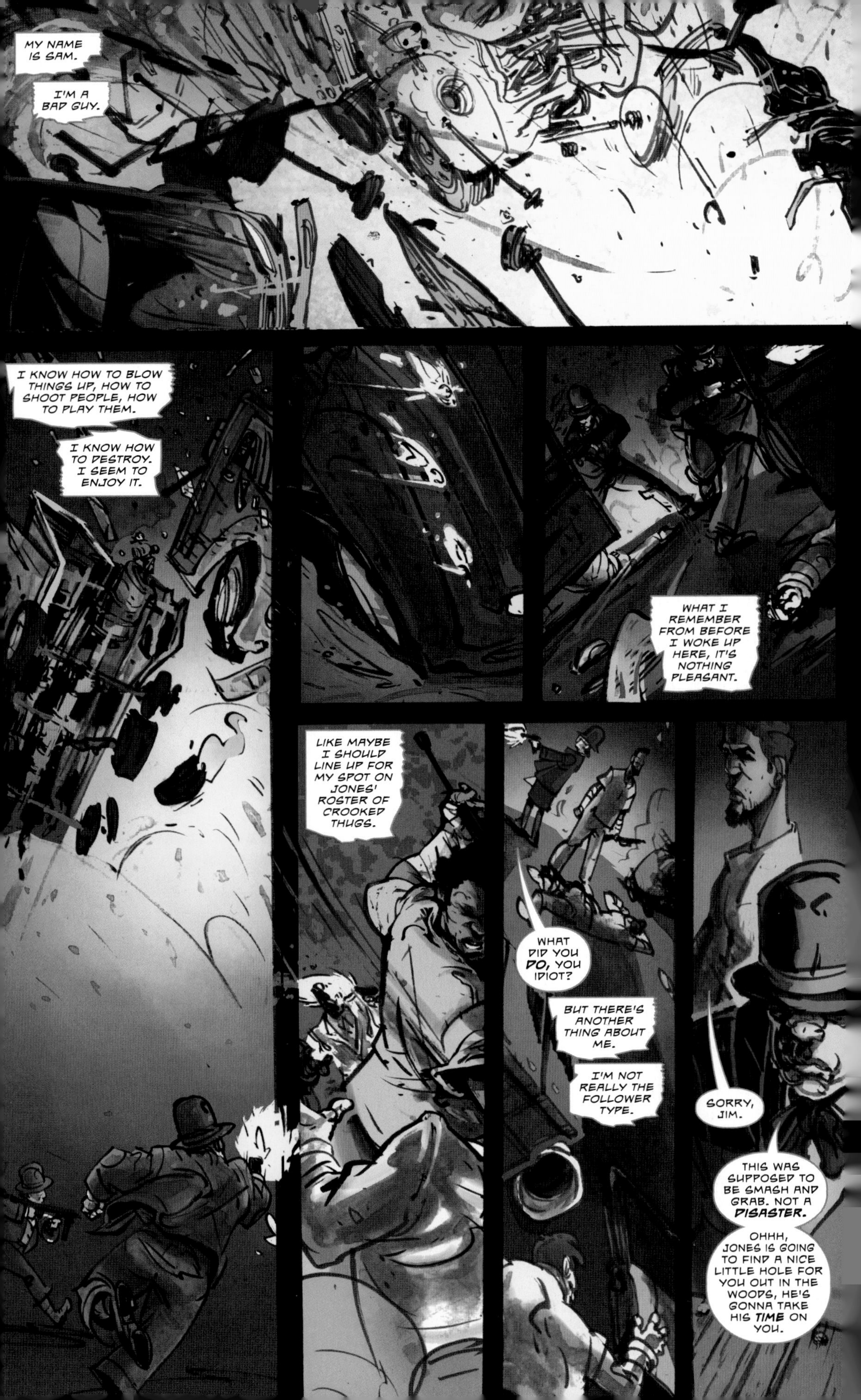
MY NAME IS SAM.
I'M A BAD GUY.
I KNOW HOW TO BLOW THINGS UP, HOW TO SHOOT PEOPLE, HOW TO PLAY THEM.
I KNOW HOW TO DESTROY. I SEEM TO ENJOY IT.
WHAT I REMEMBER FROM BEFORE I WOKE UP HERE, IT'S NOTHING PLEASANT.
LIKE MAYBE I SHOULD LINE UP FOR MY SPOT ON JONES' ROSTER OF CROOKED THUGS.
WHAT DID YOU DO, YOU IDIOT?
BUT THERE'S ANOTHER THING ABOUT ME.
I'M NOT REALLY THE FOLLOWER TYPE.
SORRY, JIM.
THIS WAS SUPPOSED TO BE SMASH AND GRAB. NOT A DISASTER.
OHHH, JONES IS GOING TO FIND A NICE LITTLE HOLE FOR YOU OUT IN THE WOODS, HE'S GONNA TAKE HIS TIME ON YOU.

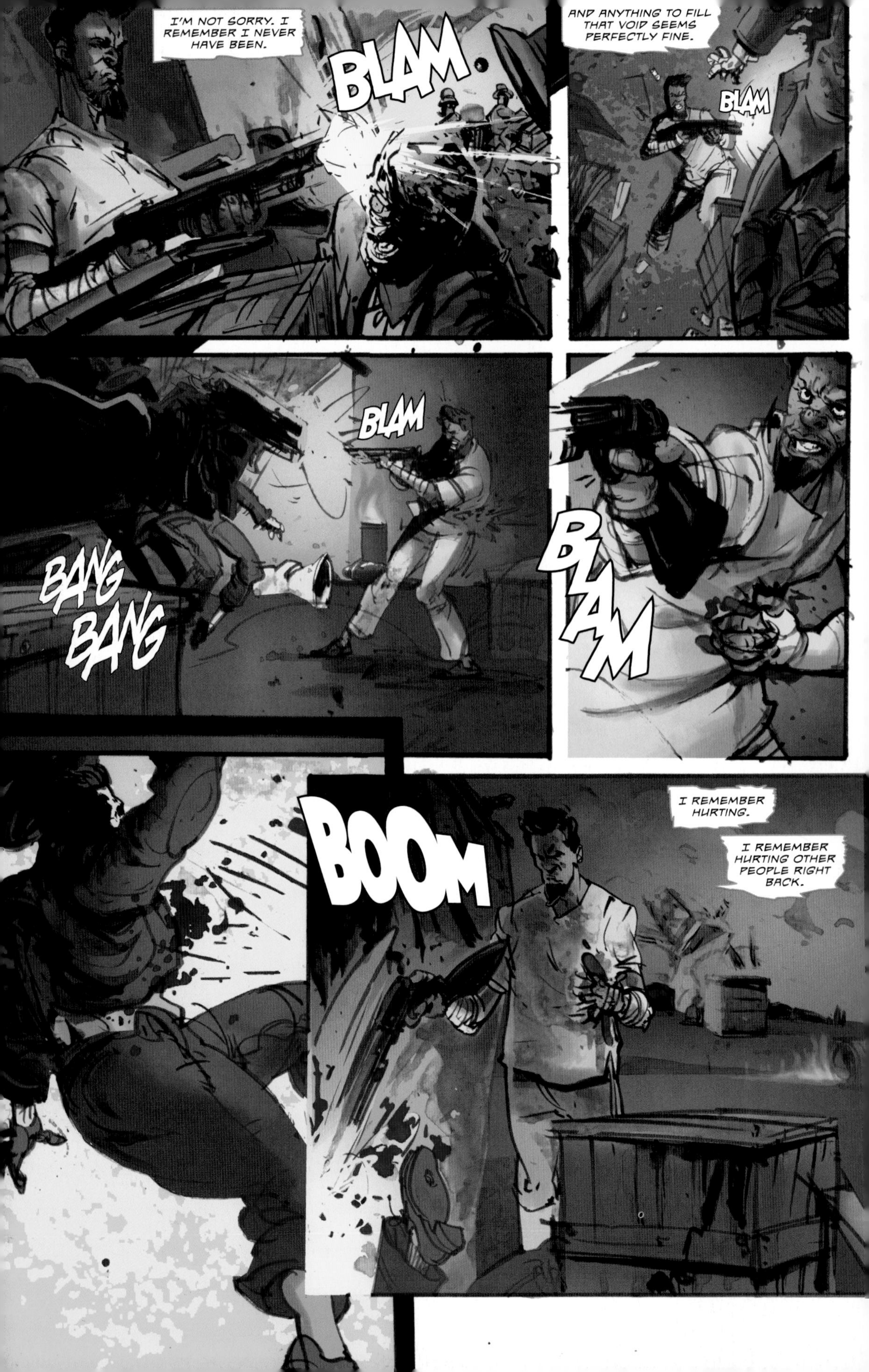
I'M NOT SORRY. I REMEMBER I NEVER HAVE BEEN.
BLAM
AND ANYTHING TO FILL THAT VOID SEEMS PERFECTLY FINE.
BLAM
BLAM
BANG BANG
BLAM
BOOM
I REMEMBER HURTING.
I REMEMBER HURTING OTHER PEOPLE RIGHT BACK.

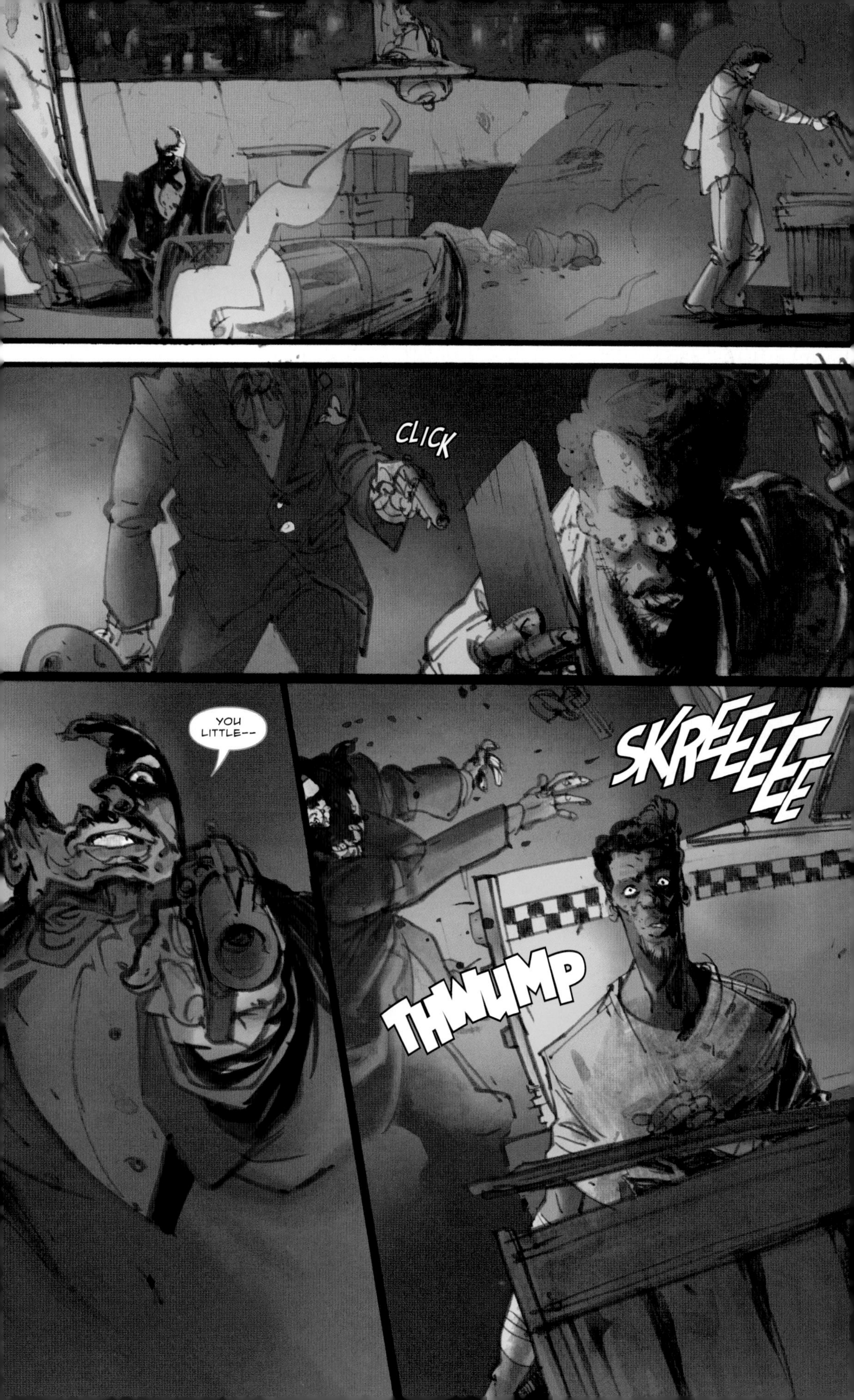
CLICK
YOU LITTLE--
SKREEEEEE
THWUMP

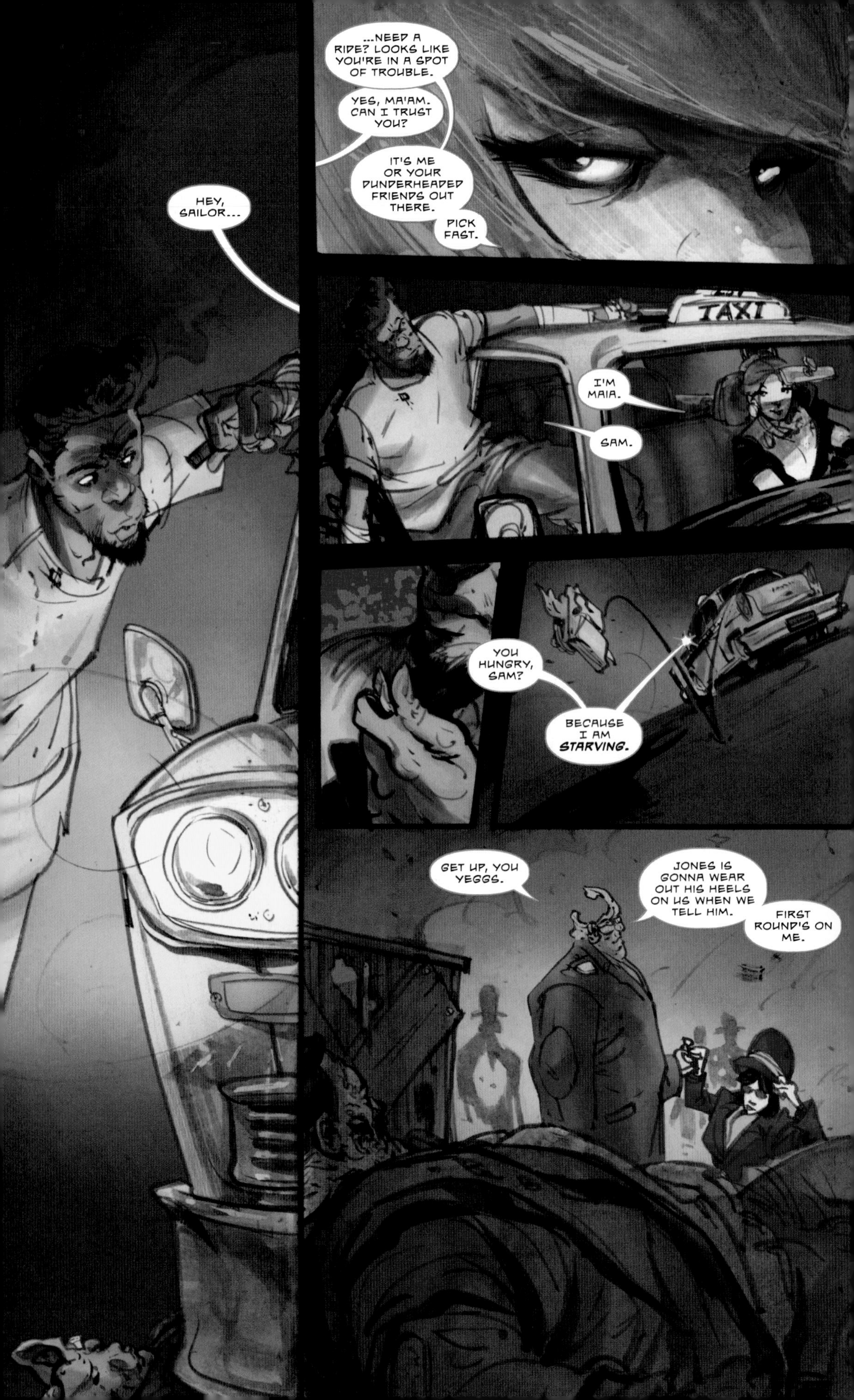
HEY, SAILOR...
...NEED A RIDE? LOOKS LIKE YOU'RE IN A SPOT OF TROUBLE.
YES, MA'AM. CAN I TRUST YOU?
IT'S ME OR YOUR DUNDERHEADED FRIENDS OUT THERE.
PICK FAST.
TAXI
I'M MAIA.
SAM.
YOU HUNGRY, SAM?
BECAUSE I AM STARVING.
GET UP, YOU YEGGS.
JONES IS GONNA WEAR OUT HIS HEELS ON US WHEN WE TELL HIM.
FIRST ROUND'S ON ME.

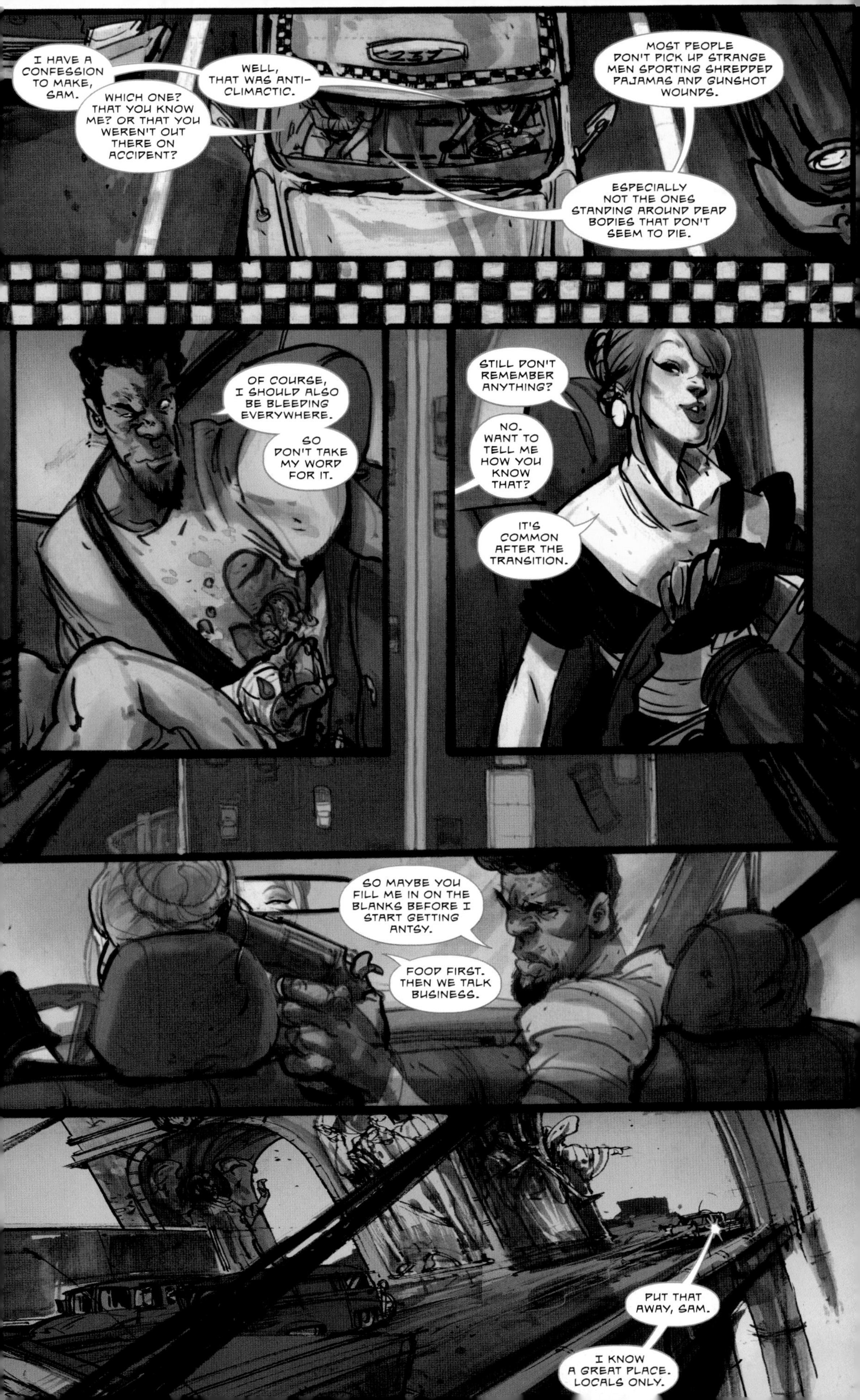
I HAVE A CONFESSION TO MAKE, SAM.
WELL, THAT WAS ANTI-CLIMACTIC.
WHICH ONE? THAT YOU KNOW ME? OR THAT YOU WEREN'T OUT THERE ON ACCIDENT?
MOST PEOPLE DON'T PICK UP STRANGE MEN SPORTING SHREDDED PAJAMAS AND GUNSHOT WOUNDS.
ESPECIALLY NOT THE ONES STANDING AROUND DEAD BODIES THAT DON'T SEEM TO DIE.
OF COURSE, I SHOULD ALSO BE BLEEDING EVERYWHERE.
SO DON'T TAKE MY WORD FOR IT.
STILL DON'T REMEMBER ANYTHING?
NO. WANT TO TELL ME HOW YOU KNOW THAT?
IT'S COMMON AFTER THE TRANSITION.
SO MAYBE YOU FILL ME IN ON THE BLANKS BEFORE I START GETTING ANTSY.
FOOD FIRST. THEN WE TALK BUSINESS.
PUT THAT AWAY, SAM.
I KNOW A GREAT PLACE. LOCALS ONLY.

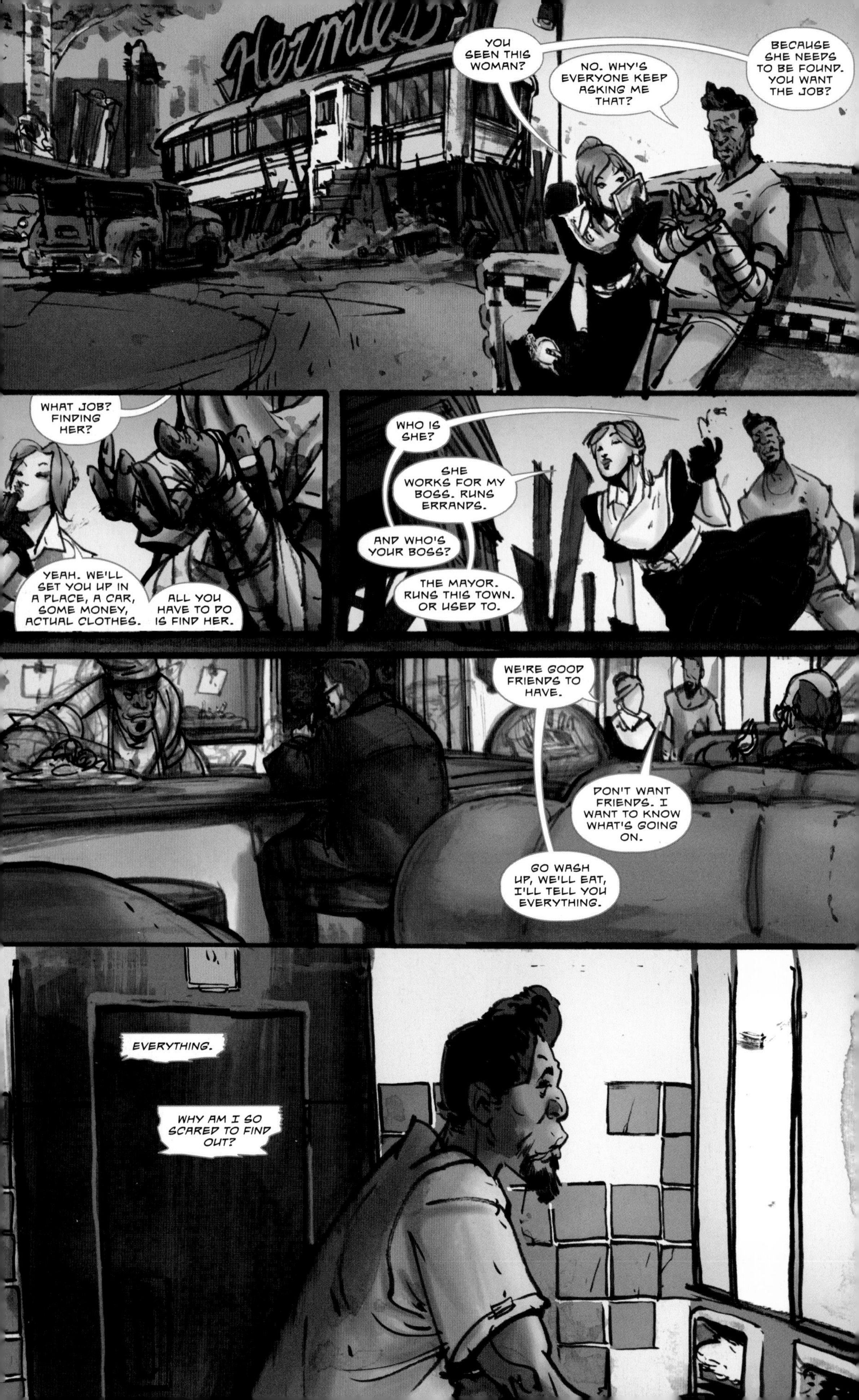
Hermes
YOU SEEN THIS WOMAN?
NO. WHY'S EVERYONE KEEP ASKING ME THAT?
BECAUSE SHE NEEDS TO BE FOUND. YOU WANT THE JOB?
WHAT JOB? FINDING HER?
YEAH. WE'LL SET YOU UP IN A PLACE, A CAR, SOME MONEY, ACTUAL CLOTHES.
ALL YOU HAVE TO DO IS FIND HER.
WHO IS SHE?
SHE WORKS FOR MY BOSS. RUNS ERRANDS.
AND WHO'S YOUR BOSS?
THE MAYOR. RUNS THIS TOWN. OR USED TO.
WE'RE GOOD FRIENDS TO HAVE.
DON'T WANT FRIENDS. I WANT TO KNOW WHAT'S GOING ON.
GO WASH UP, WE'LL EAT, I'LL TELL YOU EVERYTHING.
EVERYTHING.
WHY AM I SO SCARED TO FIND OUT?

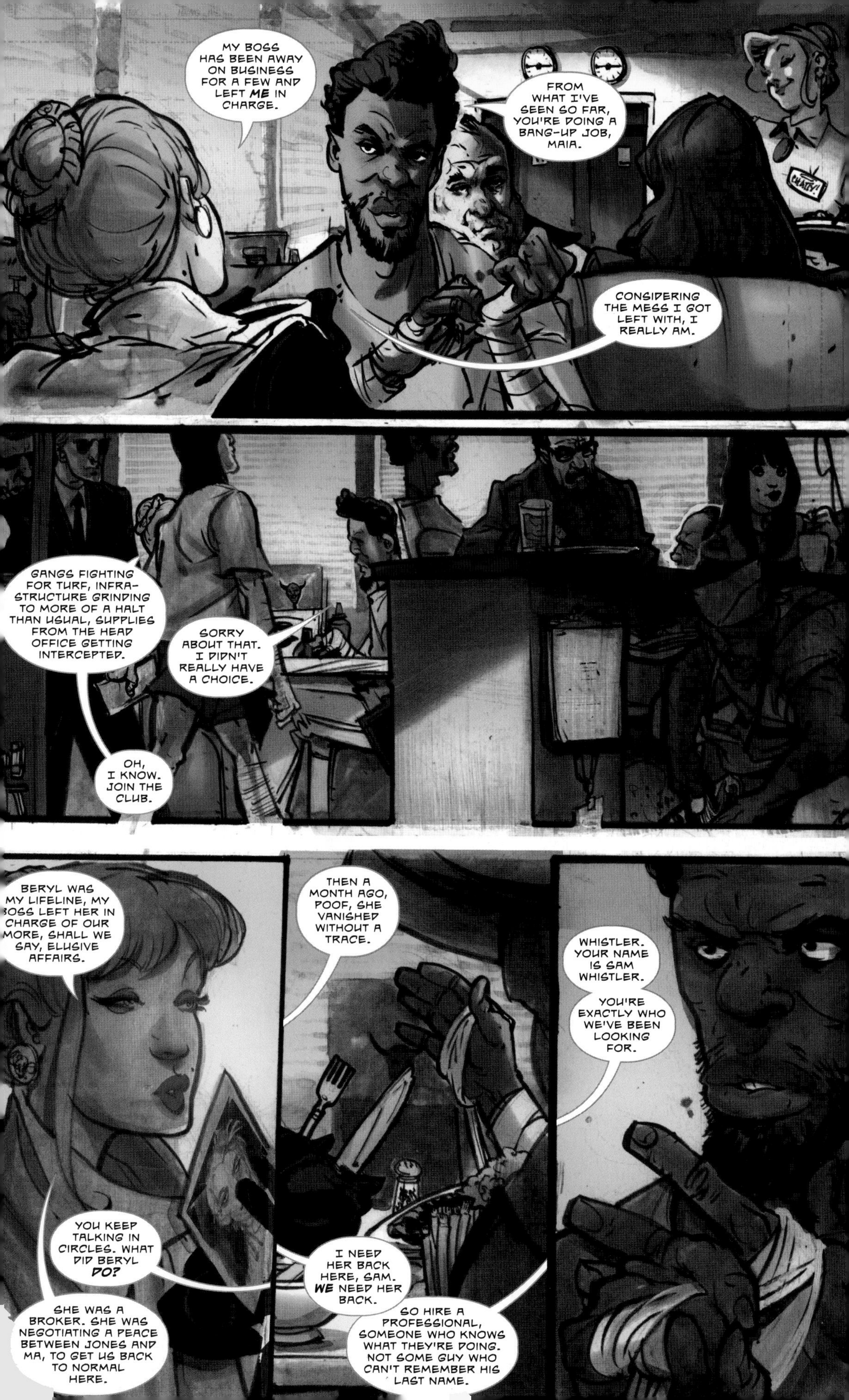
MY BOSS HAS BEEN AWAY ON BUSINESS FOR A FEW AND LEFT *ME* IN CHARGE.
FROM WHAT I'VE SEEN SO FAR, YOU'RE DOING A BANG-UP JOB, MAIA.
CONSIDERING THE MESS I GOT LEFT WITH, I REALLY AM.
GANGS FIGHTING FOR TURF, INFRA-STRUCTURE GRINDING TO MORE OF A HALT THAN USUAL, SUPPLIES FROM THE HEAD OFFICE GETTING INTERCEPTED.
SORRY ABOUT THAT. I DIDN'T REALLY HAVE A CHOICE.
OH, I KNOW. JOIN THE CLUB.
BERYL WAS MY LIFELINE, MY BOSS LEFT HER IN CHARGE OF OUR MORE, SHALL WE SAY, ELUSIVE AFFAIRS.
THEN A MONTH AGO, POOF, SHE VANISHED WITHOUT A TRACE.
WHISTLER. YOUR NAME IS SAM WHISTLER.
YOU'RE EXACTLY WHO WE'VE BEEN LOOKING FOR.
YOU KEEP TALKING IN CIRCLES. WHAT DID BERYL *DO?*
SHE WAS A BROKER. SHE WAS NEGOTIATING A PEACE BETWEEN JONES AND MA, TO GET US BACK TO NORMAL HERE.
I NEED HER BACK HERE, SAM. *WE* NEED HER BACK.
SO HIRE A PROFESSIONAL, SOMEONE WHO KNOWS WHAT THEY'RE DOING. NOT SOME GUY WHO CAN'T REMEMBER HIS LAST NAME.

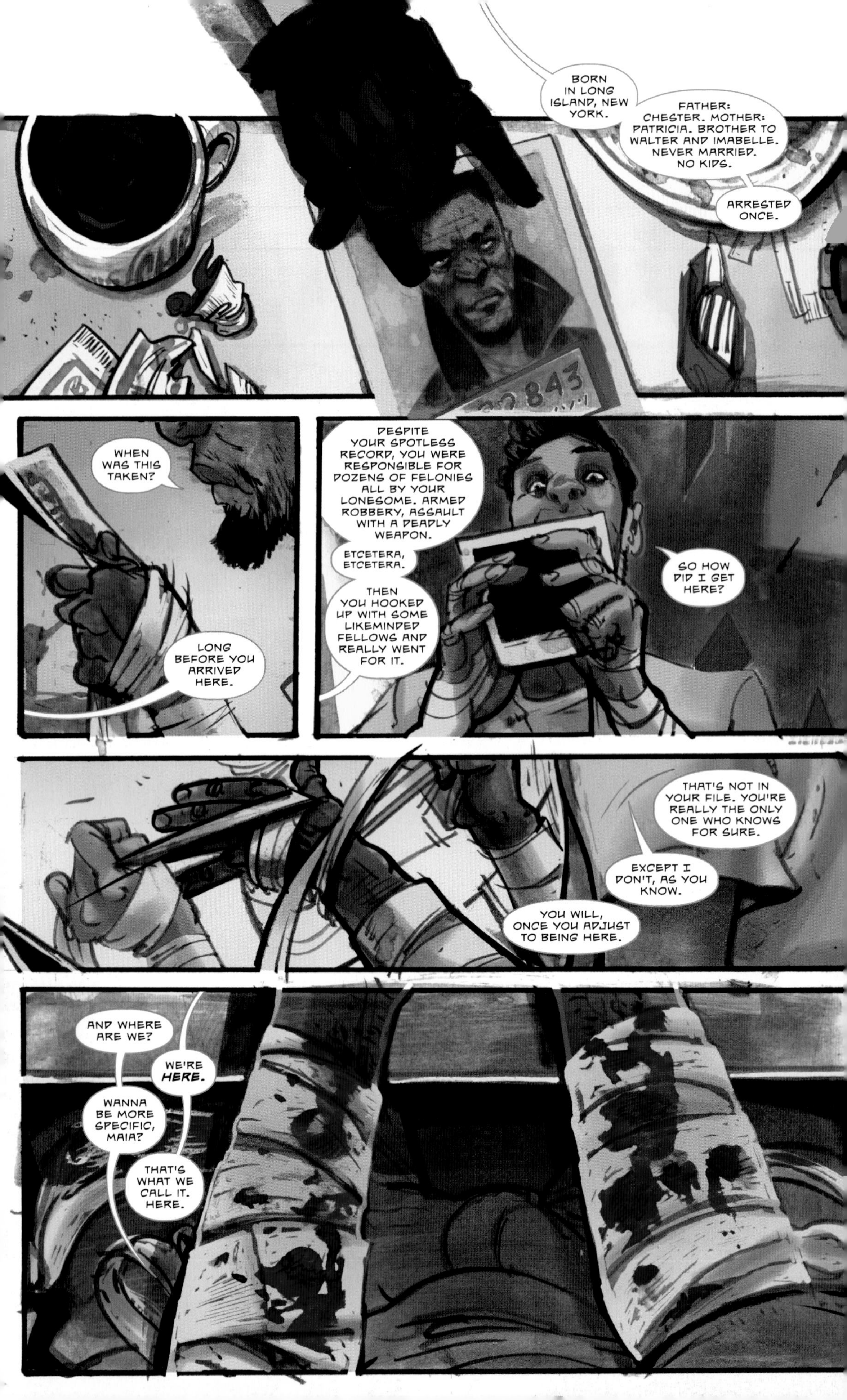
BORN IN LONG ISLAND, NEW YORK.
FATHER: CHESTER. MOTHER: PATRICIA. BROTHER TO WALTER AND IMABELLE. NEVER MARRIED. NO KIDS.
ARRESTED ONCE.
WHEN WAS THIS TAKEN?
LONG BEFORE YOU ARRIVED HERE.
DESPITE YOUR SPOTLESS RECORD, YOU WERE RESPONSIBLE FOR DOZENS OF FELONIES ALL BY YOUR LONESOME. ARMED ROBBERY, ASSAULT WITH A DEADLY WEAPON.
ETCETERA, ETCETERA.
THEN YOU HOOKED UP WITH SOME LIKEMINDED FELLOWS AND REALLY WENT FOR IT.
SO HOW DID I GET HERE?
THAT'S NOT IN YOUR FILE. YOU'RE REALLY THE ONLY ONE WHO KNOWS FOR SURE.
EXCEPT I DON'T, AS YOU KNOW.
YOU WILL, ONCE YOU ADJUST TO BEING HERE.
AND WHERE ARE WE?
WE'RE *HERE.*
WANNA BE MORE SPECIFIC, MAIA?
THAT'S WHAT WE CALL IT. HERE.

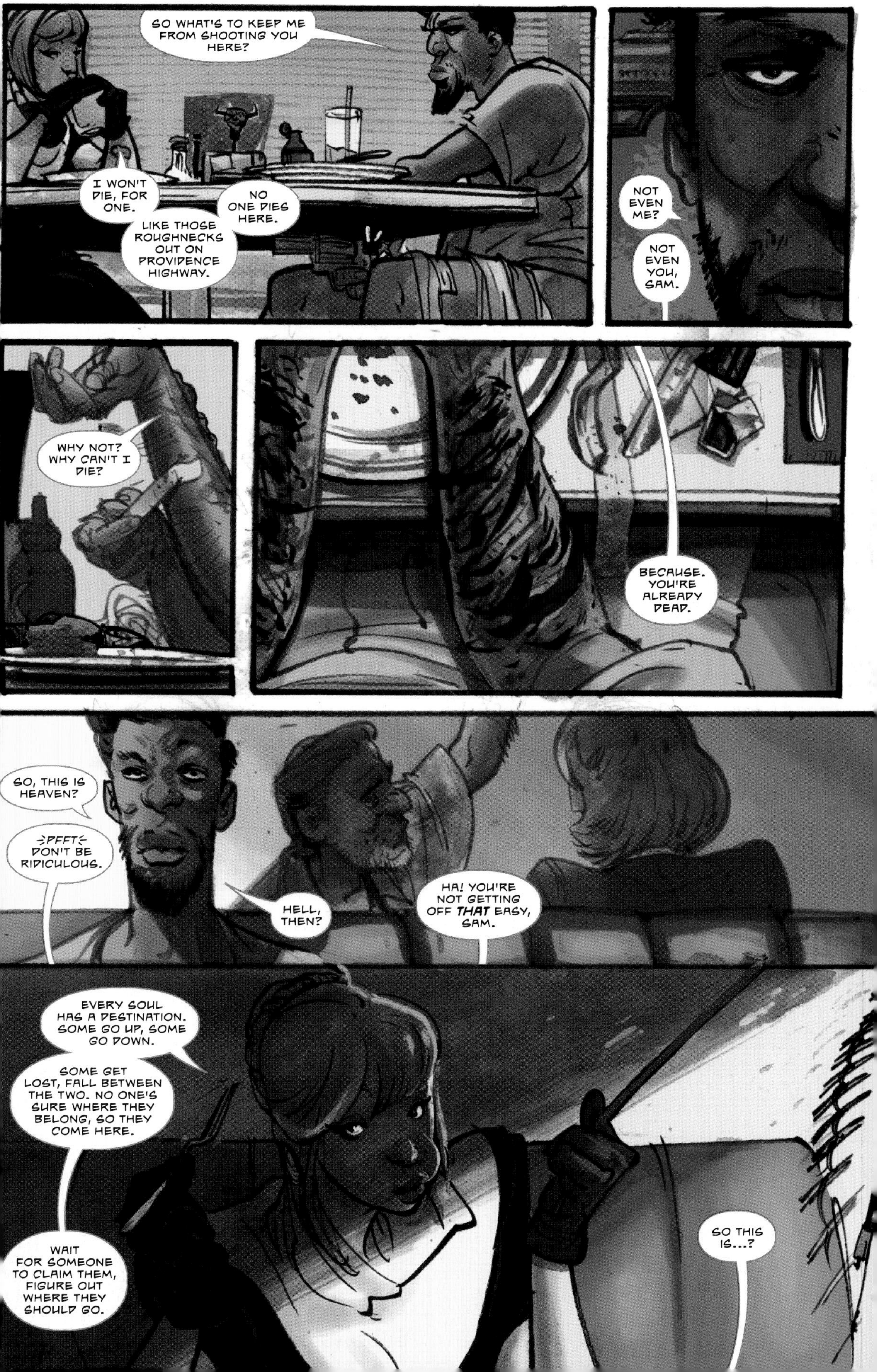
SO WHAT'S TO KEEP ME FROM SHOOTING YOU HERE?
I WON'T DIE, FOR ONE.
LIKE THOSE ROUGHNECKS OUT ON PROVIDENCE HIGHWAY.
NO ONE DIES HERE.
NOT EVEN ME?
NOT EVEN YOU, SAM.
WHY NOT? WHY CAN'T I DIE?
BECAUSE. YOU'RE ALREADY DEAD.
SO, THIS IS HEAVEN?
PFFT DON'T BE RIDICULOUS.
HELL, THEN?
HA! YOU'RE NOT GETTING OFF THAT EASY, SAM.
EVERY SOUL HAS A DESTINATION. SOME GO UP, SOME GO DOWN.
SOME GET LOST, FALL BETWEEN THE TWO. NO ONE'S SURE WHERE THEY BELONG, SO THEY COME HERE.
WAIT FOR SOMEONE TO CLAIM THEM, FIGURE OUT WHERE THEY SHOULD GO.
SO THIS IS...?

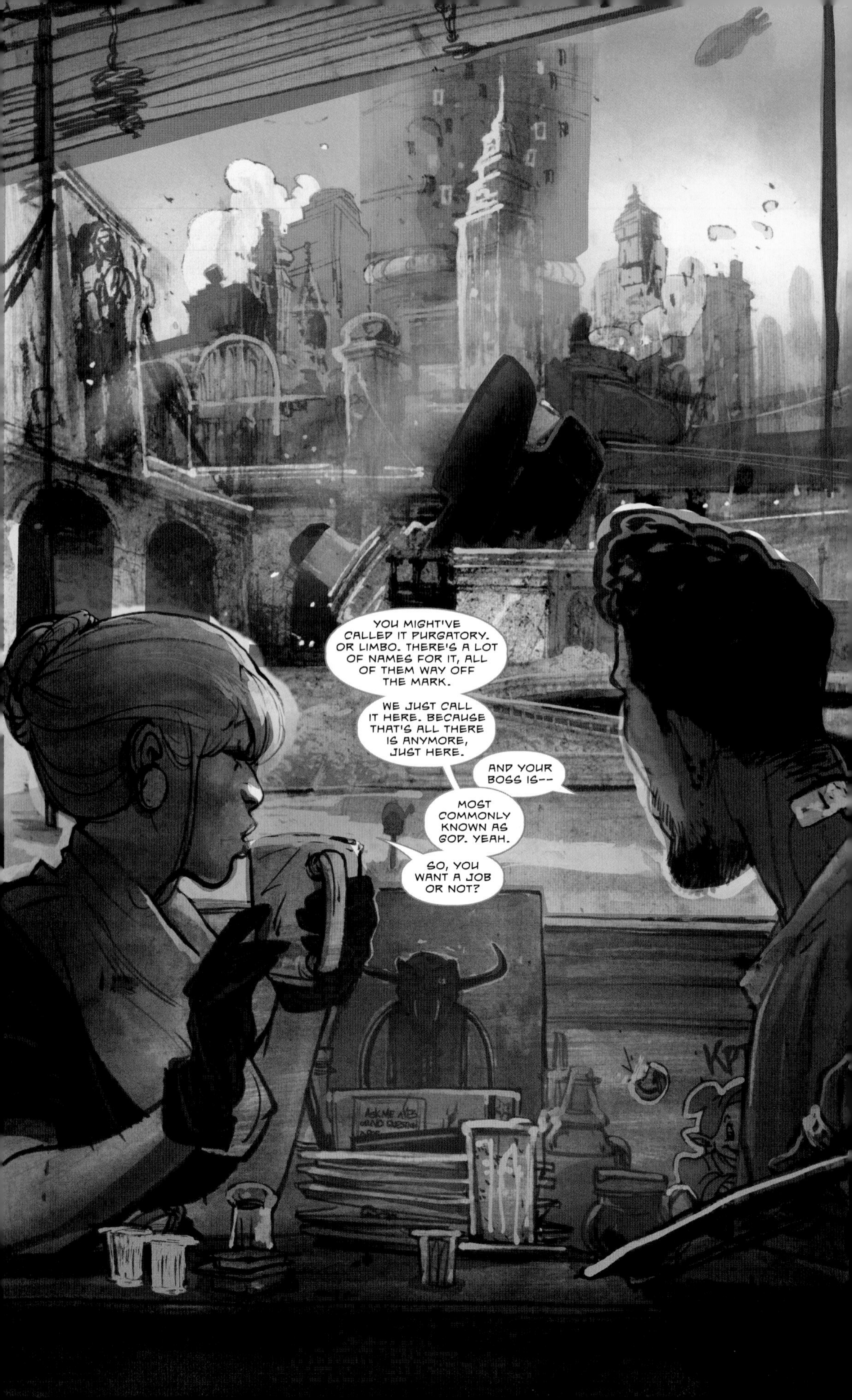
YOU MIGHT'VE CALLED IT PURGATORY. OR LIMBO. THERE'S A LOT OF NAMES FOR IT, ALL OF THEM WAY OFF THE MARK.
WE JUST CALL IT HERE. BECAUSE THAT'S ALL THERE IS ANYMORE, JUST HERE.
AND YOUR BOSS IS--
MOST COMMONLY KNOWN AS GOD. YEAH.
SO, YOU WANT A JOB OR NOT?

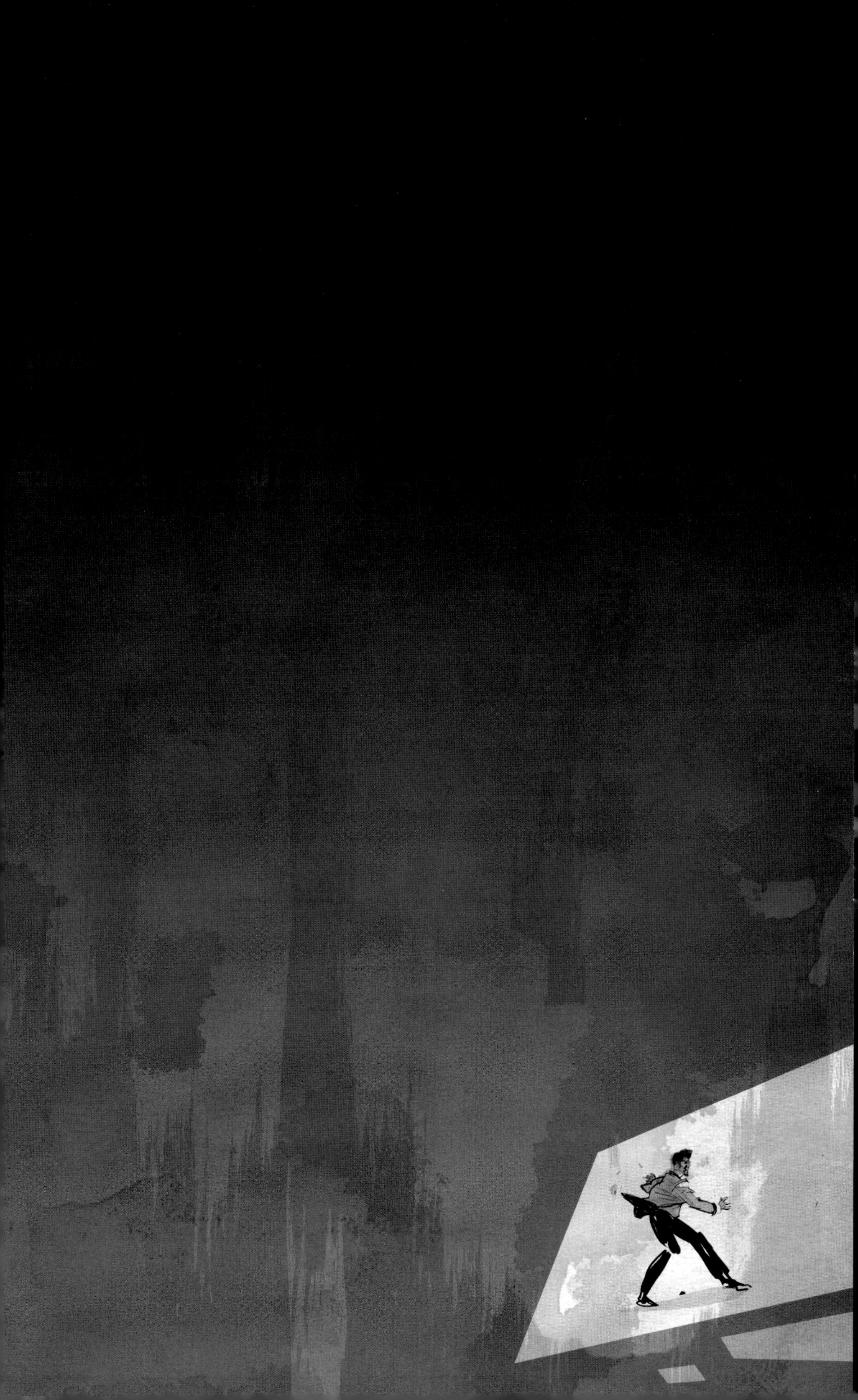

EPISODE TWO

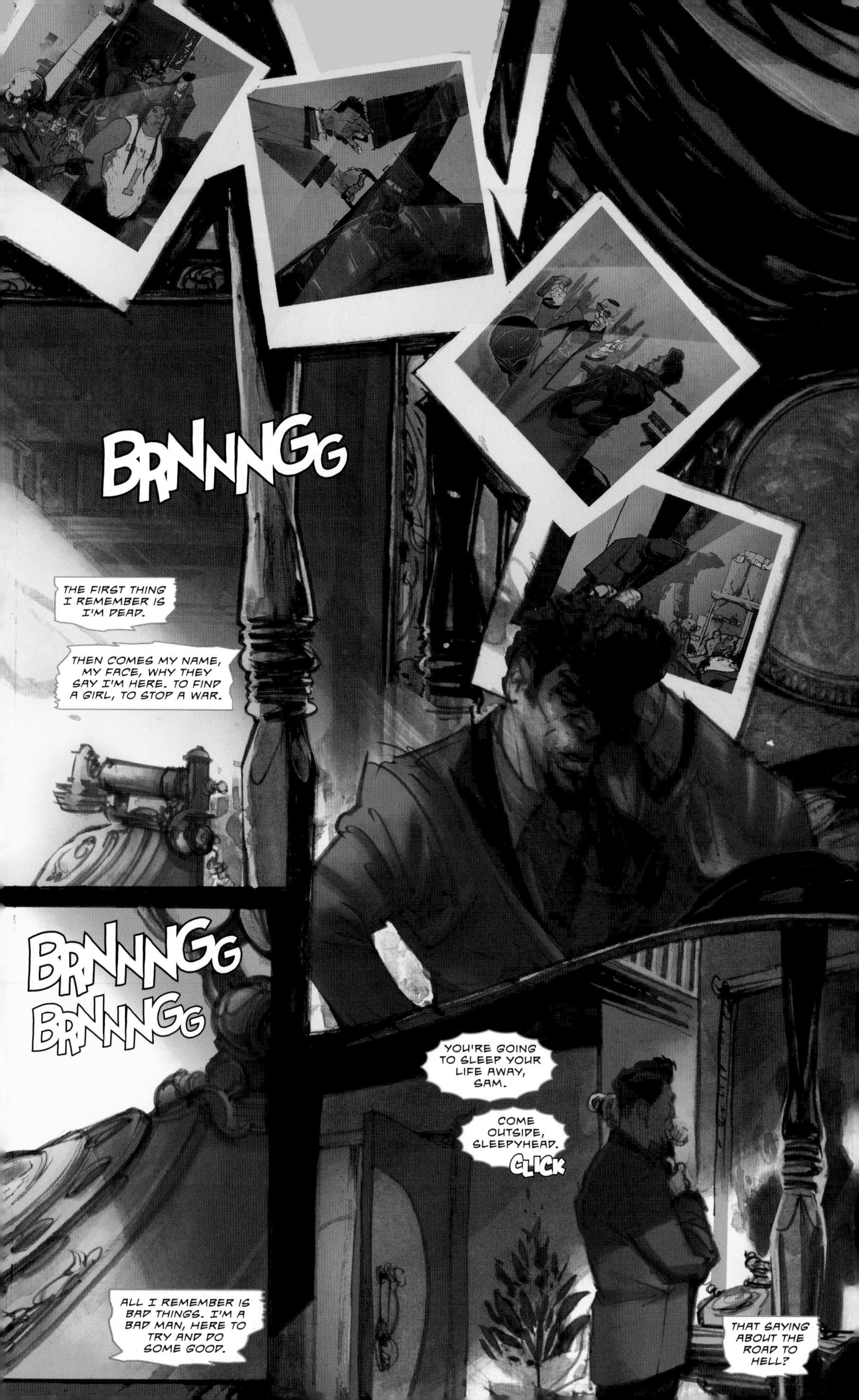
BRNNNGG
THE FIRST THING I REMEMBER IS I'M DEAD.
THEN COMES MY NAME, MY FACE, WHY THEY SAY I'M HERE. TO FIND A GIRL, TO STOP A WAR.
BRNNNGG
BRNNNGG
YOU'RE GOING TO SLEEP YOUR LIFE AWAY, SAM.
COME OUTSIDE, SLEEPYHEAD.
CLICK
ALL I REMEMBER IS BAD THINGS. I'M A BAD MAN, HERE TO TRY AND DO SOME GOOD.
THAT SAYING ABOUT THE ROAD TO HELL?

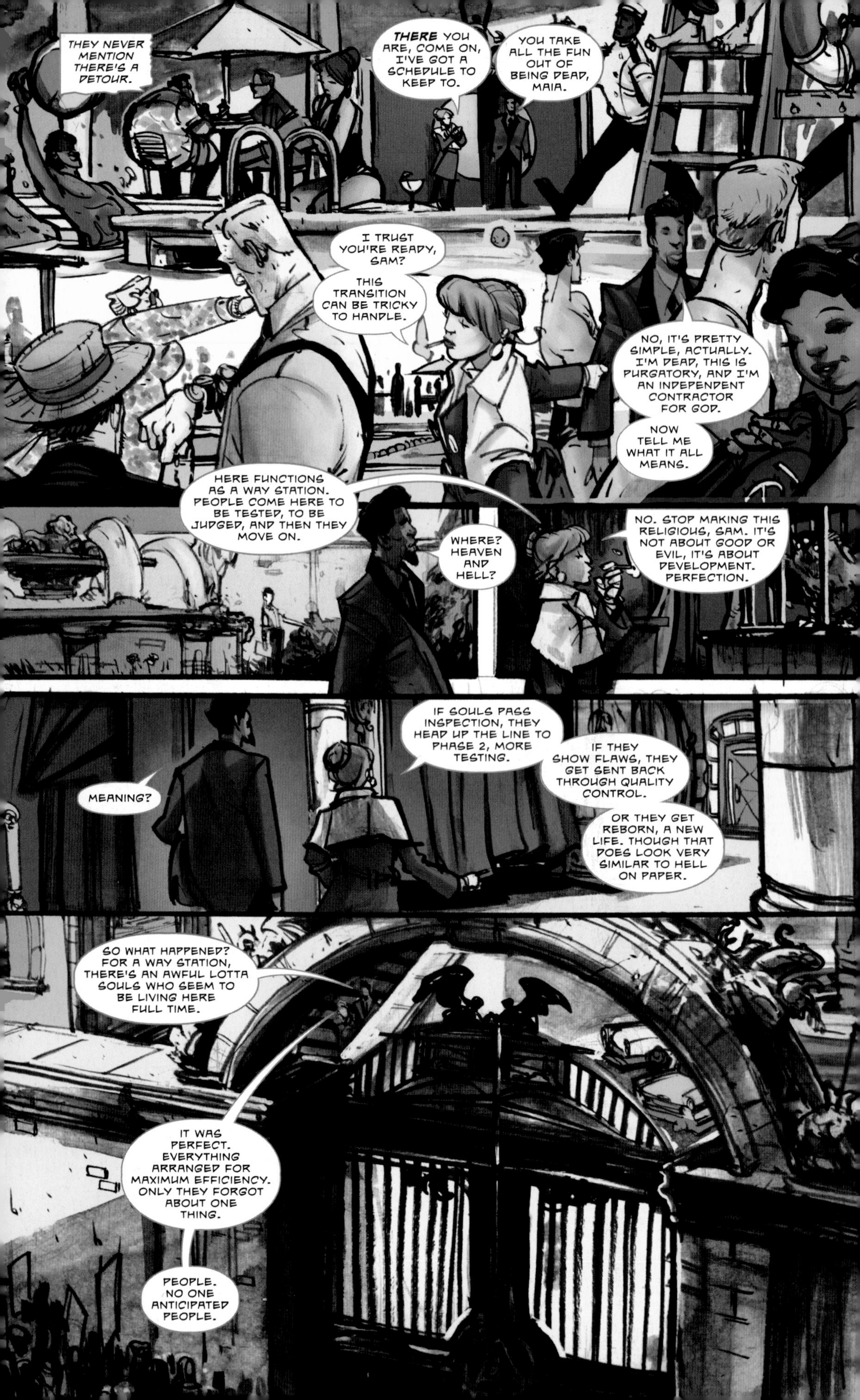
THEY NEVER MENTION THERE'S A DETOUR.
THERE YOU ARE, COME ON, I'VE GOT A SCHEDULE TO KEEP TO.
YOU TAKE ALL THE FUN OUT OF BEING DEAD, MAIA.
I TRUST YOU'RE READY, SAM?
THIS TRANSITION CAN BE TRICKY TO HANDLE.
NO, IT'S PRETTY SIMPLE, ACTUALLY. I'M DEAD, THIS IS PURGATORY, AND I'M AN INDEPENDENT CONTRACTOR FOR GOD.
NOW TELL ME WHAT IT ALL MEANS.
HERE FUNCTIONS AS A WAY STATION. PEOPLE COME HERE TO BE TESTED, TO BE JUDGED, AND THEN THEY MOVE ON.
WHERE? HEAVEN AND HELL?
NO. STOP MAKING THIS RELIGIOUS, SAM. IT'S NOT ABOUT GOOD OR EVIL, IT'S ABOUT DEVELOPMENT. PERFECTION.
MEANING?
IF SOULS PASS INSPECTION, THEY HEAD UP THE LINE TO PHASE 2, MORE TESTING.
IF THEY SHOW FLAWS, THEY GET SENT BACK THROUGH QUALITY CONTROL.
OR THEY GET REBORN, A NEW LIFE. THOUGH THAT DOES LOOK VERY SIMILAR TO HELL ON PAPER.
SO WHAT HAPPENED? FOR A WAY STATION, THERE'S AN AWFUL LOTTA SOULS WHO SEEM TO BE LIVING HERE FULL TIME.
IT WAS PERFECT. EVERYTHING ARRANGED FOR MAXIMUM EFFICIENCY. ONLY THEY FORGOT ABOUT ONE THING.
PEOPLE. NO ONE ANTICIPATED PEOPLE.

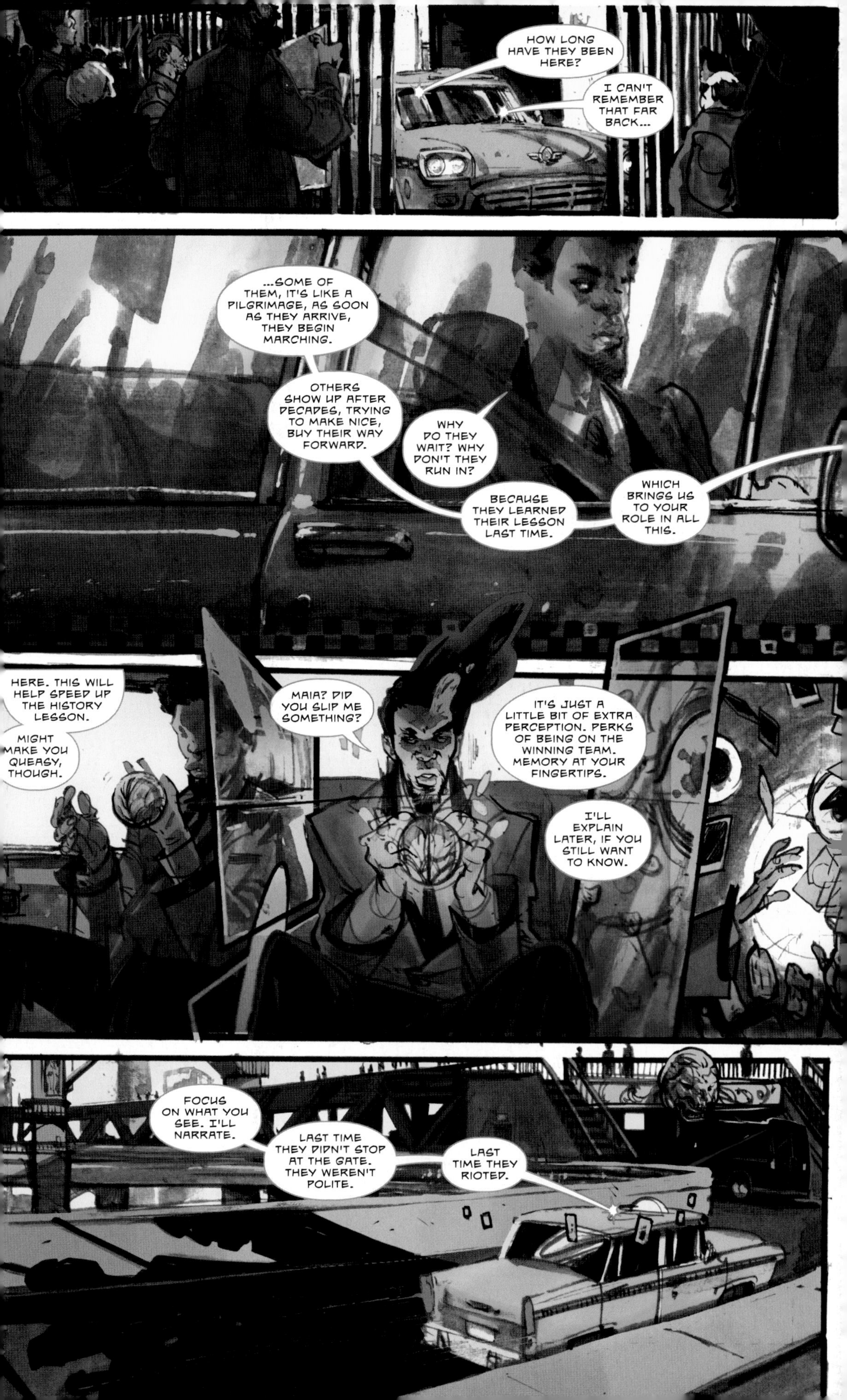
HOW LONG HAVE THEY BEEN HERE?
I CAN'T REMEMBER THAT FAR BACK...
...SOME OF THEM, IT'S LIKE A PILGRIMAGE, AS SOON AS THEY ARRIVE, THEY BEGIN MARCHING.
OTHERS SHOW UP AFTER DECADES, TRYING TO MAKE NICE, BUY THEIR WAY FORWARD.
WHY DO THEY WAIT? WHY DON'T THEY RUN IN?
BECAUSE THEY LEARNED THEIR LESSON LAST TIME.
WHICH BRINGS US TO YOUR ROLE IN ALL THIS.
HERE. THIS WILL HELP SPEED UP THE HISTORY LESSON.
MIGHT MAKE YOU QUEASY, THOUGH.
MAIA? DID YOU SLIP ME SOMETHING?
IT'S JUST A LITTLE BIT OF EXTRA PERCEPTION. PERKS OF BEING ON THE WINNING TEAM. MEMORY AT YOUR FINGERTIPS.
I'LL EXPLAIN LATER, IF YOU STILL WANT TO KNOW.
FOCUS ON WHAT YOU SEE. I'LL NARRATE.
LAST TIME THEY DIDN'T STOP AT THE GATE. THEY WEREN'T POLITE.
LAST TIME THEY RIOTED.

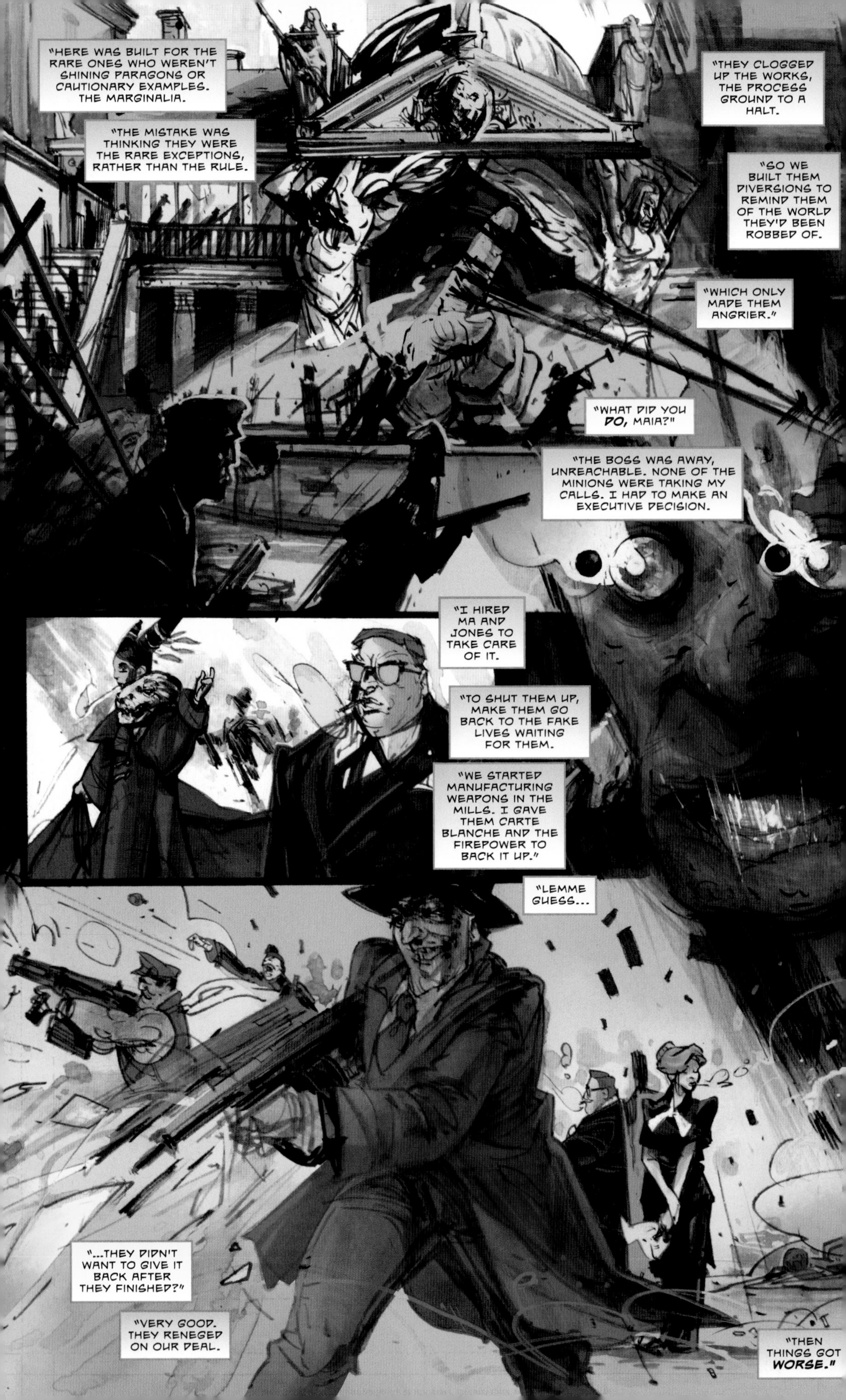

"HERE WAS BUILT FOR THE RARE ONES WHO WEREN'T SHINING PARAGONS OR CAUTIONARY EXAMPLES. THE MARGINALIA.
"THE MISTAKE WAS THINKING THEY WERE THE RARE EXCEPTIONS, RATHER THAN THE RULE.
"THEY CLOGGED UP THE WORKS, THE PROCESS GROUND TO A HALT.
"SO WE BUILT THEM DIVERSIONS TO REMIND THEM OF THE WORLD THEY'D BEEN ROBBED OF.
"WHICH ONLY MADE THEM ANGRIER."
"WHAT DID YOU DO, MAIA?"
"THE BOSS WAS AWAY, UNREACHABLE. NONE OF THE MINIONS WERE TAKING MY CALLS. I HAD TO MAKE AN EXECUTIVE DECISION.
"I HIRED MA AND JONES TO TAKE CARE OF IT.
"TO SHUT THEM UP, MAKE THEM GO BACK TO THE FAKE LIVES WAITING FOR THEM.
"WE STARTED MANUFACTURING WEAPONS IN THE MILLS. I GAVE THEM CARTE BLANCHE AND THE FIREPOWER TO BACK IT UP."
"LEMME GUESS...
"...THEY DIDN'T WANT TO GIVE IT BACK AFTER THEY FINISHED?"
"VERY GOOD. THEY RENEGED ON OUR DEAL.
"THEN THINGS GOT WORSE."

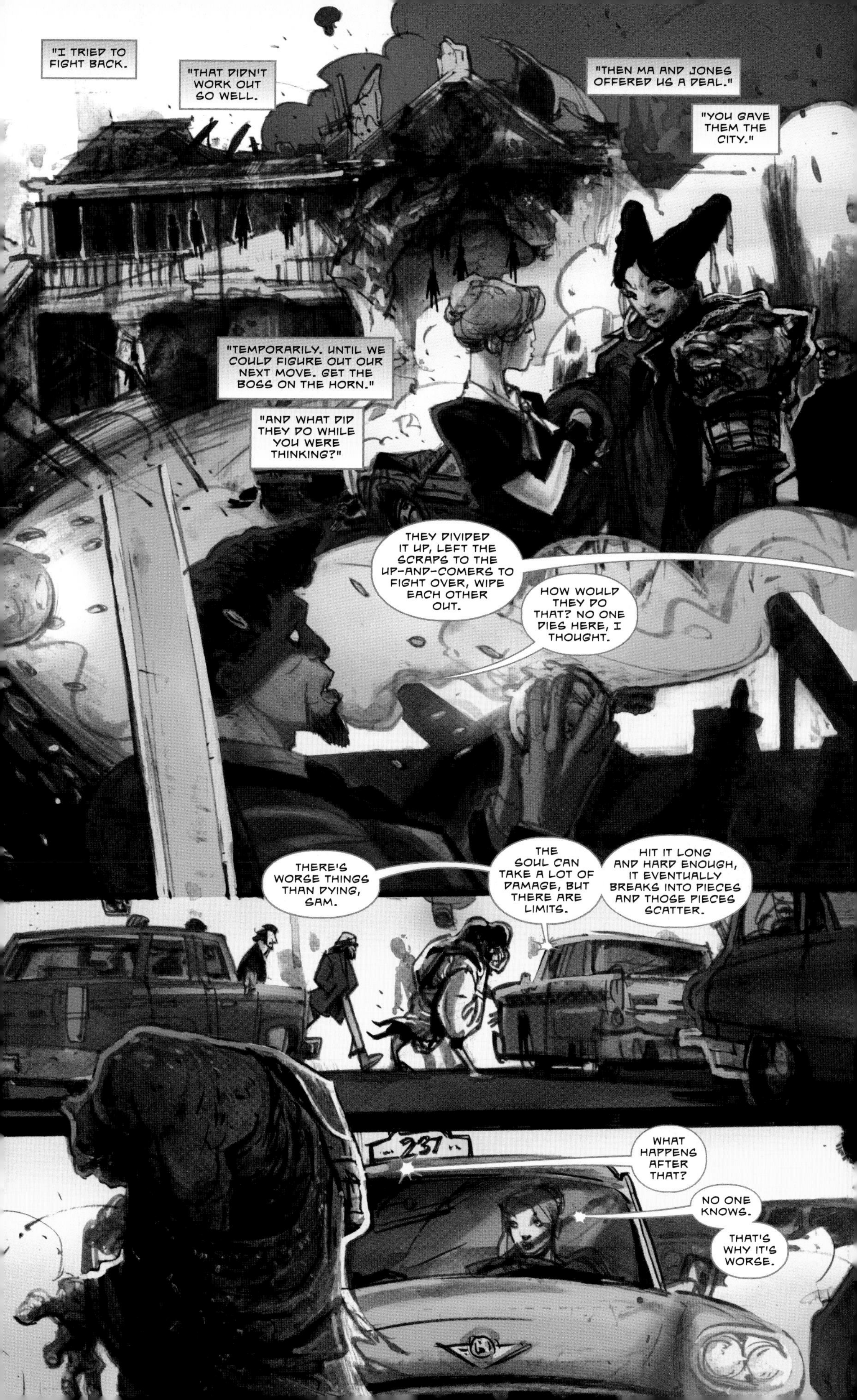
"I TRIED TO FIGHT BACK.
"THAT DIDN'T WORK OUT SO WELL.
"THEN MA AND JONES OFFERED US A DEAL."
"YOU GAVE THEM THE CITY."
"TEMPORARILY. UNTIL WE COULD FIGURE OUT OUR NEXT MOVE. GET THE BOSS ON THE HORN."
"AND WHAT DID THEY DO WHILE YOU WERE THINKING?"
THEY DIVIDED IT UP, LEFT THE SCRAPS TO THE UP-AND-COMERS TO FIGHT OVER, WIPE EACH OTHER OUT.
HOW WOULD THEY DO THAT? NO ONE DIES HERE, I THOUGHT.
THERE'S WORSE THINGS THAN DYING, SAM.
THE SOUL CAN TAKE A LOT OF DAMAGE, BUT THERE ARE LIMITS.
HIT IT LONG AND HARD ENOUGH, IT EVENTUALLY BREAKS INTO PIECES AND THOSE PIECES SCATTER.
WHAT HAPPENS AFTER THAT?
NO ONE KNOWS.
THAT'S WHY IT'S WORSE.

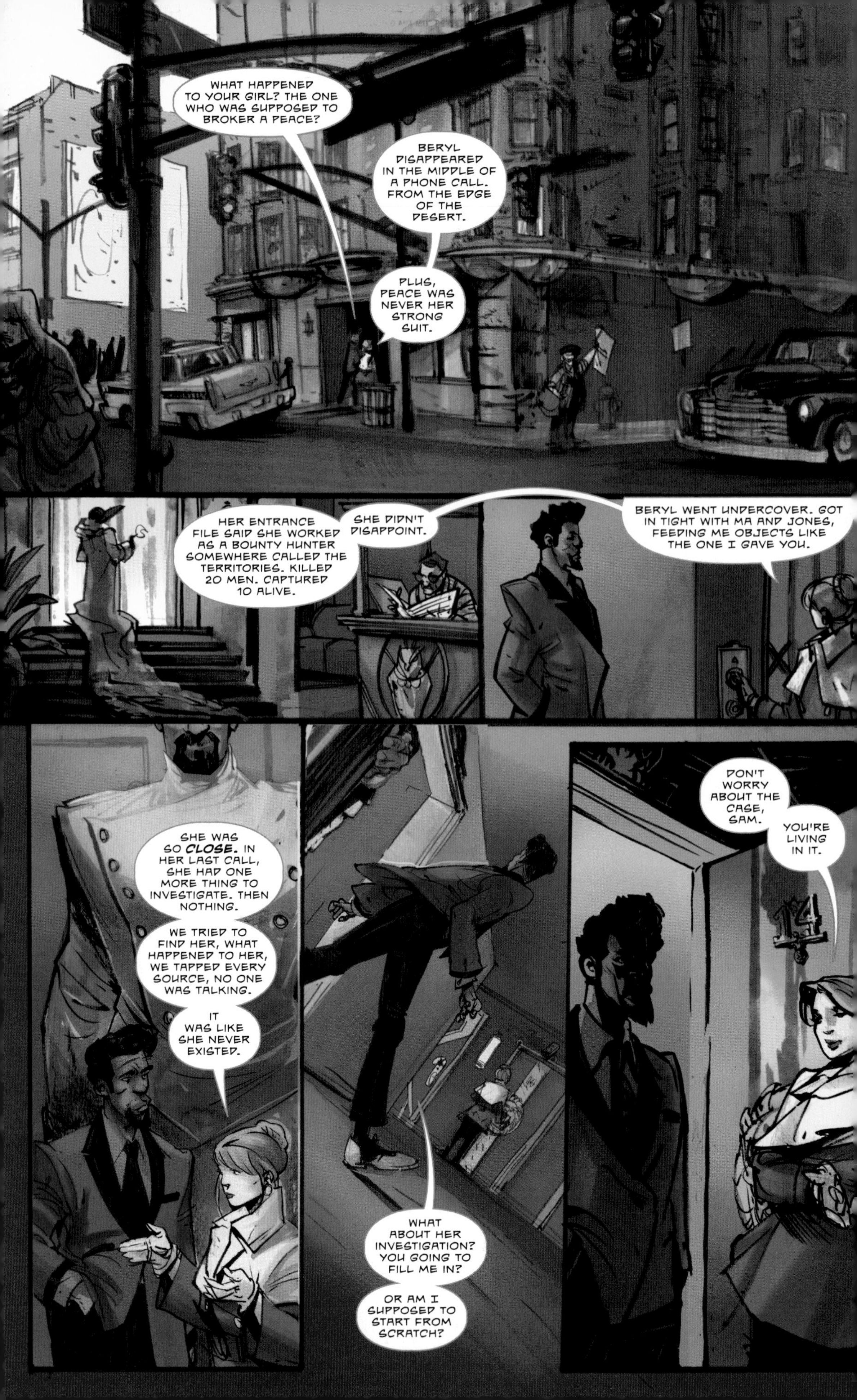
WHAT HAPPENED TO YOUR GIRL? THE ONE WHO WAS SUPPOSED TO BROKER A PEACE?
BERYL DISAPPEARED IN THE MIDDLE OF A PHONE CALL. FROM THE EDGE OF THE DESERT.
PLUS, PEACE WAS NEVER HER STRONG SUIT.
HER ENTRANCE FILE SAID SHE WORKED AS A BOUNTY HUNTER SOMEWHERE CALLED THE TERRITORIES. KILLED 20 MEN. CAPTURED 10 ALIVE.
SHE DIDN'T DISAPPOINT.
BERYL WENT UNDERCOVER. GOT IN TIGHT WITH MA AND JONES, FEEDING ME OBJECTS LIKE THE ONE I GAVE YOU.
SHE WAS SO **CLOSE.** IN HER LAST CALL, SHE HAD ONE MORE THING TO INVESTIGATE. THEN NOTHING.
WE TRIED TO FIND HER, WHAT HAPPENED TO HER, WE TAPPED EVERY SOURCE, NO ONE WAS TALKING.
IT WAS LIKE SHE NEVER EXISTED.
WHAT ABOUT HER INVESTIGATION? YOU GOING TO FILL ME IN?
OR AM I SUPPOSED TO START FROM SCRATCH?
DON'T WORRY ABOUT THE CASE, SAM.
YOU'RE LIVING IN IT.
14

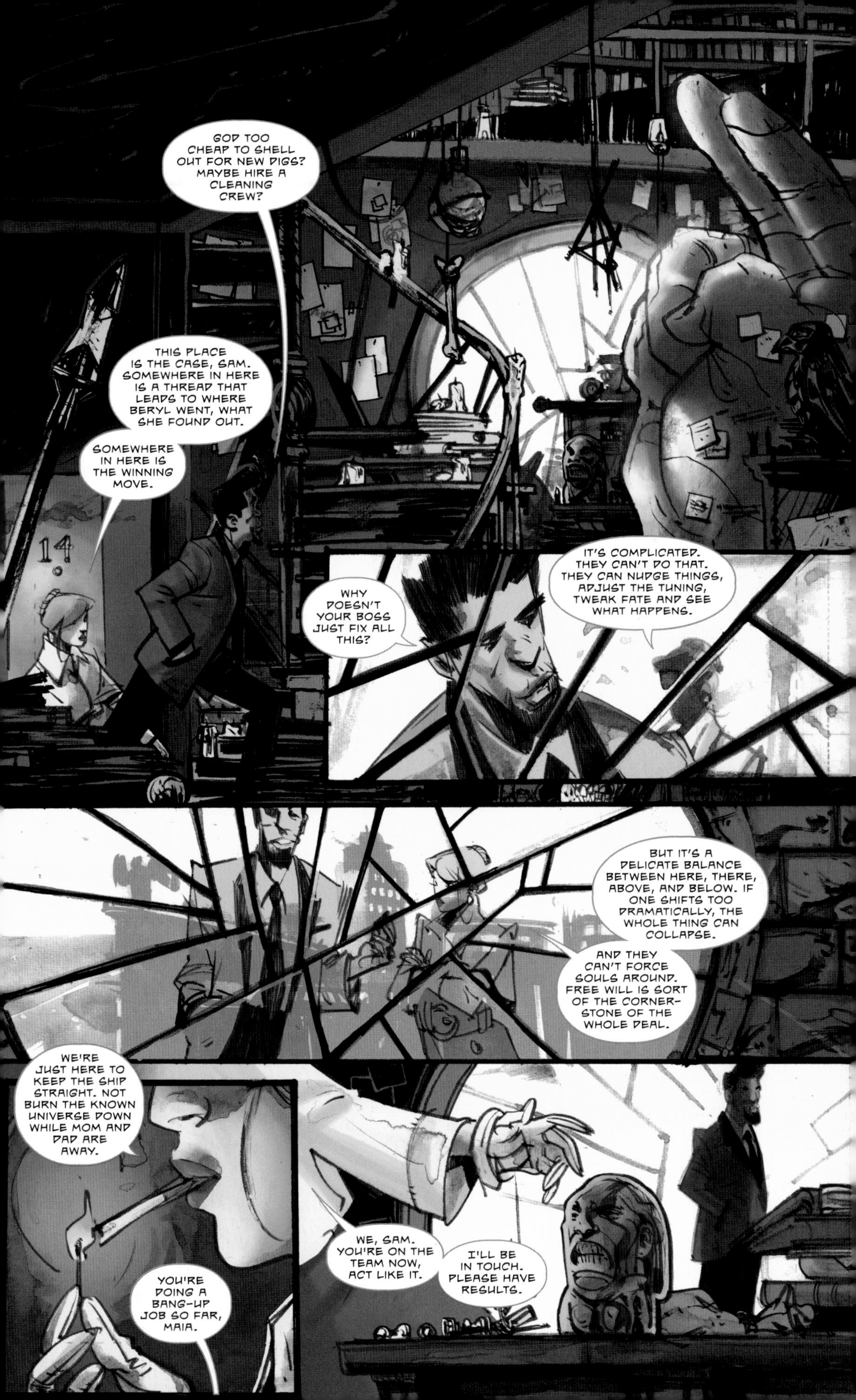
GOD TOO CHEAP TO SHELL OUT FOR NEW DIGS? MAYBE HIRE A CLEANING CREW?
THIS PLACE IS THE CASE, SAM. SOMEWHERE IN HERE IS A THREAD THAT LEADS TO WHERE BERYL WENT, WHAT SHE FOUND OUT.
SOMEWHERE IN HERE IS THE WINNING MOVE.
14
WHY DOESN'T YOUR BOSS JUST FIX ALL THIS?
IT'S COMPLICATED. THEY CAN'T DO THAT. THEY CAN NUDGE THINGS, ADJUST THE TUNING, TWEAK FATE AND SEE WHAT HAPPENS.
BUT IT'S A DELICATE BALANCE BETWEEN HERE, THERE, ABOVE, AND BELOW. IF ONE SHIFTS TOO DRAMATICALLY, THE WHOLE THING CAN COLLAPSE.
AND THEY CAN'T FORCE SOULS AROUND. FREE WILL IS SORT OF THE CORNER-STONE OF THE WHOLE DEAL.
WE'RE JUST HERE TO KEEP THE SHIP STRAIGHT. NOT BURN THE KNOWN UNIVERSE DOWN WHILE MOM AND DAD ARE AWAY.
YOU'RE DOING A BANG-UP JOB SO FAR, MAIA.
WE, SAM. YOU'RE ON THE TEAM NOW, ACT LIKE IT.
I'LL BE IN TOUCH. PLEASE HAVE RESULTS.

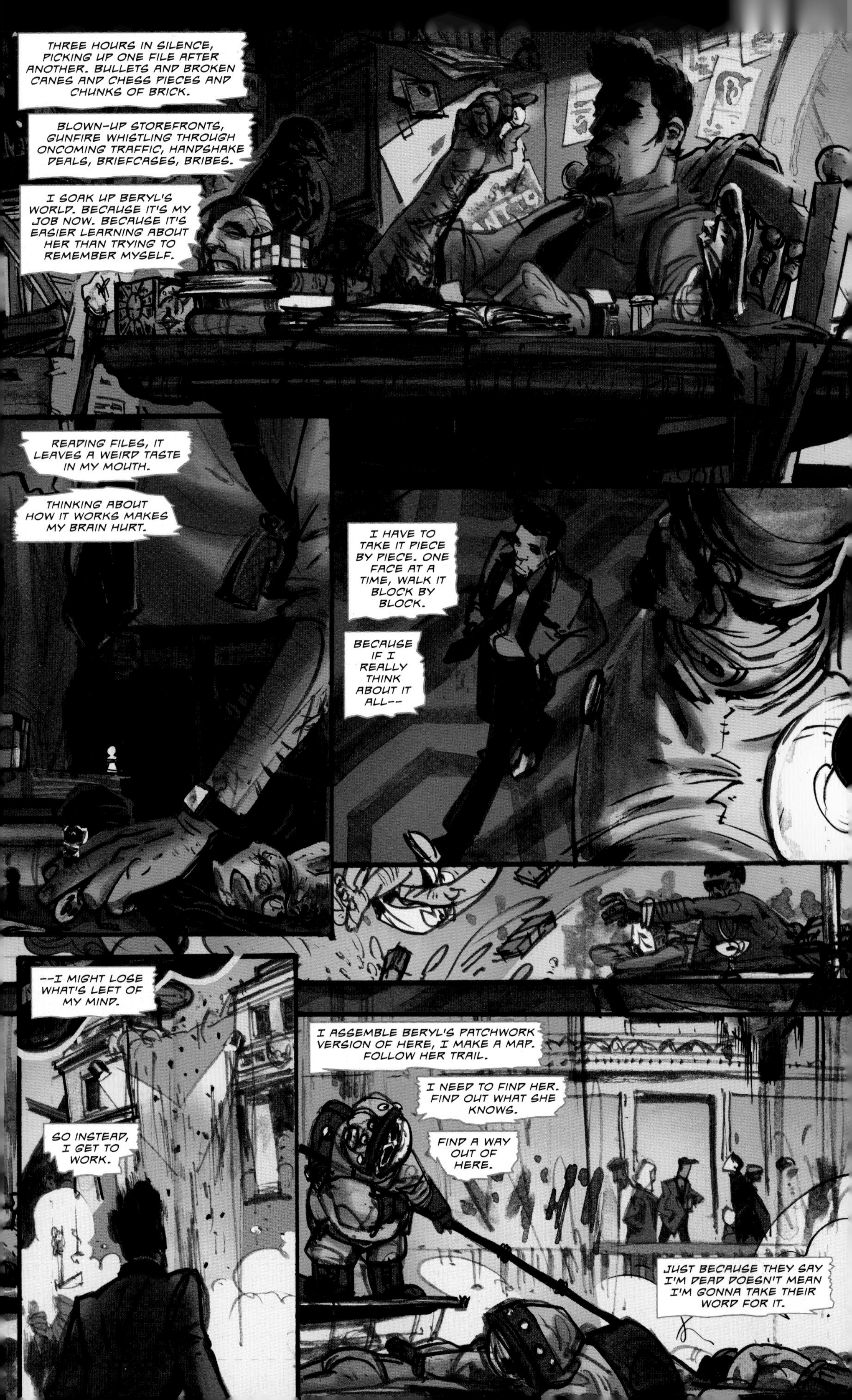
THREE HOURS IN SILENCE, PICKING UP ONE FILE AFTER ANOTHER. BULLETS AND BROKEN CANES AND CHESS PIECES AND CHUNKS OF BRICK.
BLOWN-UP STOREFRONTS, GUNFIRE WHISTLING THROUGH ONCOMING TRAFFIC, HANDSHAKE DEALS, BRIEFCASES, BRIBES.
I SOAK UP BERYL'S WORLD. BECAUSE IT'S MY JOB NOW. BECAUSE IT'S EASIER LEARNING ABOUT HER THAN TRYING TO REMEMBER MYSELF.
READING FILES, IT LEAVES A WEIRD TASTE IN MY MOUTH.
THINKING ABOUT HOW IT WORKS MAKES MY BRAIN HURT.
I HAVE TO TAKE IT PIECE BY PIECE. ONE FACE AT A TIME, WALK IT BLOCK BY BLOCK.
BECAUSE IF I REALLY THINK ABOUT IT ALL--
--I MIGHT LOSE WHAT'S LEFT OF MY MIND.
SO INSTEAD, I GET TO WORK.
I ASSEMBLE BERYL'S PATCHWORK VERSION OF HERE, I MAKE A MAP. FOLLOW HER TRAIL.
I NEED TO FIND HER. FIND OUT WHAT SHE KNOWS.
FIND A WAY OUT OF HERE.
JUST BECAUSE THEY SAY I'M DEAD DOESN'T MEAN I'M GONNA TAKE THEIR WORD FOR IT.

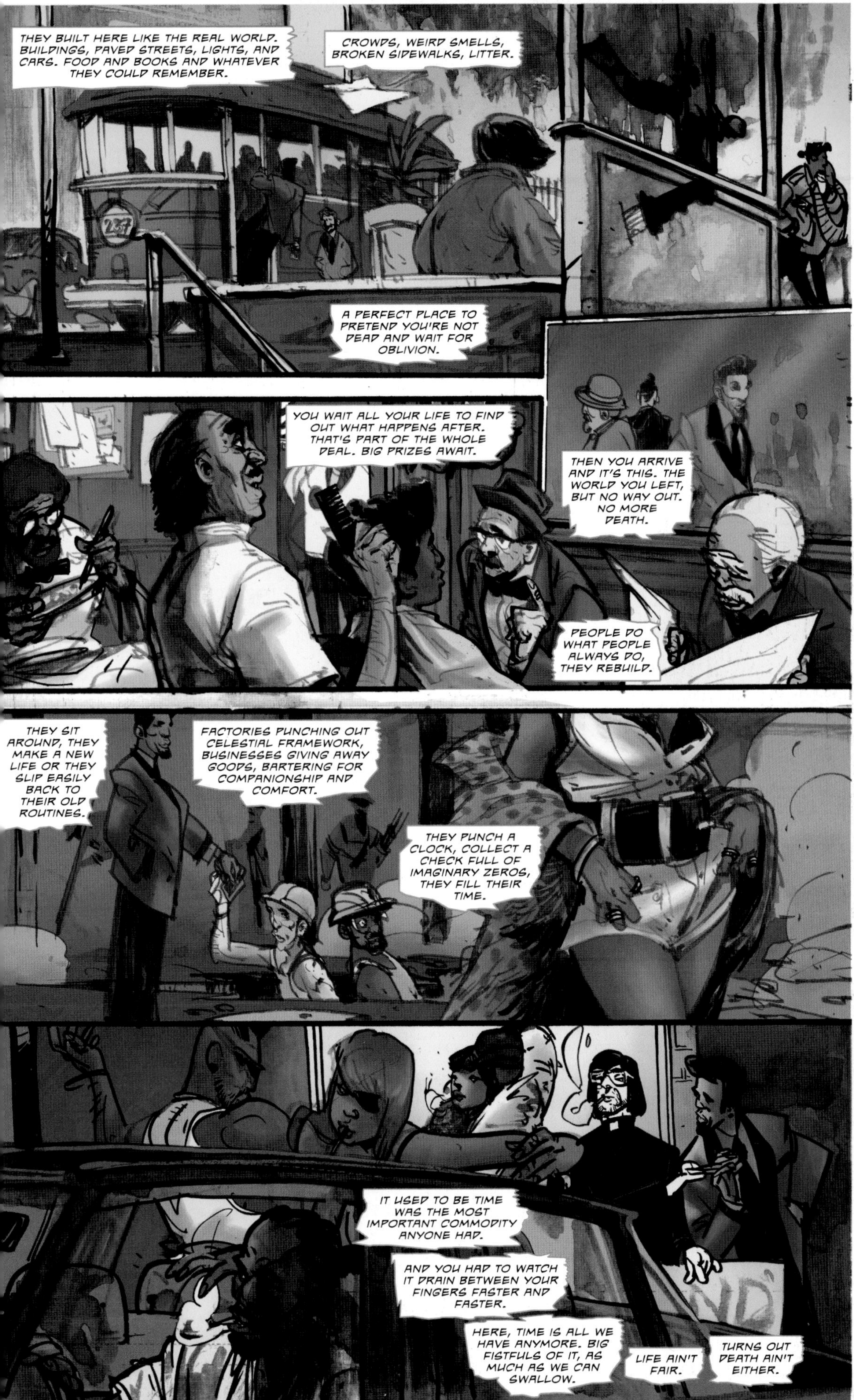
THEY BUILT HERE LIKE THE REAL WORLD. BUILDINGS, PAVED STREETS, LIGHTS, AND CARS. FOOD AND BOOKS AND WHATEVER THEY COULD REMEMBER.
CROWDS, WEIRD SMELLS, BROKEN SIDEWALKS, LITTER.
A PERFECT PLACE TO PRETEND YOU'RE NOT DEAD AND WAIT FOR OBLIVION.
YOU WAIT ALL YOUR LIFE TO FIND OUT WHAT HAPPENS AFTER. THAT'S PART OF THE WHOLE DEAL. BIG PRIZES AWAIT.
THEN YOU ARRIVE AND IT'S THIS. THE WORLD YOU LEFT, BUT NO WAY OUT. NO MORE DEATH.
PEOPLE DO WHAT PEOPLE ALWAYS DO, THEY REBUILD.
THEY SIT AROUND, THEY MAKE A NEW LIFE OR THEY SLIP EASILY BACK TO THEIR OLD ROUTINES.
FACTORIES PUNCHING OUT CELESTIAL FRAMEWORK, BUSINESSES GIVING AWAY GOODS, BARTERING FOR COMPANIONSHIP AND COMFORT.
THEY PUNCH A CLOCK, COLLECT A CHECK FULL OF IMAGINARY ZEROS, THEY FILL THEIR TIME.
IT USED TO BE TIME WAS THE MOST IMPORTANT COMMODITY ANYONE HAD.
AND YOU HAD TO WATCH IT DRAIN BETWEEN YOUR FINGERS FASTER AND FASTER.
HERE, TIME IS ALL WE HAVE ANYMORE. BIG FISTFULS OF IT, AS MUCH AS WE CAN SWALLOW.
LIFE AIN'T FAIR.
TURNS OUT DEATH AIN'T EITHER.

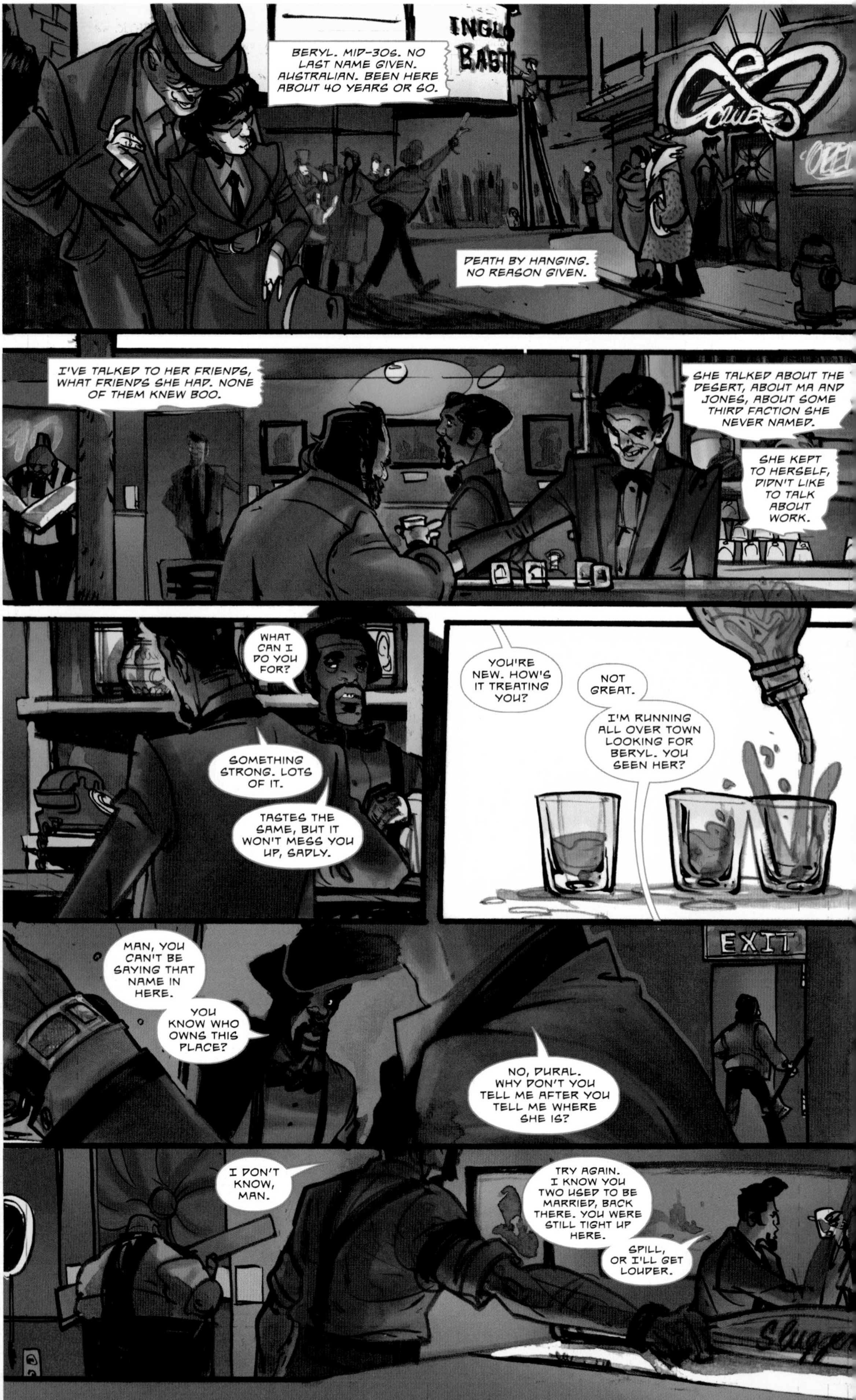
BERYL. MID-30s. NO LAST NAME GIVEN. AUSTRALIAN. BEEN HERE ABOUT 40 YEARS OR SO.
DEATH BY HANGING. NO REASON GIVEN.
I'VE TALKED TO HER FRIENDS, WHAT FRIENDS SHE HAD. NONE OF THEM KNEW BOO.
SHE TALKED ABOUT THE DESERT, ABOUT MA AND JONES, ABOUT SOME THIRD FACTION SHE NEVER NAMED.
SHE KEPT TO HERSELF, DIDN'T LIKE TO TALK ABOUT WORK.
WHAT CAN I DO YOU FOR?
SOMETHING STRONG. LOTS OF IT.
TASTES THE SAME, BUT IT WON'T MESS YOU UP, SADLY.
YOU'RE NEW. HOW'S IT TREATING YOU?
NOT GREAT.
I'M RUNNING ALL OVER TOWN LOOKING FOR BERYL. YOU SEEN HER?
MAN, YOU CAN'T BE SAYING THAT NAME IN HERE.
YOU KNOW WHO OWNS THIS PLACE?
NO, DURAL. WHY DON'T YOU TELL ME AFTER YOU TELL ME WHERE SHE IS?
EXIT
I DON'T KNOW, MAN.
TRY AGAIN. I KNOW YOU TWO USED TO BE MARRIED, BACK THERE. YOU WERE STILL TIGHT UP HERE.
SPILL, OR I'LL GET LOUDER.

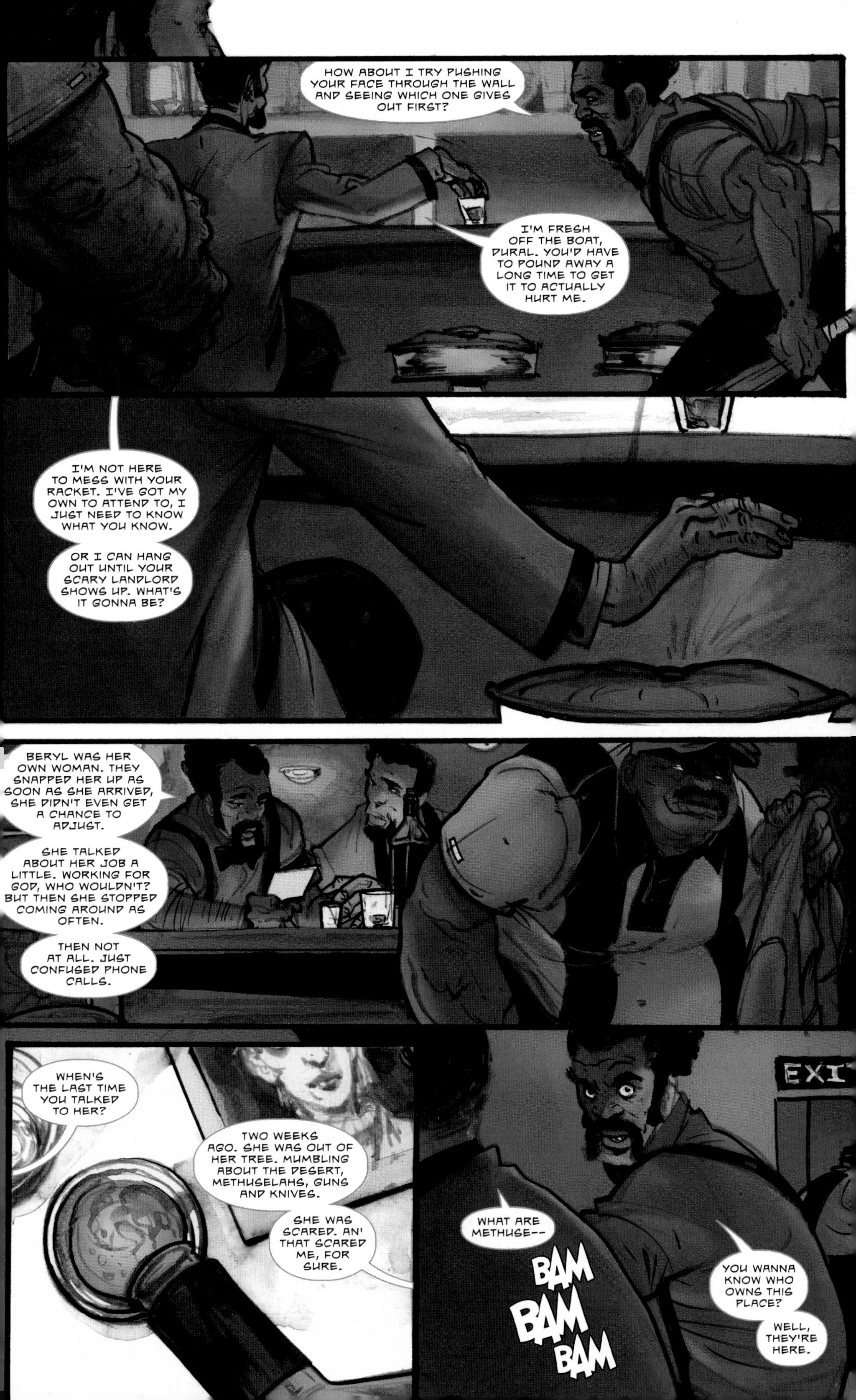
HOW ABOUT I TRY PUSHING YOUR FACE THROUGH THE WALL AND SEEING WHICH ONE GIVES OUT FIRST?
I'M FRESH OFF THE BOAT, DURAL. YOU'D HAVE TO POUND AWAY A LONG TIME TO GET IT TO ACTUALLY HURT ME.
I'M NOT HERE TO MESS WITH YOUR RACKET. I'VE GOT MY OWN TO ATTEND TO, I JUST NEED TO KNOW WHAT YOU KNOW.
OR I CAN HANG OUT UNTIL YOUR SCARY LANDLORD SHOWS UP. WHAT'S IT GONNA BE?
BERYL WAS HER OWN WOMAN. THEY SNAPPED HER UP AS SOON AS SHE ARRIVED, SHE DIDN'T EVEN GET A CHANCE TO ADJUST.
SHE TALKED ABOUT HER JOB A LITTLE. WORKING FOR GOD, WHO WOULDN'T? BUT THEN SHE STOPPED COMING AROUND AS OFTEN.
THEN NOT AT ALL. JUST CONFUSED PHONE CALLS.
WHEN'S THE LAST TIME YOU TALKED TO HER?
TWO WEEKS AGO. SHE WAS OUT OF HER TREE. MUMBLING ABOUT THE DESERT, METHUSELAHS, GUNS AND KNIVES.
SHE WAS SCARED. AN' THAT SCARED ME, FOR SURE.
EXIT
WHAT ARE METHUSE--
BAM
BAM
BAM
YOU WANNA KNOW WHO OWNS THIS PLACE?
WELL, THEY'RE HERE.

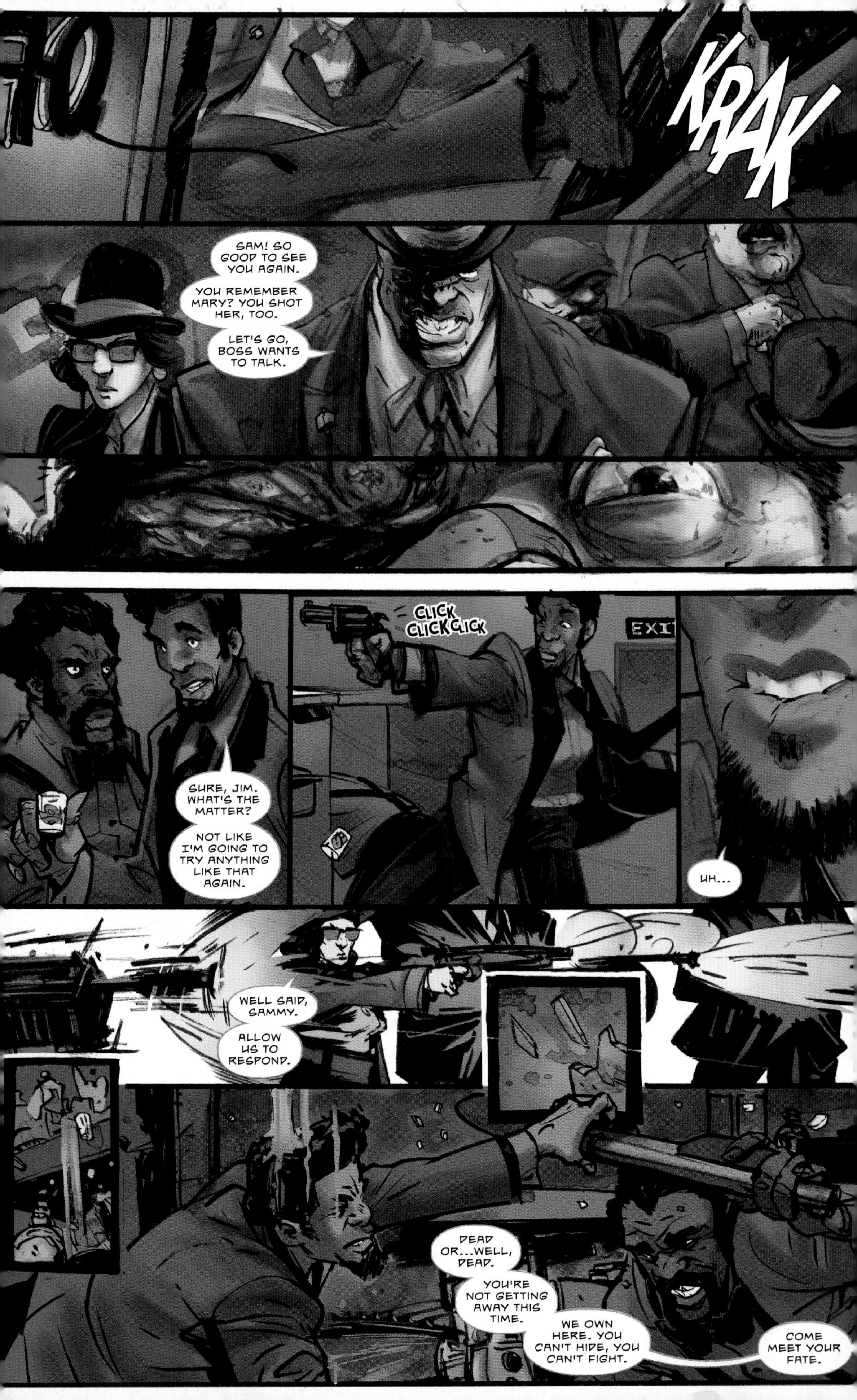
KRAK
SAM! SO GOOD TO SEE YOU AGAIN.
YOU REMEMBER MARY? YOU SHOT HER, TOO.
LET'S GO, BOSS WANTS TO TALK.
SURE, JIM. WHAT'S THE MATTER?
NOT LIKE I'M GOING TO TRY ANYTHING LIKE THAT AGAIN.
CLICK CLICK CLICK
EXIT
UH...
WELL SAID, SAMMY.
ALLOW US TO RESPOND.
DEAD OR...WELL, DEAD.
YOU'RE NOT GETTING AWAY THIS TIME.
WE OWN HERE. YOU CAN'T HIDE, YOU CAN'T FIGHT.
COME MEET YOUR FATE.

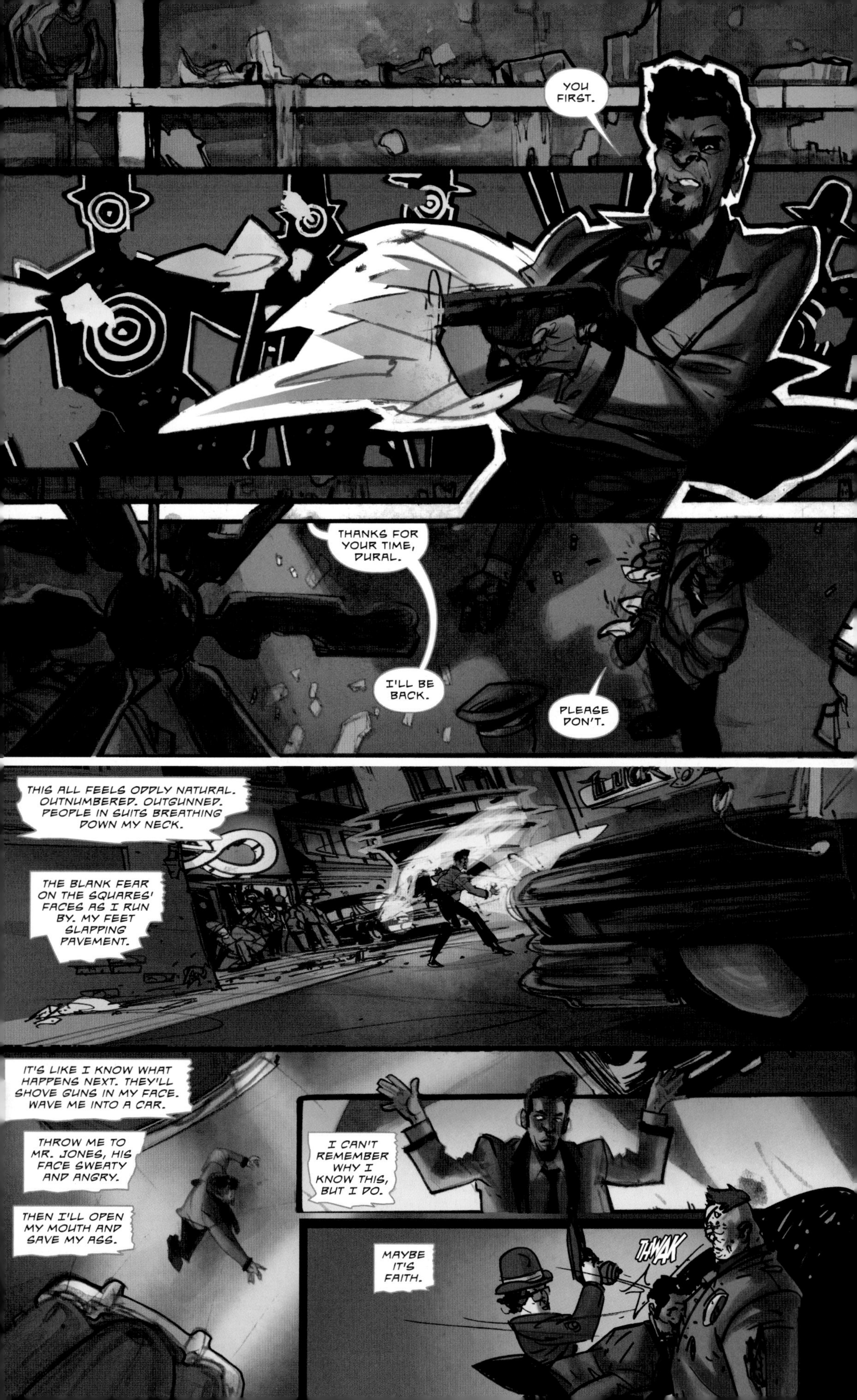

YOU FIRST.
THANKS FOR YOUR TIME, DURAL.
I'LL BE BACK.
PLEASE DON'T.
THIS ALL FEELS ODDLY NATURAL. OUTNUMBERED. OUTGUNNED. PEOPLE IN SUITS BREATHING DOWN MY NECK.
THE BLANK FEAR ON THE SQUARES' FACES AS I RUN BY. MY FEET SLAPPING PAVEMENT.
IT'S LIKE I KNOW WHAT HAPPENS NEXT. THEY'LL SHOVE GUNS IN MY FACE. WAVE ME INTO A CAR.
THROW ME TO MR. JONES, HIS FACE SWEATY AND ANGRY.
THEN I'LL OPEN MY MOUTH AND SAVE MY ASS.
I CAN'T REMEMBER WHY I KNOW THIS, BUT I DO.
MAYBE IT'S FAITH.
THWAK

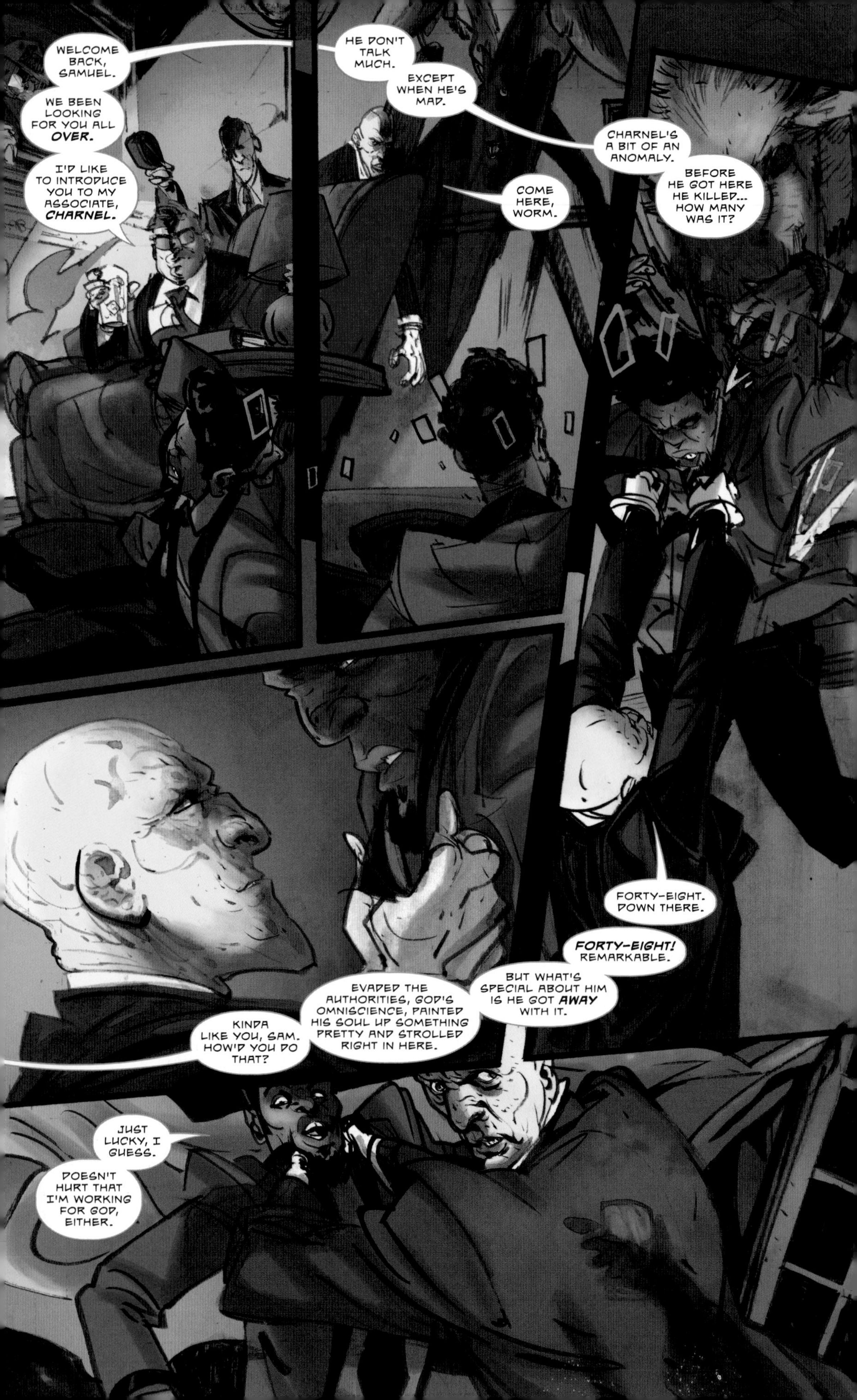
WELCOME BACK, SAMUEL.
WE BEEN LOOKING FOR YOU ALL **OVER.**
I'D LIKE TO INTRODUCE YOU TO MY ASSOCIATE, **CHARNEL.**
HE DON'T TALK MUCH.
EXCEPT WHEN HE'S MAD.
COME HERE, WORM.
CHARNEL'S A BIT OF AN ANOMALY.
BEFORE HE GOT HERE HE KILLED... HOW MANY WAS IT?
FORTY-EIGHT. DOWN THERE.
FORTY-EIGHT! REMARKABLE.
BUT WHAT'S SPECIAL ABOUT HIM IS HE GOT **AWAY** WITH IT.
EVADED THE AUTHORITIES, GOD'S OMNISCIENCE, PAINTED HIS SOUL UP SOMETHING PRETTY AND STROLLED RIGHT IN HERE.
KINDA LIKE YOU, SAM. HOW'D YOU DO THAT?
JUST LUCKY, I GUESS.
DOESN'T HURT THAT I'M WORKING FOR GOD, EITHER.

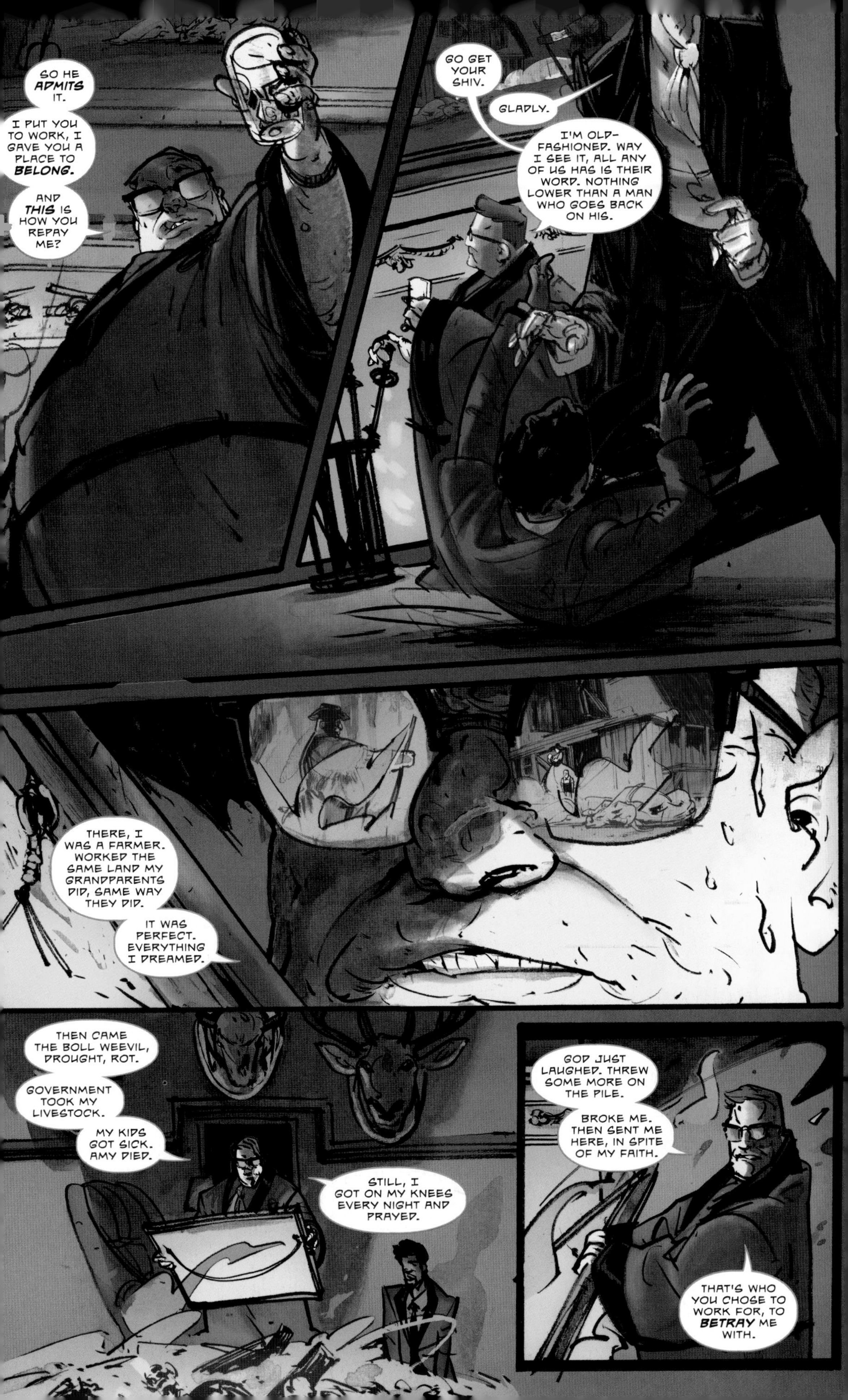
SO HE ADMITS IT.
I PUT YOU TO WORK, I GAVE YOU A PLACE TO BELONG.
AND THIS IS HOW YOU REPAY ME?
GO GET YOUR SHIV.
GLADLY.
I'M OLD-FASHIONED. WAY I SEE IT, ALL ANY OF US HAS IS THEIR WORD. NOTHING LOWER THAN A MAN WHO GOES BACK ON HIS.
THERE, I WAS A FARMER. WORKED THE SAME LAND MY GRANDPARENTS DID, SAME WAY THEY DID.
IT WAS PERFECT. EVERYTHING I DREAMED.
THEN CAME THE BOLL WEEVIL, DROUGHT, ROT.
GOVERNMENT TOOK MY LIVESTOCK.
MY KIDS GOT SICK. AMY DIED.
STILL, I GOT ON MY KNEES EVERY NIGHT AND PRAYED.
GOD JUST LAUGHED. THREW SOME MORE ON THE PILE.
BROKE ME. THEN SENT ME HERE, IN SPITE OF MY FAITH.
THAT'S WHO YOU CHOSE TO WORK FOR, TO BETRAY ME WITH.

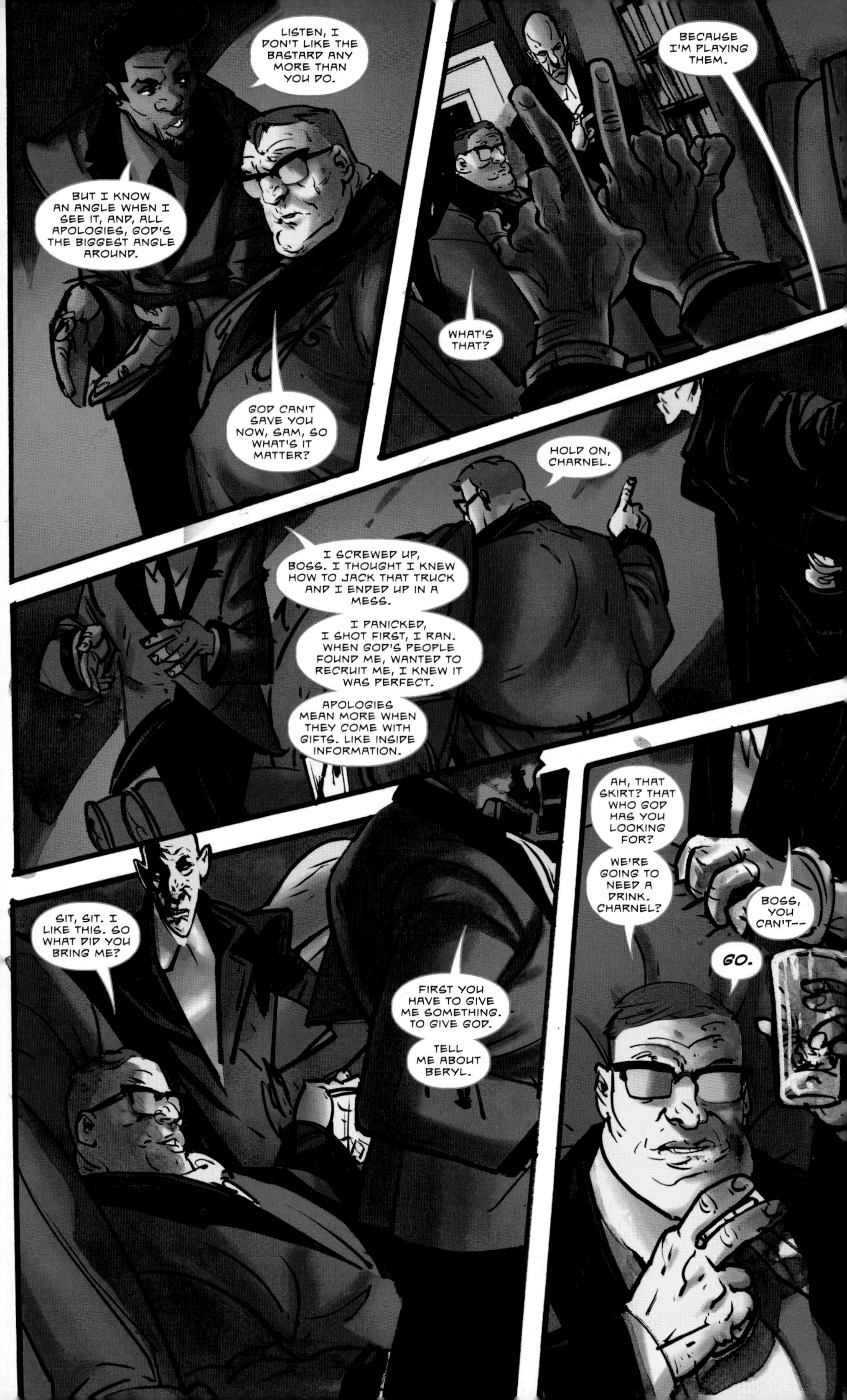

LISTEN, I DON'T LIKE THE BASTARD ANY MORE THAN YOU DO.
BUT I KNOW AN ANGLE WHEN I SEE IT, AND, ALL APOLOGIES, GOD'S THE BIGGEST ANGLE AROUND.
GOD CAN'T SAVE YOU NOW, SAM, SO WHAT'S IT MATTER?
BECAUSE I'M PLAYING THEM.
WHAT'S THAT?
HOLD ON, CHARNEL.
I SCREWED UP, BOSS. I THOUGHT I KNEW HOW TO JACK THAT TRUCK AND I ENDED UP IN A MESS.
I PANICKED, I SHOT FIRST, I RAN. WHEN GOD'S PEOPLE FOUND ME, WANTED TO RECRUIT ME, I KNEW IT WAS PERFECT.
APOLOGIES MEAN MORE WHEN THEY COME WITH GIFTS. LIKE INSIDE INFORMATION.
SIT, SIT. I LIKE THIS. SO WHAT DID YOU BRING ME?
FIRST YOU HAVE TO GIVE ME SOMETHING. TO GIVE GOD.
TELL ME ABOUT BERYL.
AH, THAT SKIRT? THAT WHO GOD HAS YOU LOOKING FOR?
WE'RE GOING TO NEED A DRINK. CHARNEL?
BOSS, YOU CAN'T--
GO.

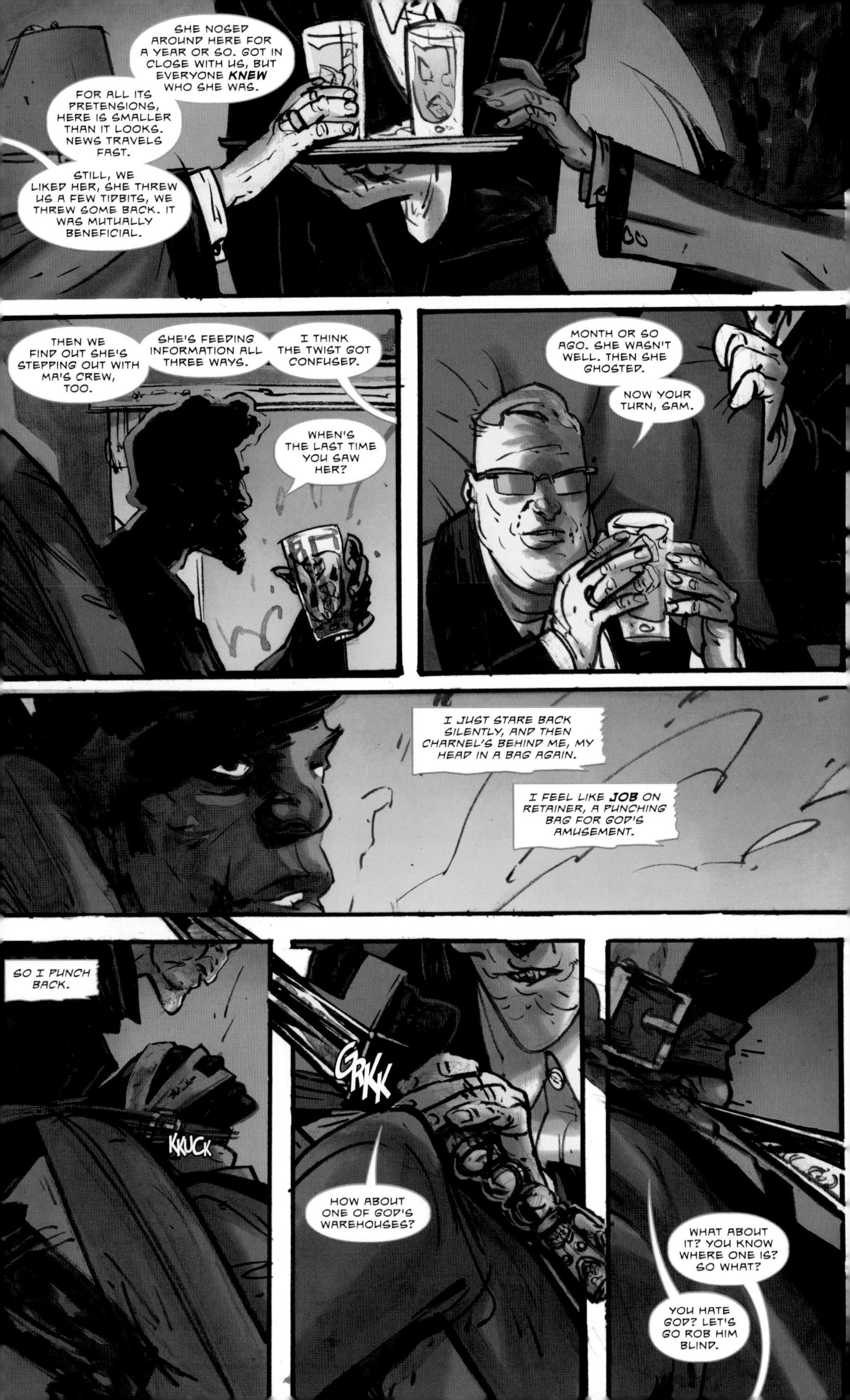

SHE NOSED AROUND HERE FOR A YEAR OR SO. GOT IN CLOSE WITH US, BUT EVERYONE KNEW WHO SHE WAS.
FOR ALL ITS PRETENSIONS, HERE IS SMALLER THAN IT LOOKS. NEWS TRAVELS FAST.
STILL, WE LIKED HER, SHE THREW US A FEW TIDBITS, WE THREW SOME BACK. IT WAS MUTUALLY BENEFICIAL.
THEN WE FIND OUT SHE'S STEPPING OUT WITH MA'S CREW, TOO.
SHE'S FEEDING INFORMATION ALL THREE WAYS.
I THINK THE TWIST GOT CONFUSED.
WHEN'S THE LAST TIME YOU SAW HER?
MONTH OR SO AGO. SHE WASN'T WELL. THEN SHE GHOSTED.
NOW YOUR TURN, SAM.
I JUST STARE BACK SILENTLY, AND THEN CHARNEL'S BEHIND ME, MY HEAD IN A BAG AGAIN.
I FEEL LIKE JOB ON RETAINER, A PUNCHING BAG FOR GOD'S AMUSEMENT.
SO I PUNCH BACK.
KKUCK
GRKK
HOW ABOUT ONE OF GOD'S WAREHOUSES?
WHAT ABOUT IT? YOU KNOW WHERE ONE IS? SO WHAT?
YOU HATE GOD? LET'S GO ROB HIM BLIND.

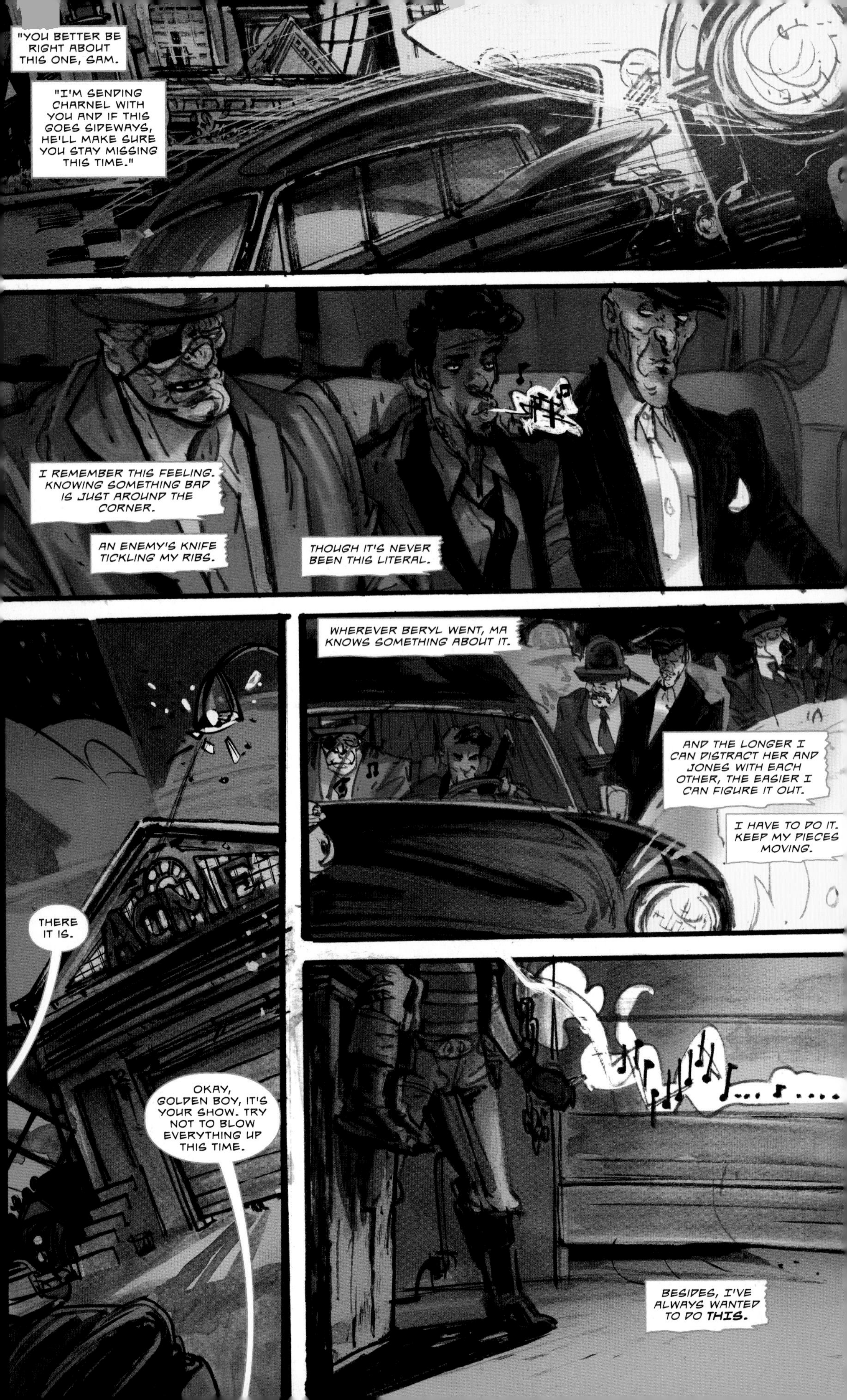
"YOU BETTER BE RIGHT ABOUT THIS ONE, SAM.
"I'M SENDING CHARNEL WITH YOU AND IF THIS GOES SIDEWAYS, HE'LL MAKE SURE YOU STAY MISSING THIS TIME."
I REMEMBER THIS FEELING. KNOWING SOMETHING BAD IS JUST AROUND THE CORNER.
AN ENEMY'S KNIFE TICKLING MY RIBS.
THOUGH IT'S NEVER BEEN THIS LITERAL.
THERE IT IS.
OKAY, GOLDEN BOY, IT'S YOUR SHOW. TRY NOT TO BLOW EVERYTHING UP THIS TIME.
WHEREVER BERYL WENT, MA KNOWS SOMETHING ABOUT IT.
AND THE LONGER I CAN DISTRACT HER AND JONES WITH EACH OTHER, THE EASIER I CAN FIGURE IT OUT.
I HAVE TO DO IT. KEEP MY PIECES MOVING.
BESIDES, I'VE ALWAYS WANTED TO DO THIS.

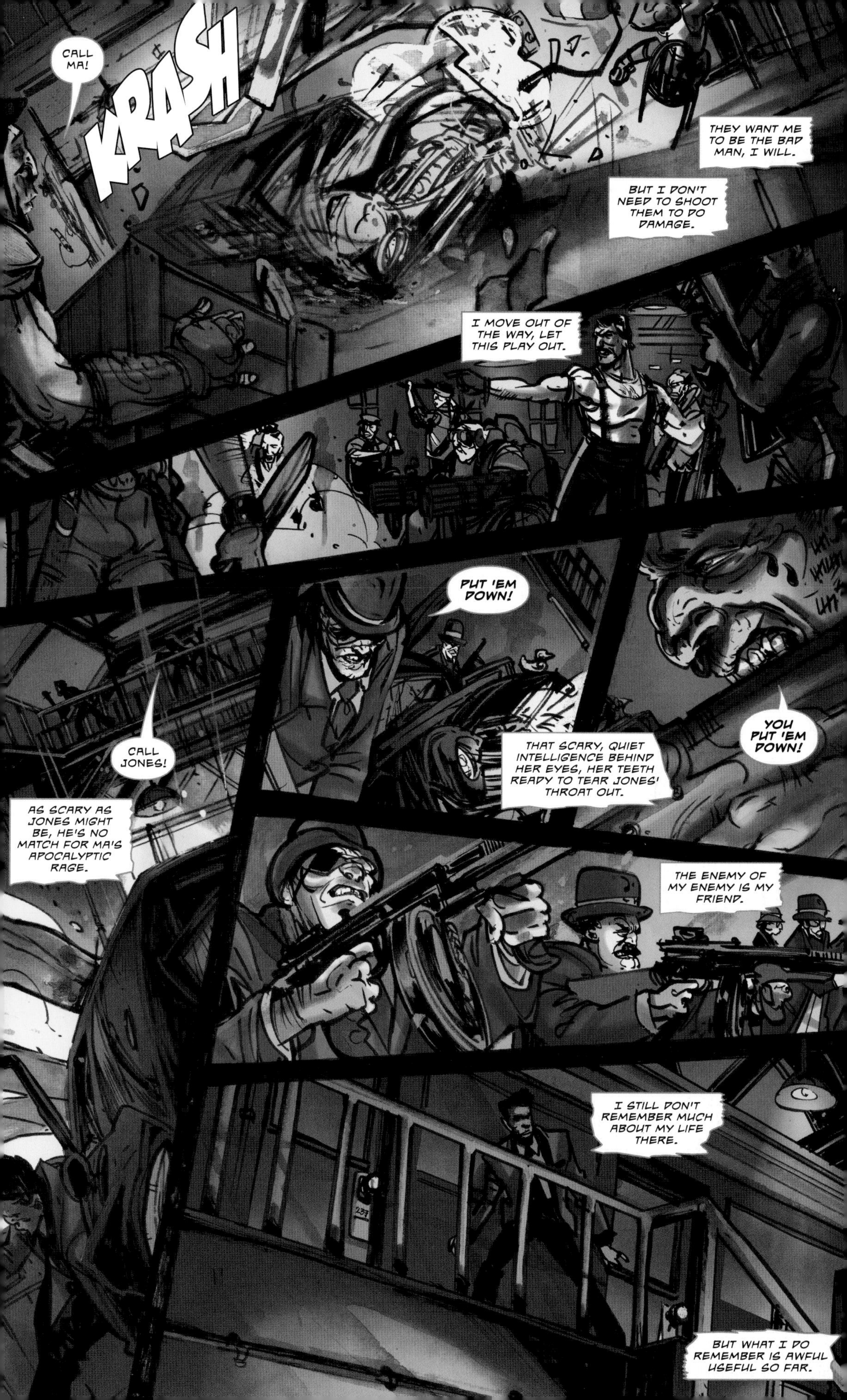
CALL MA!
KRASH
THEY WANT ME TO BE THE BAD MAN, I WILL.
BUT I DON'T NEED TO SHOOT THEM TO DO DAMAGE.
I MOVE OUT OF THE WAY, LET THIS PLAY OUT.
PUT 'EM DOWN!
YOU PUT 'EM DOWN!
THAT SCARY, QUIET INTELLIGENCE BEHIND HER EYES, HER TEETH READY TO TEAR JONES' THROAT OUT.
CALL JONES!
AS SCARY AS JONES MIGHT BE, HE'S NO MATCH FOR MA'S APOCALYPTIC RAGE.
THE ENEMY OF MY ENEMY IS MY FRIEND.
I STILL DON'T REMEMBER MUCH ABOUT MY LIFE THERE.
BUT WHAT I DO REMEMBER IS AWFUL USEFUL SO FAR.

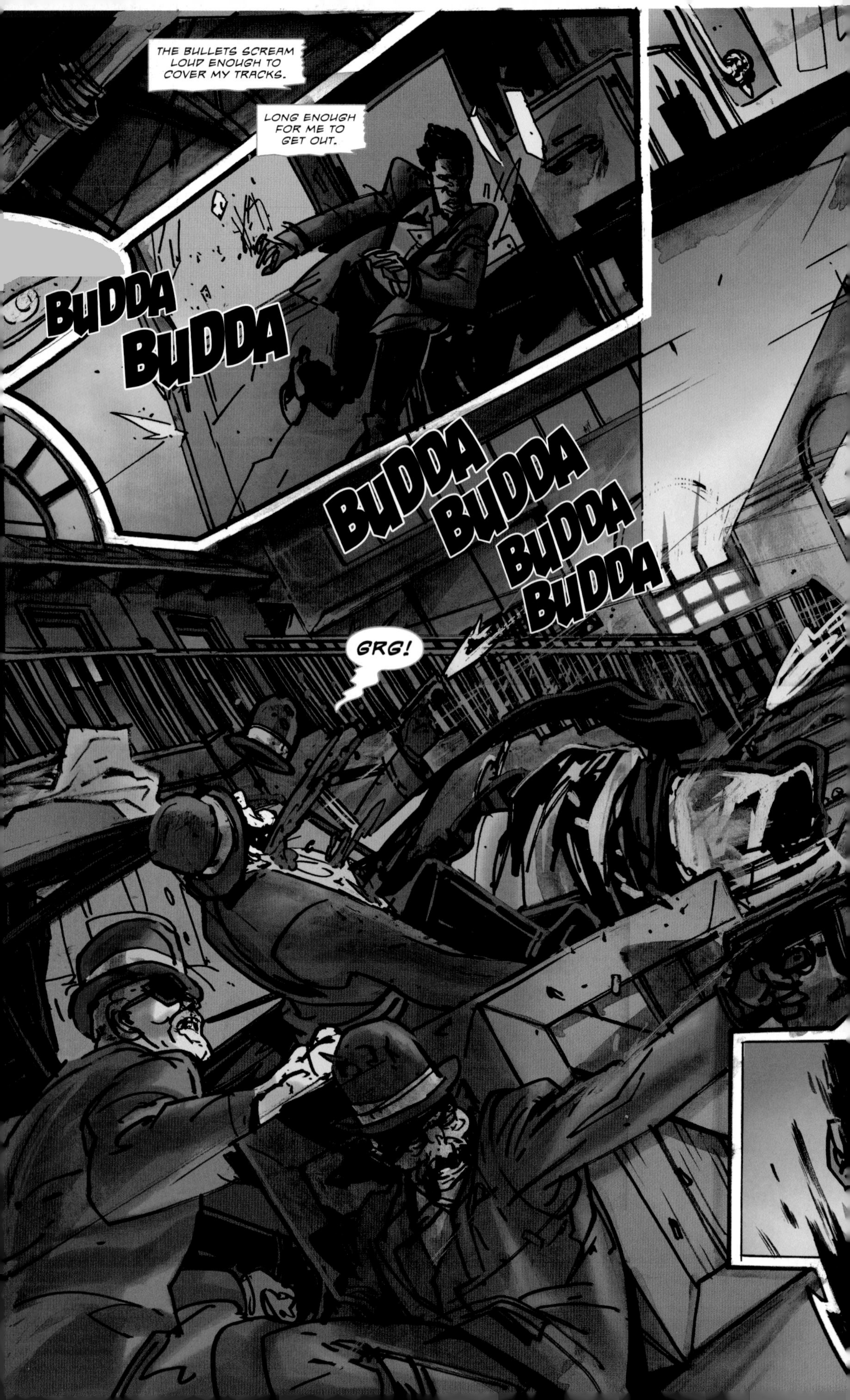
THE BULLETS SCREAM LOUD ENOUGH TO COVER MY TRACKS.
LONG ENOUGH FOR ME TO GET OUT.
BuDDA BuDDA
BuDDA BuDDA BuDDA BuDDA
GRG!

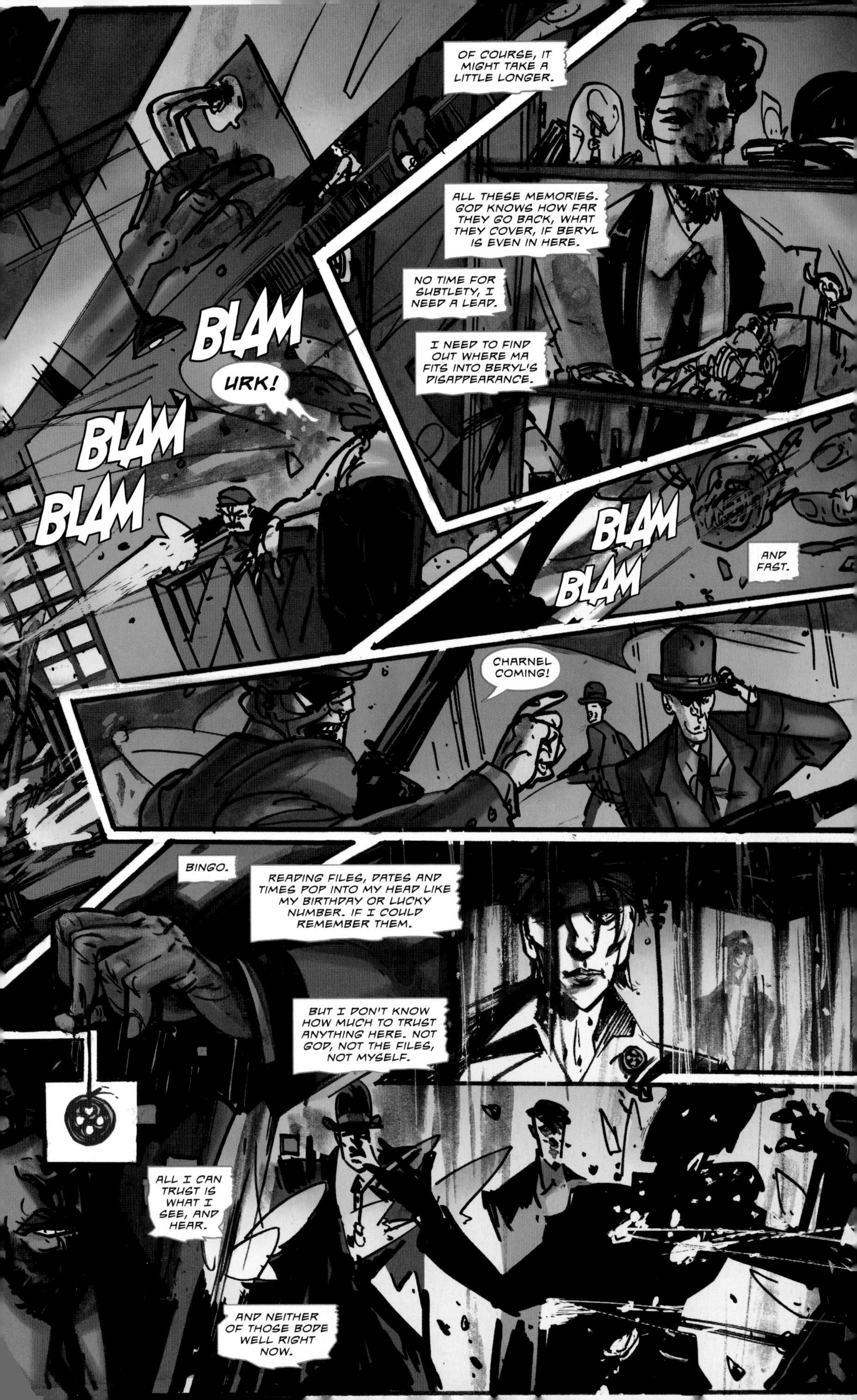

OF COURSE, IT MIGHT TAKE A LITTLE LONGER.
ALL THESE MEMORIES. GOD KNOWS HOW FAR THEY GO BACK, WHAT THEY COVER, IF BERYL IS EVEN IN HERE.
NO TIME FOR SUBTLETY, I NEED A LEAD.
I NEED TO FIND OUT WHERE MA FITS INTO BERYL'S DISAPPEARANCE.
BLAM
URK!
BLAM
BLAM
BLAM
BLAM
AND FAST.
CHARNEL COMING!
BINGO.
READING FILES, DATES AND TIMES POP INTO MY HEAD LIKE MY BIRTHDAY OR LUCKY NUMBER. IF I COULD REMEMBER THEM.
BUT I DON'T KNOW HOW MUCH TO TRUST ANYTHING HERE. NOT GOD, NOT THE FILES, NOT MYSELF.
ALL I CAN TRUST IS WHAT I SEE, AND HEAR.
AND NEITHER OF THOSE BODE WELL RIGHT NOW.

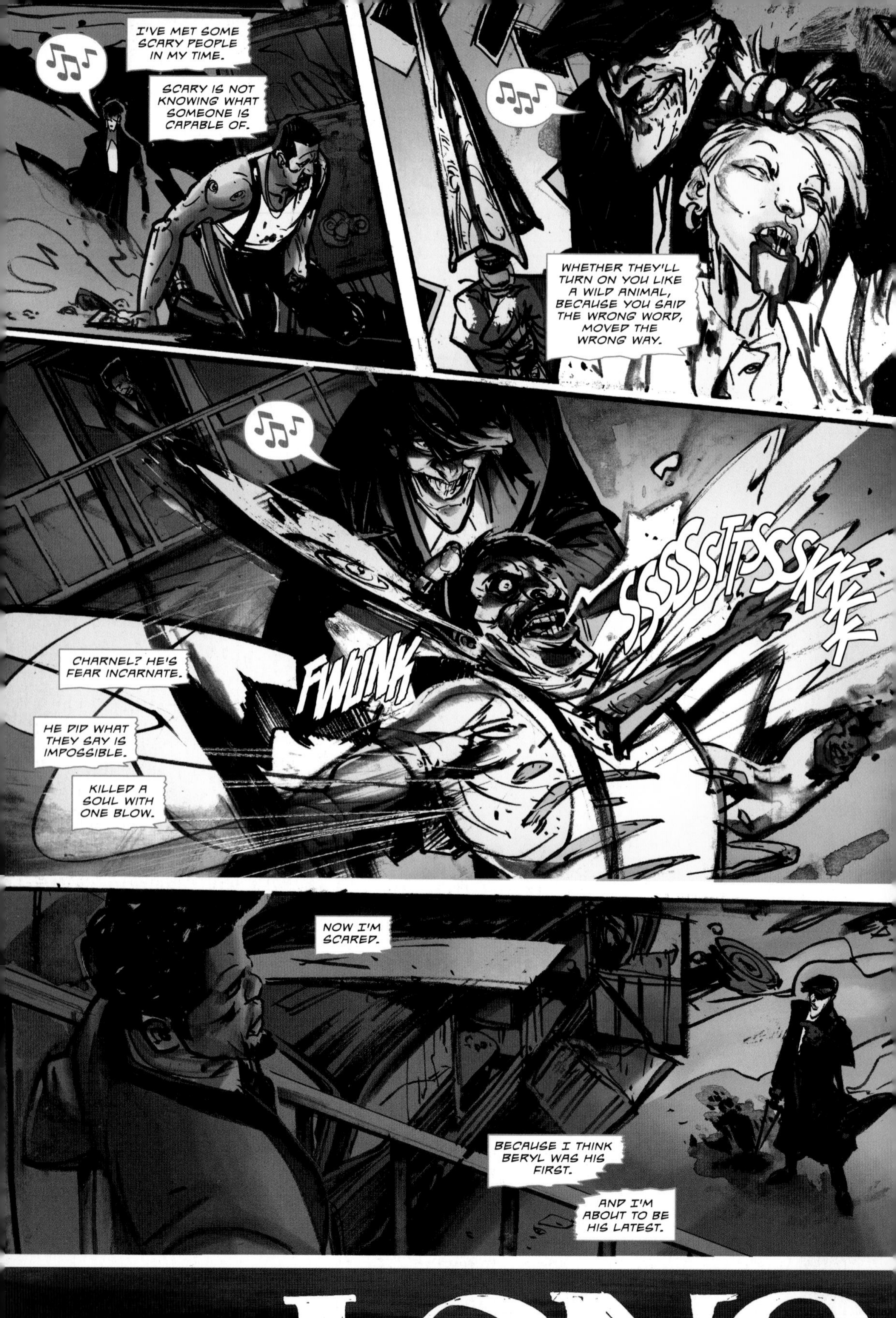
I'VE MET SOME SCARY PEOPLE IN MY TIME.
SCARY IS NOT KNOWING WHAT SOMEONE IS CAPABLE OF.
WHETHER THEY'LL TURN ON YOU LIKE A WILD ANIMAL, BECAUSE YOU SAID THE WRONG WORD, MOVED THE WRONG WAY.
FWUNK
CHARNEL? HE'S FEAR INCARNATE.
HE DID WHAT THEY SAY IS IMPOSSIBLE.
KILLED A SOUL WITH ONE BLOW.
NOW I'M SCARED.
BECAUSE I THINK BERYL WAS HIS FIRST.
AND I'M ABOUT TO BE HIS LATEST.

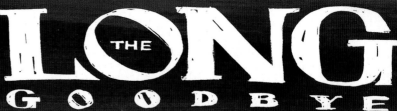

EPISODE 2:
SEBELA & VISIONS

THE LONG GOODBYE

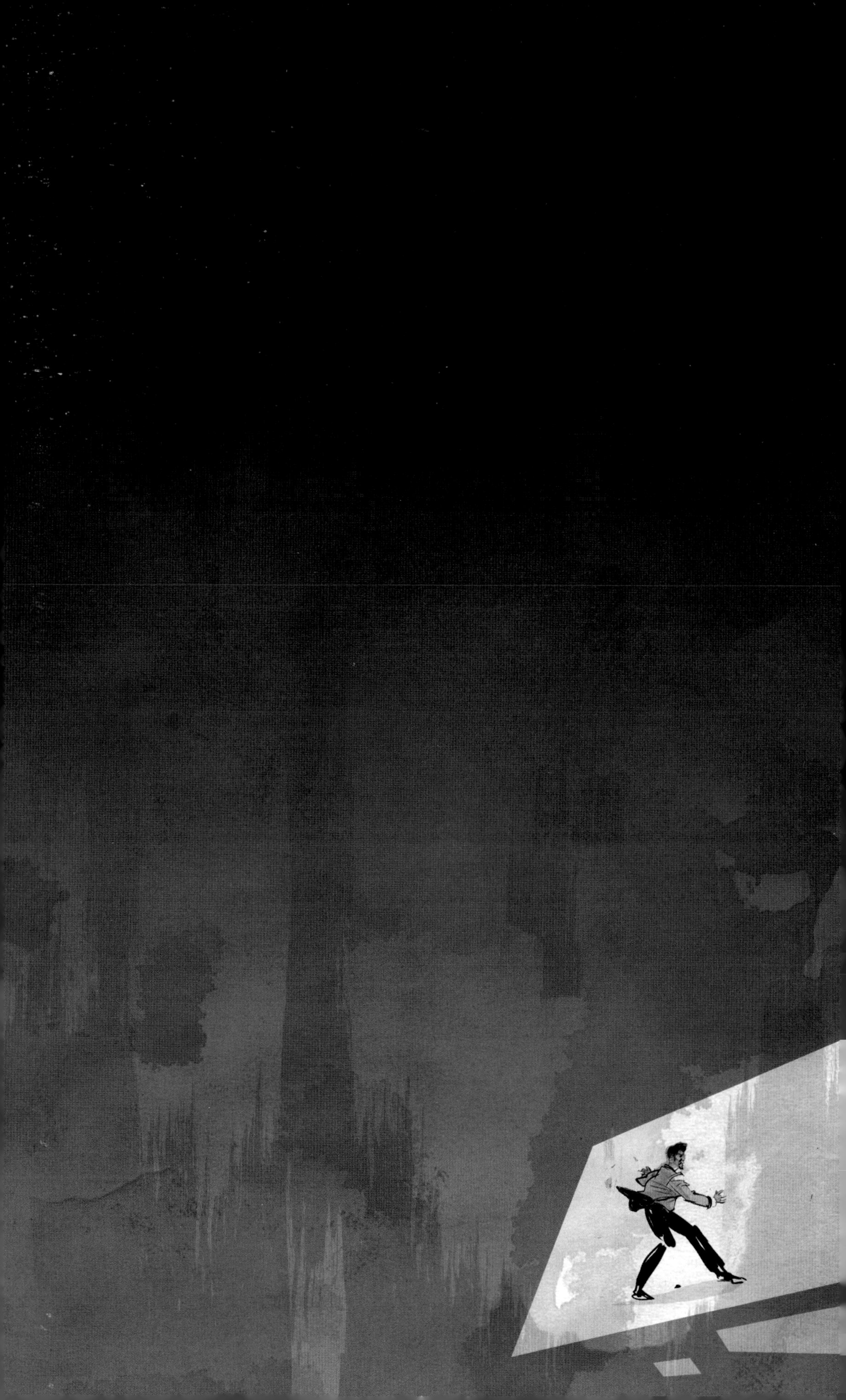

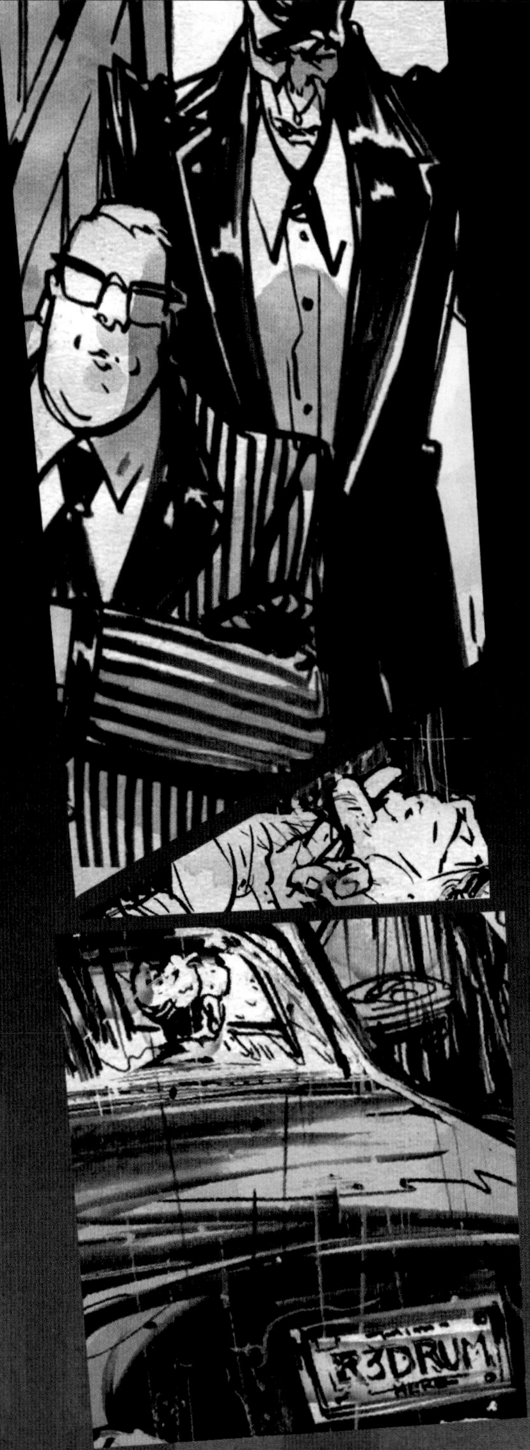
R3DRUM

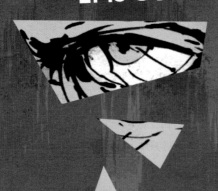

EPISODE THREE

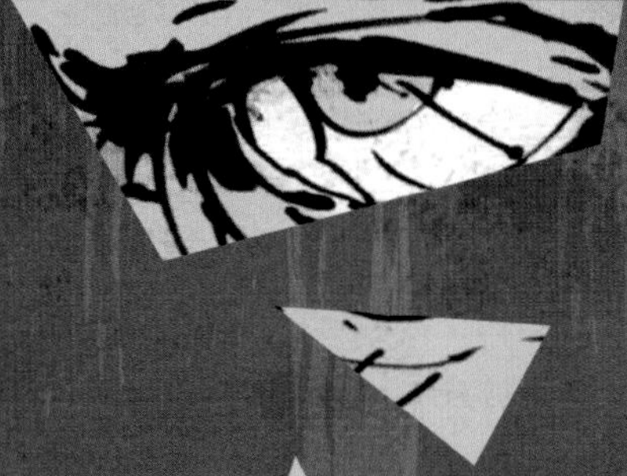

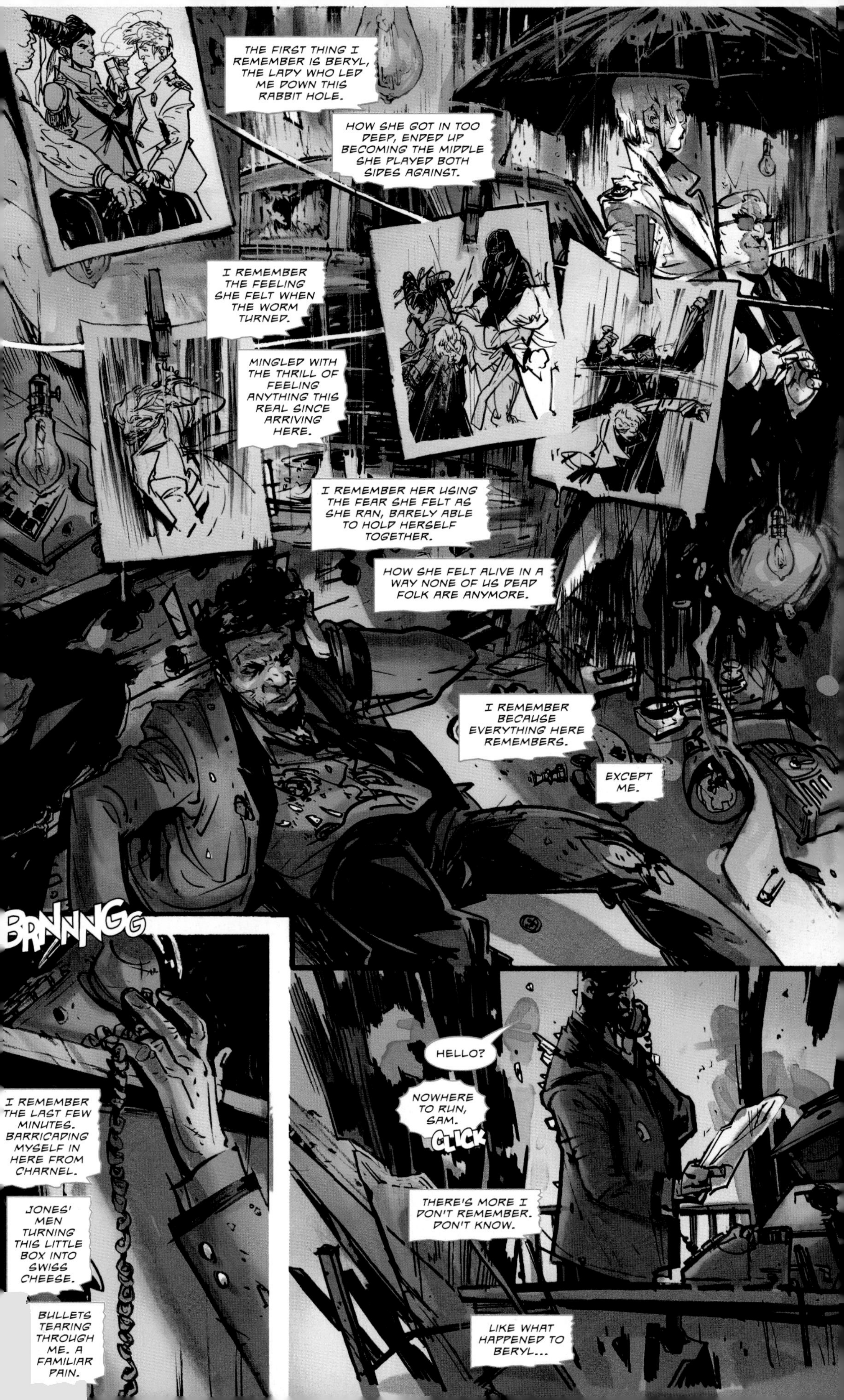
THE FIRST THING I REMEMBER IS BERYL, THE LADY WHO LED ME DOWN THIS RABBIT HOLE.
HOW SHE GOT IN TOO DEEP, ENDED UP BECOMING THE MIDDLE SHE PLAYED BOTH SIDES AGAINST.
I REMEMBER THE FEELING SHE FELT WHEN THE WORM TURNED.
MINGLED WITH THE THRILL OF FEELING ANYTHING THIS REAL SINCE ARRIVING HERE.
I REMEMBER HER USING THE FEAR SHE FELT AS SHE RAN, BARELY ABLE TO HOLD HERSELF TOGETHER.
HOW SHE FELT ALIVE IN A WAY NONE OF US DEAD FOLK ARE ANYMORE.
I REMEMBER BECAUSE EVERYTHING HERE REMEMBERS.
EXCEPT ME.
BRNNNGG
I REMEMBER THE LAST FEW MINUTES. BARRICADING MYSELF IN HERE FROM CHARNEL.
JONES' MEN TURNING THIS LITTLE BOX INTO SWISS CHEESE.
BULLETS TEARING THROUGH ME. A FAMILIAR PAIN.
HELLO?
NOWHERE TO RUN, SAM.
CLICK
THERE'S MORE I DON'T REMEMBER. DON'T KNOW.
LIKE WHAT HAPPENED TO BERYL...

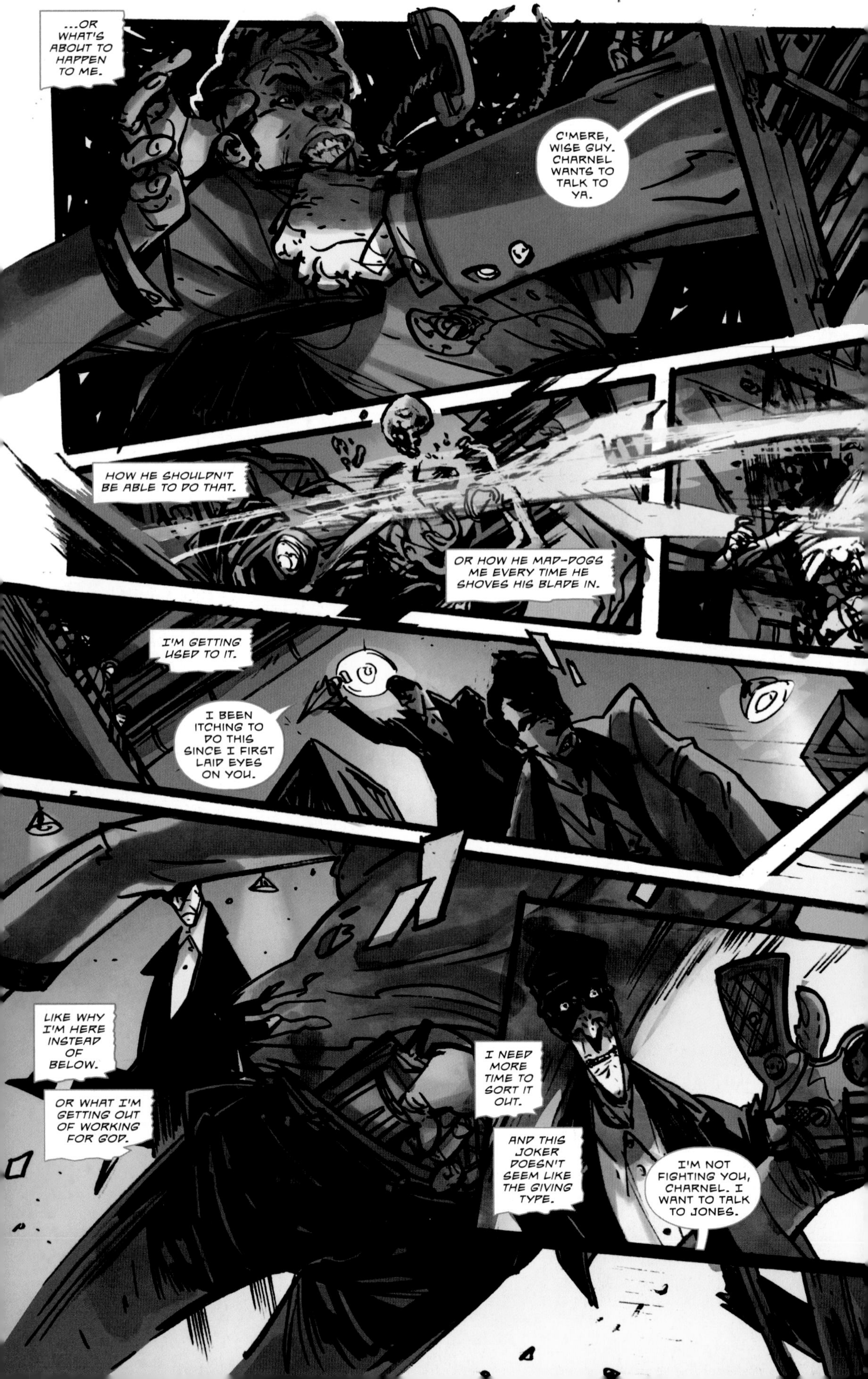
...OR WHAT'S ABOUT TO HAPPEN TO ME.
C'MERE, WISE GUY. CHARNEL WANTS TO TALK TO YA.
HOW HE SHOULDN'T BE ABLE TO DO THAT.
OR HOW HE MAD-DOGS ME EVERY TIME HE SHOVES HIS BLADE IN.
I'M GETTING USED TO IT.
I BEEN ITCHING TO DO THIS SINCE I FIRST LAID EYES ON YOU.
LIKE WHY I'M HERE INSTEAD OF BELOW.
OR WHAT I'M GETTING OUT OF WORKING FOR GOD.
I NEED MORE TIME TO SORT IT OUT.
AND THIS JOKER DOESN'T SEEM LIKE THE GIVING TYPE.
I'M NOT FIGHTING YOU, CHARNEL. I WANT TO TALK TO JONES.

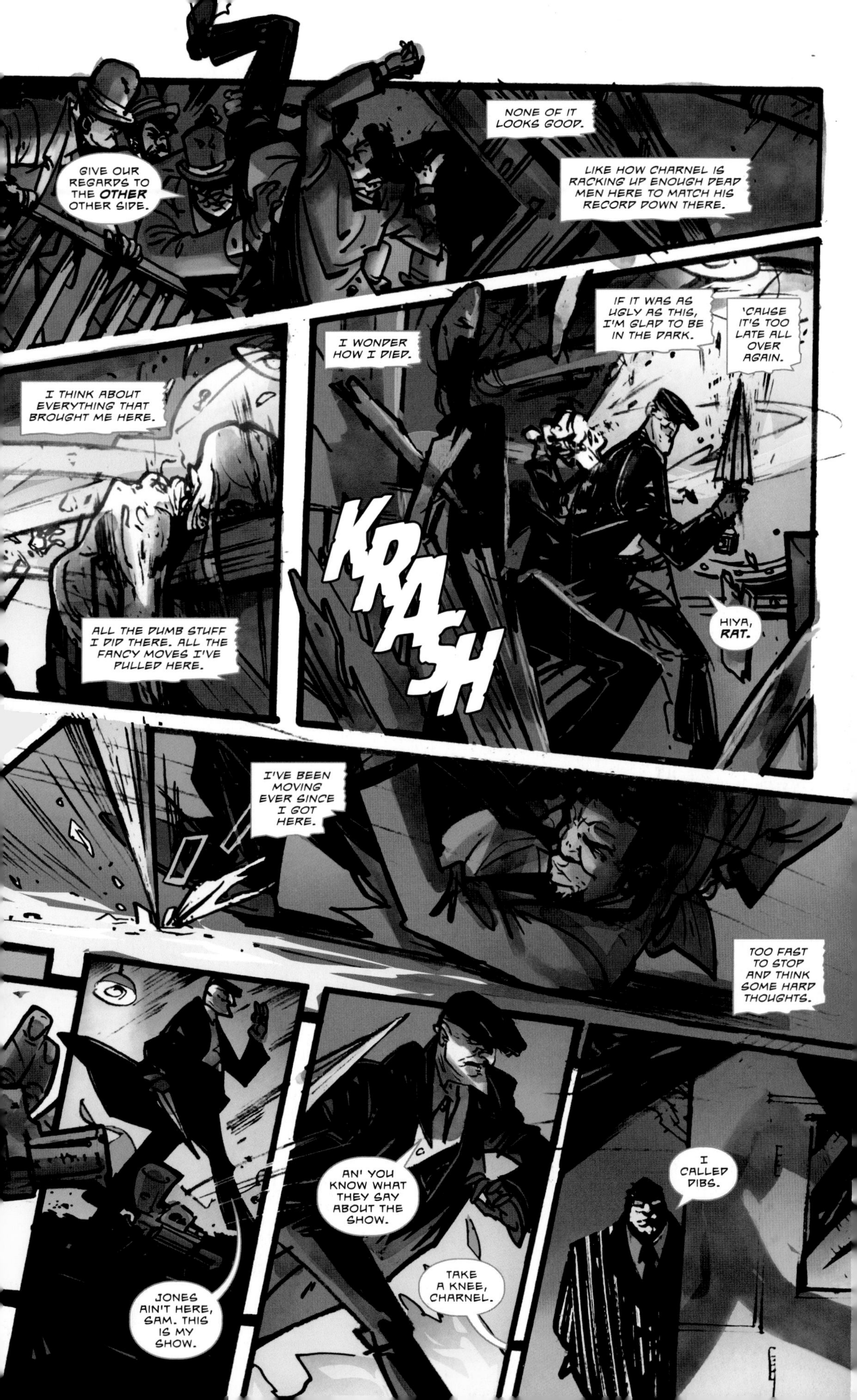

NONE OF IT LOOKS GOOD.
LIKE HOW CHARNEL IS RACKING UP ENOUGH DEAD MEN HERE TO MATCH HIS RECORD DOWN THERE.
GIVE OUR REGARDS TO THE OTHER OTHER SIDE.
I THINK ABOUT EVERYTHING THAT BROUGHT ME HERE.
ALL THE DUMB STUFF I DID THERE. ALL THE FANCY MOVES I'VE PULLED HERE.
I WONDER HOW I DIED.
IF IT WAS AS UGLY AS THIS, I'M GLAD TO BE IN THE DARK.
'CAUSE IT'S TOO LATE ALL OVER AGAIN.
KRASH
HIYA, RAT.
I'VE BEEN MOVING EVER SINCE I GOT HERE.
TOO FAST TO STOP AND THINK SOME HARD THOUGHTS.
JONES AIN'T HERE, SAM. THIS IS MY SHOW.
AN' YOU KNOW WHAT THEY SAY ABOUT THE SHOW.
TAKE A KNEE, CHARNEL.
I CALLED DIBS.

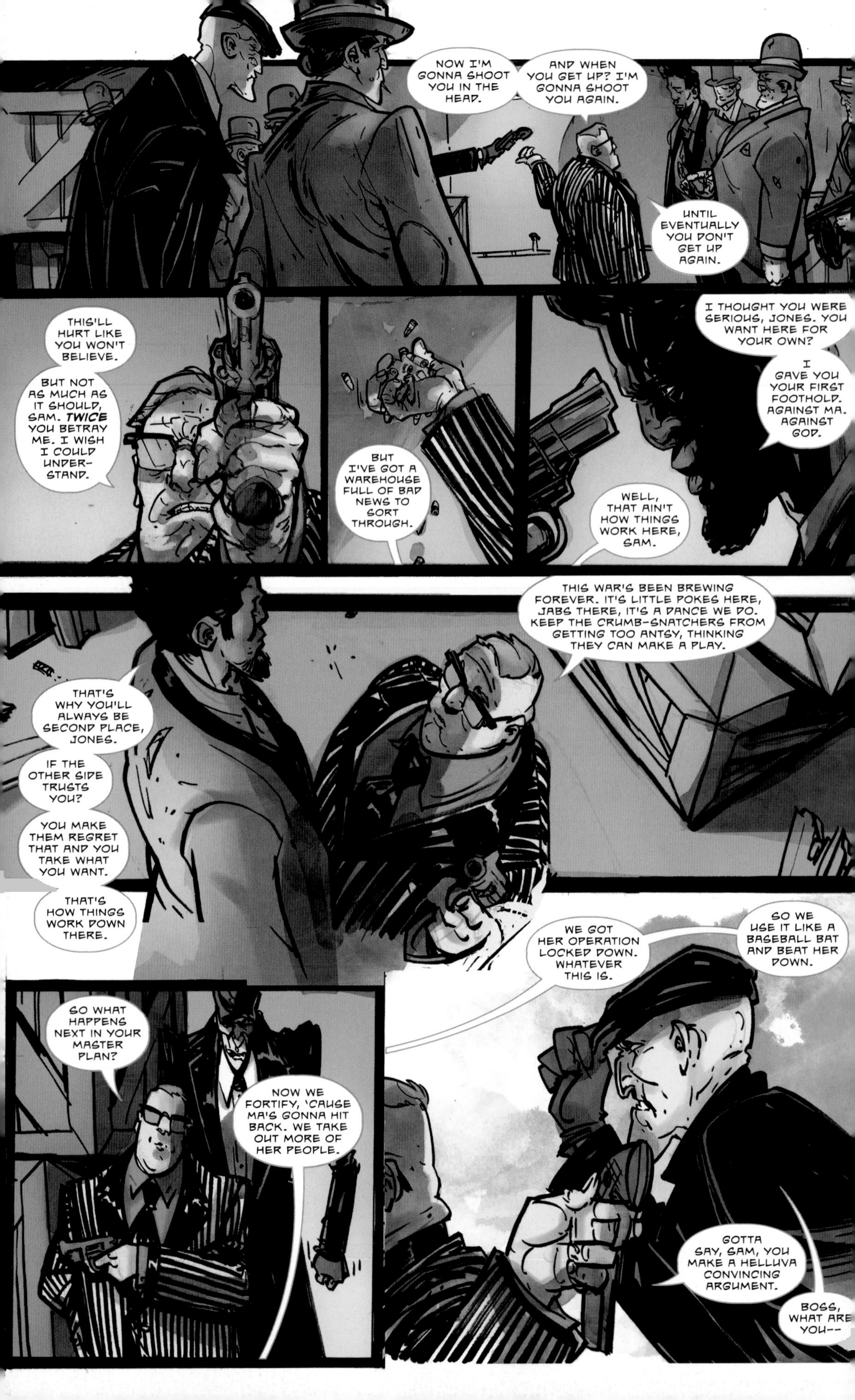
NOW I'M GONNA SHOOT YOU IN THE HEAD.
AND WHEN YOU GET UP? I'M GONNA SHOOT YOU AGAIN.
UNTIL EVENTUALLY YOU DON'T GET UP AGAIN.
THIS'LL HURT LIKE YOU WON'T BELIEVE.
BUT NOT AS MUCH AS IT SHOULD, SAM. TWICE YOU BETRAY ME. I WISH I COULD UNDER- STAND.
BUT I'VE GOT A WAREHOUSE FULL OF BAD NEWS TO SORT THROUGH.
I THOUGHT YOU WERE SERIOUS, JONES. YOU WANT HERE FOR YOUR OWN?
I GAVE YOU YOUR FIRST FOOTHOLD. AGAINST MA. AGAINST GOD.
WELL, THAT AIN'T HOW THINGS WORK HERE, SAM.
THIS WAR'S BEEN BREWING FOREVER. IT'S LITTLE POKES HERE, JABS THERE, IT'S A DANCE WE DO. KEEP THE CRUMB-SNATCHERS FROM GETTING TOO ANTSY, THINKING THEY CAN MAKE A PLAY.
THAT'S WHY YOU'LL ALWAYS BE SECOND PLACE, JONES.
IF THE OTHER SIDE TRUSTS YOU?
YOU MAKE THEM REGRET THAT AND YOU TAKE WHAT YOU WANT.
THAT'S HOW THINGS WORK DOWN THERE.
SO WHAT HAPPENS NEXT IN YOUR MASTER PLAN?
NOW WE FORTIFY, 'CAUSE MA'S GONNA HIT BACK. WE TAKE OUT MORE OF HER PEOPLE.
WE GOT HER OPERATION LOCKED DOWN. WHATEVER THIS IS.
SO WE USE IT LIKE A BASEBALL BAT AND BEAT HER DOWN.
GOTTA SAY, SAM, YOU MAKE A HELLUVA CONVINCING ARGUMENT.
BOSS, WHAT ARE YOU--

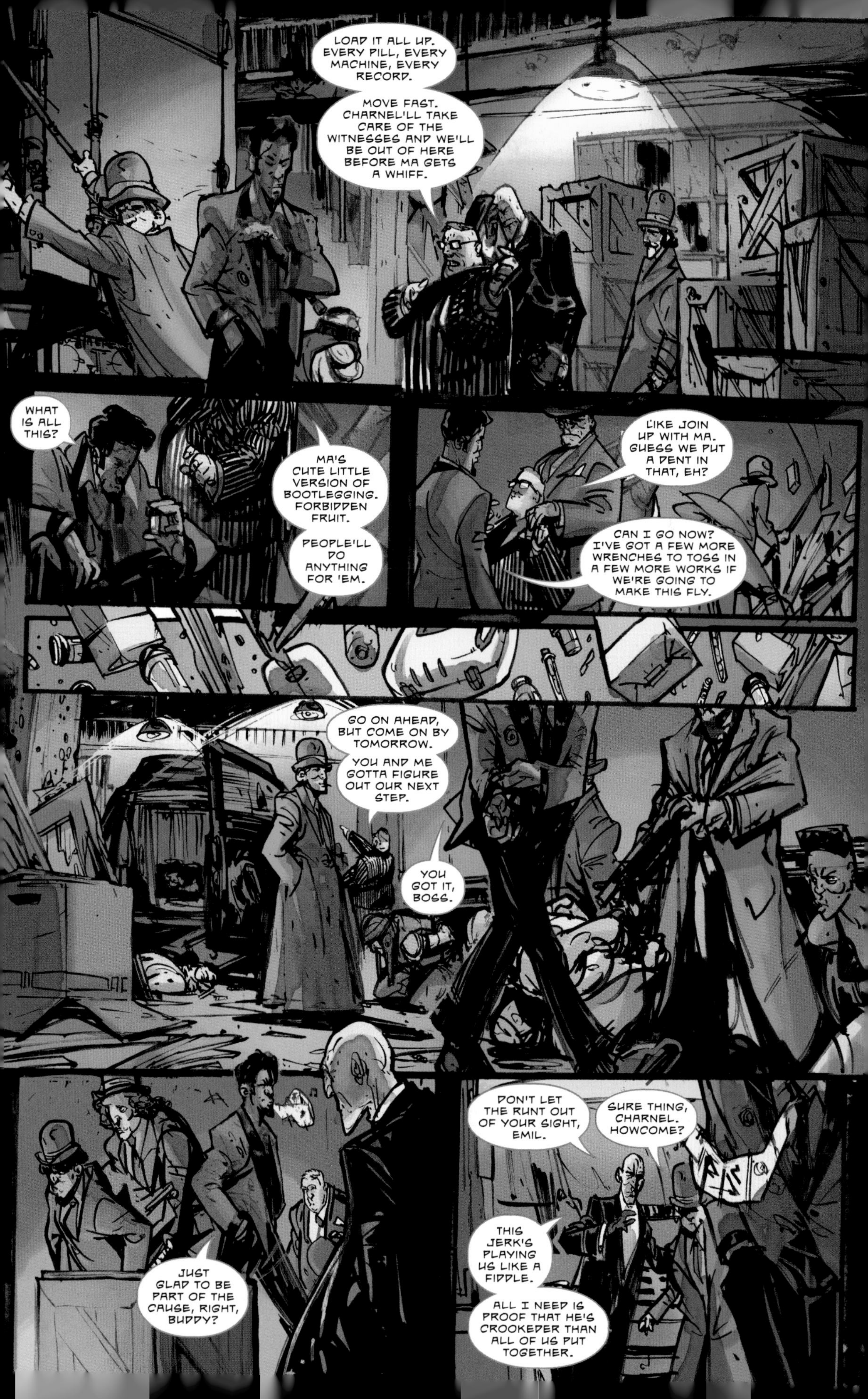
LOAD IT ALL UP. EVERY PILL, EVERY MACHINE, EVERY RECORD.
MOVE FAST. CHARNEL'LL TAKE CARE OF THE WITNESSES AND WE'LL BE OUT OF HERE BEFORE MA GETS A WHIFF.
WHAT IS ALL THIS?
MA'S CUTE LITTLE VERSION OF BOOTLEGGING. FORBIDDEN FRUIT.
PEOPLE'LL DO ANYTHING FOR 'EM.
LIKE JOIN UP WITH MA. GUESS WE PUT A DENT IN THAT, EH?
CAN I GO NOW? I'VE GOT A FEW MORE WRENCHES TO TOSS IN A FEW MORE WORKS IF WE'RE GOING TO MAKE THIS FLY.
GO ON AHEAD, BUT COME ON BY TOMORROW.
YOU AND ME GOTTA FIGURE OUT OUR NEXT STEP.
YOU GOT IT, BOSS.
JUST GLAD TO BE PART OF THE CAUSE, RIGHT, BUDDY?
DON'T LET THE RUNT OUT OF YOUR SIGHT, EMIL.
SURE THING, CHARNEL. HOWCOME?
THIS JERK'S PLAYING US LIKE A FIDDLE.
ALL I NEED IS PROOF THAT HE'S CROOKEDER THAN ALL OF US PUT TOGETHER.

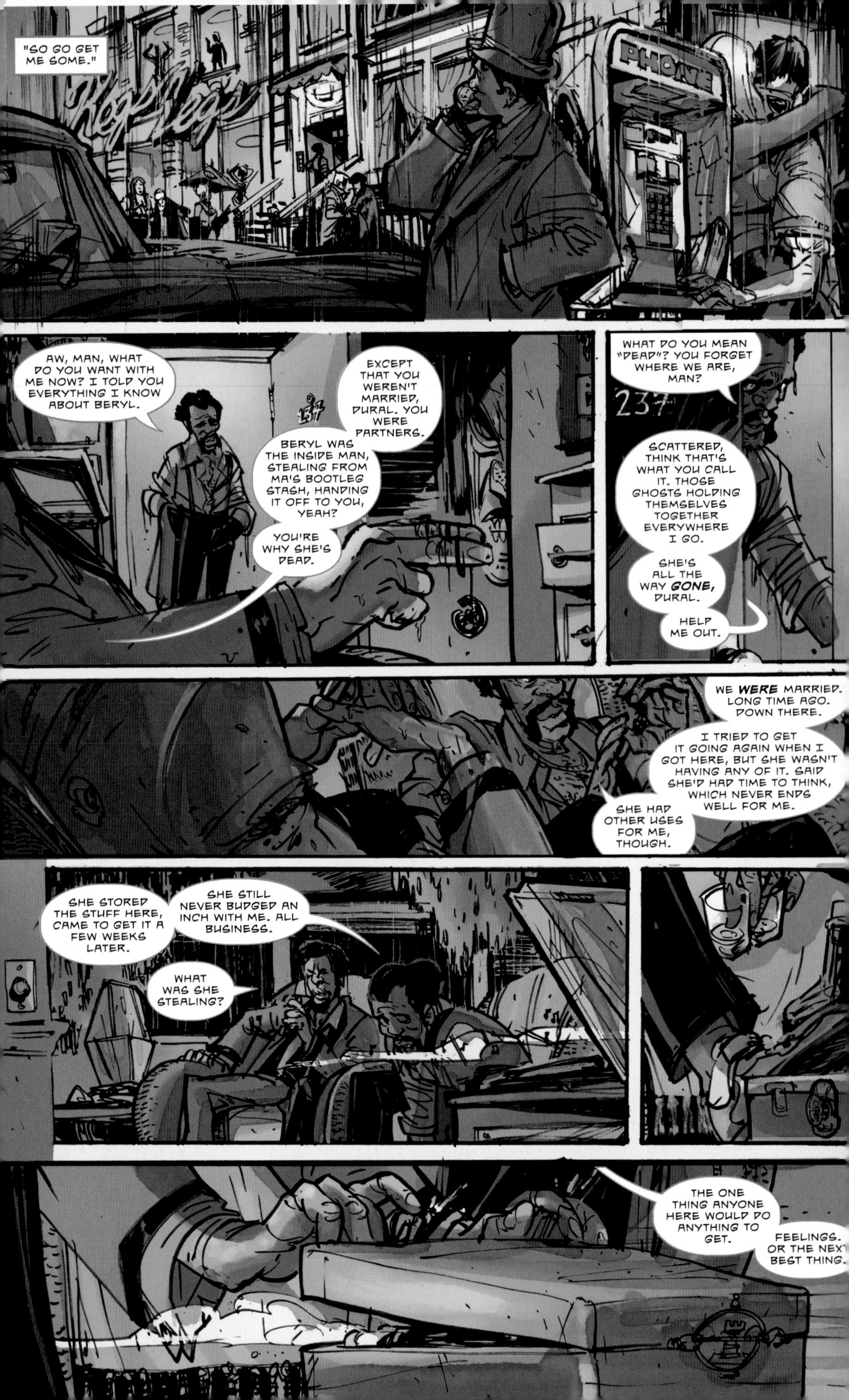
"SO GO GET ME SOME."
Keg's Legs
PHONE
AW, MAN, WHAT DO YOU WANT WITH ME NOW? I TOLD YOU EVERYTHING I KNOW ABOUT BERYL.
EXCEPT THAT YOU WEREN'T MARRIED, DURAL. YOU WERE PARTNERS.
BERYL WAS THE INSIDE MAN, STEALING FROM MA'S BOOTLEG STASH, HANDING IT OFF TO YOU, YEAH?
YOU'RE WHY SHE'S DEAD.
WHAT DO YOU MEAN "DEAD"? YOU FORGET WHERE WE ARE, MAN?
SCATTERED, THINK THAT'S WHAT YOU CALL IT. THOSE GHOSTS HOLDING THEMSELVES TOGETHER EVERYWHERE I GO.
SHE'S ALL THE WAY GONE, DURAL.
HELP ME OUT.
WE WERE MARRIED. LONG TIME AGO. DOWN THERE.
I TRIED TO GET IT GOING AGAIN WHEN I GOT HERE, BUT SHE WASN'T HAVING ANY OF IT. SAID SHE'D HAD TIME TO THINK, WHICH NEVER ENDS WELL FOR ME.
SHE HAD OTHER USES FOR ME, THOUGH.
SHE STORED THE STUFF HERE, CAME TO GET IT A FEW WEEKS LATER.
SHE STILL NEVER BUDGED AN INCH WITH ME. ALL BUSINESS.
WHAT WAS SHE STEALING?
THE ONE THING ANYONE HERE WOULD DO ANYTHING TO GET.
FEELINGS. OR THE NEXT BEST THING.

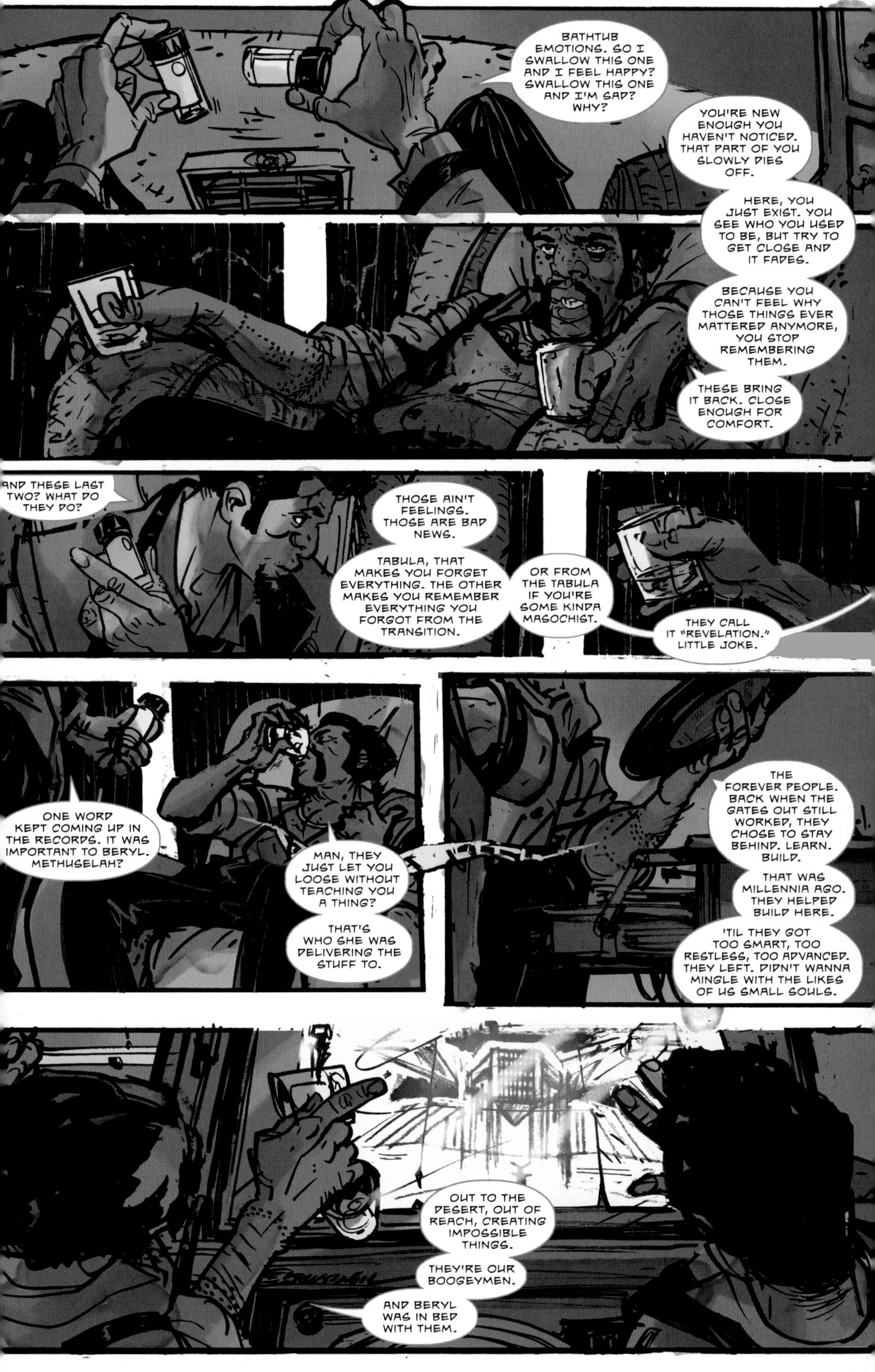
BATHTUB EMOTIONS. SO I SWALLOW THIS ONE AND I FEEL HAPPY? SWALLOW THIS ONE AND I'M SAD? WHY?
YOU'RE NEW ENOUGH YOU HAVEN'T NOTICED. THAT PART OF YOU SLOWLY DIES OFF.
HERE, YOU JUST EXIST. YOU SEE WHO YOU USED TO BE, BUT TRY TO GET CLOSE AND IT FADES.
BECAUSE YOU CAN'T FEEL WHY THOSE THINGS EVER MATTERED ANYMORE, YOU STOP REMEMBERING THEM.
THESE BRING IT BACK. CLOSE ENOUGH FOR COMFORT.
AND THESE LAST TWO? WHAT DO THEY DO?
THOSE AIN'T FEELINGS. THOSE ARE BAD NEWS.
TABULA, THAT MAKES YOU FORGET EVERYTHING. THE OTHER MAKES YOU REMEMBER EVERYTHING YOU FORGOT FROM THE TRANSITION.
OR FROM THE TABULA IF YOU'RE SOME KINDA MASOCHIST.
THEY CALL IT "REVELATION." LITTLE JOKE.
ONE WORD KEPT COMING UP IN THE RECORDS. IT WAS IMPORTANT TO BERYL. METHUSELAH?
MAN, THEY JUST LET YOU LOOSE WITHOUT TEACHING YOU A THING?
THAT'S WHO SHE WAS DELIVERING THE STUFF TO.
THE FOREVER PEOPLE. BACK WHEN THE GATES OUT STILL WORKED, THEY CHOSE TO STAY BEHIND. LEARN. BUILD.
THAT WAS MILLENNIA AGO. THEY HELPED BUILD HERE.
'TIL THEY GOT TOO SMART, TOO RESTLESS, TOO ADVANCED. THEY LEFT. DIDN'T WANNA MINGLE WITH THE LIKES OF US SMALL SOULS.
OUT TO THE DESERT, OUT OF REACH, CREATING IMPOSSIBLE THINGS.
THEY'RE OUR BOOGEYMEN.
AND BERYL WAS IN BED WITH THEM.

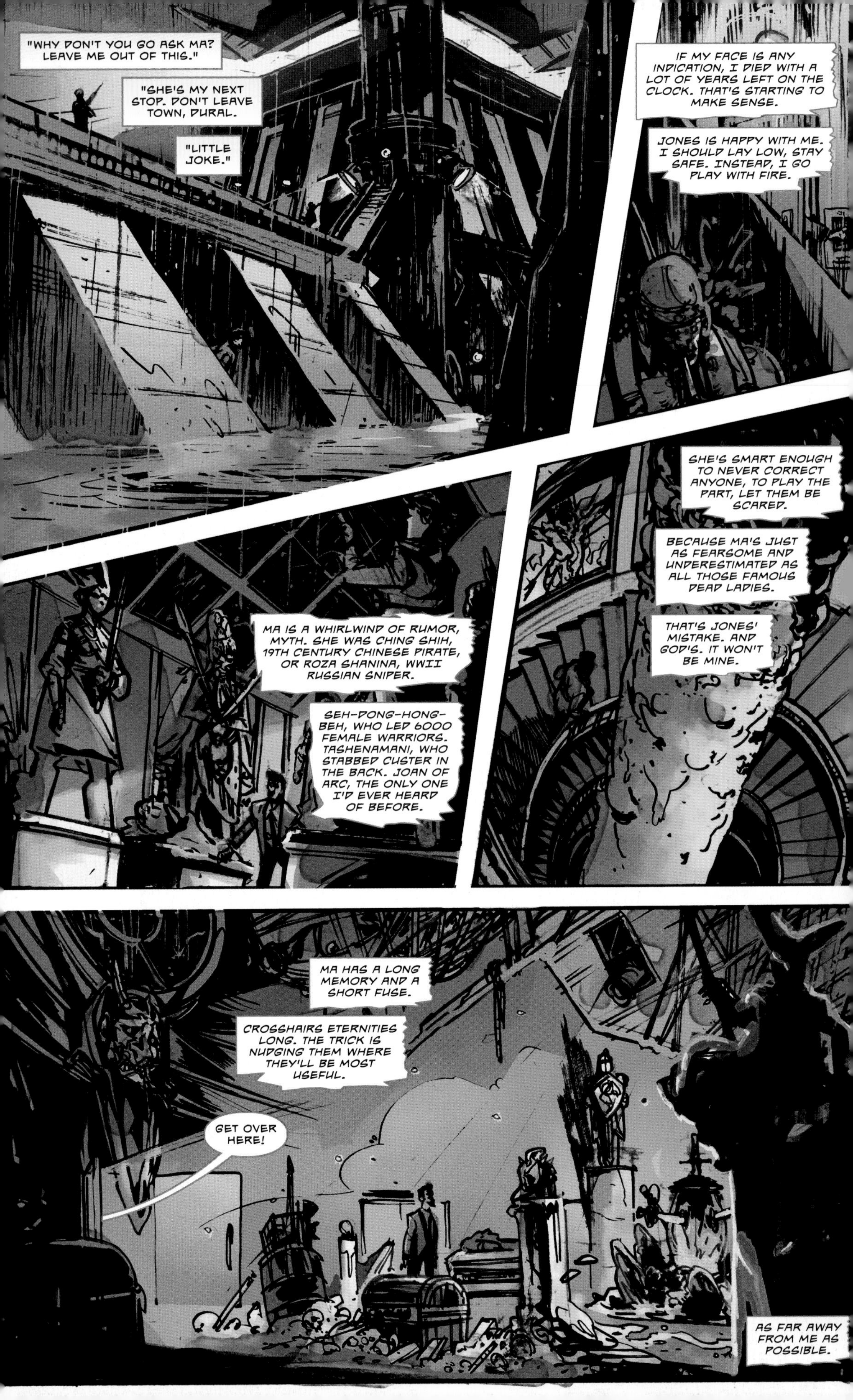
"WHY DON'T YOU GO ASK MA? LEAVE ME OUT OF THIS."
"SHE'S MY NEXT STOP. DON'T LEAVE TOWN, DURAL.
"LITTLE JOKE."
IF MY FACE IS ANY INDICATION, I DIED WITH A LOT OF YEARS LEFT ON THE CLOCK. THAT'S STARTING TO MAKE SENSE.
JONES IS HAPPY WITH ME. I SHOULD LAY LOW, STAY SAFE. INSTEAD, I GO PLAY WITH FIRE.
MA IS A WHIRLWIND OF RUMOR, MYTH. SHE WAS CHING SHIH, 19TH CENTURY CHINESE PIRATE, OR ROZA SHANINA, WWII RUSSIAN SNIPER.
SEH-DONG-HONG-BEH, WHO LED 6000 FEMALE WARRIORS. TASHENAMANI, WHO STABBED CUSTER IN THE BACK. JOAN OF ARC, THE ONLY ONE I'D EVER HEARD OF BEFORE.
SHE'S SMART ENOUGH TO NEVER CORRECT ANYONE, TO PLAY THE PART, LET THEM BE SCARED.
BECAUSE MA'S JUST AS FEARSOME AND UNDERESTIMATED AS ALL THOSE FAMOUS DEAD LADIES.
THAT'S JONES' MISTAKE. AND GOD'S. IT WON'T BE MINE.
MA HAS A LONG MEMORY AND A SHORT FUSE.
CROSSHAIRS ETERNITIES LONG. THE TRICK IS NUDGING THEM WHERE THEY'LL BE MOST USEFUL.
GET OVER HERE!
AS FAR AWAY FROM ME AS POSSIBLE.

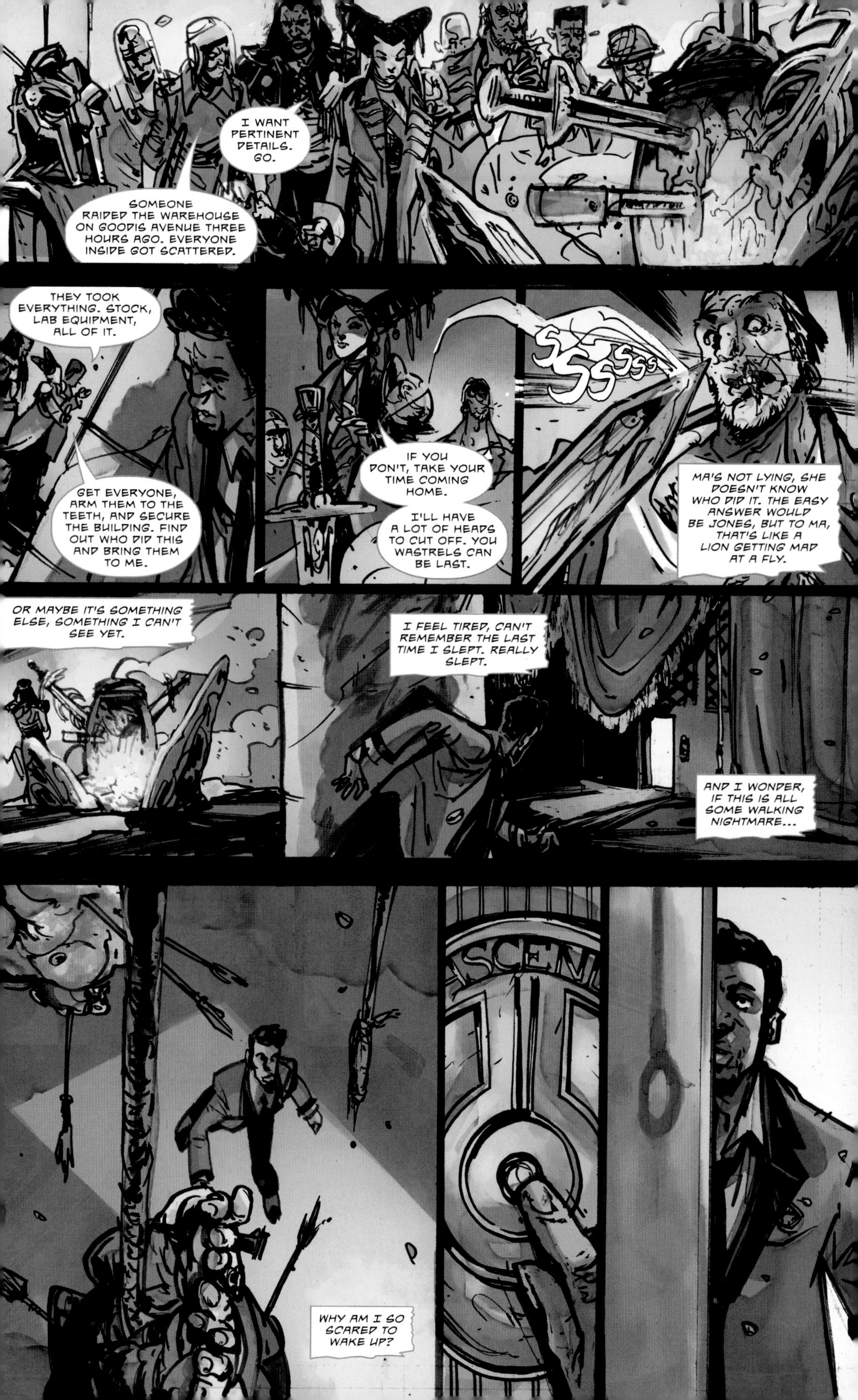
I WANT PERTINENT DETAILS. GO.
SOMEONE RAIDED THE WAREHOUSE ON GOODIS AVENUE THREE HOURS AGO. EVERYONE INSIDE GOT SCATTERED.
THEY TOOK EVERYTHING. STOCK, LAB EQUIPMENT, ALL OF IT.
GET EVERYONE, ARM THEM TO THE TEETH, AND SECURE THE BUILDING. FIND OUT WHO DID THIS AND BRING THEM TO ME.
IF YOU DON'T, TAKE YOUR TIME COMING HOME.
I'LL HAVE A LOT OF HEADS TO CUT OFF. YOU WASTRELS CAN BE LAST.
SSSSSSS
MA'S NOT LYING, SHE DOESN'T KNOW WHO DID IT. THE EASY ANSWER WOULD BE JONES, BUT TO MA, THAT'S LIKE A LION GETTING MAD AT A FLY.
OR MAYBE IT'S SOMETHING ELSE, SOMETHING I CAN'T SEE YET.
I FEEL TIRED, CAN'T REMEMBER THE LAST TIME I SLEPT. REALLY SLEPT.
AND I WONDER, IF THIS IS ALL SOME WALKING NIGHTMARE...
ASCEN
WHY AM I SO SCARED TO WAKE UP?

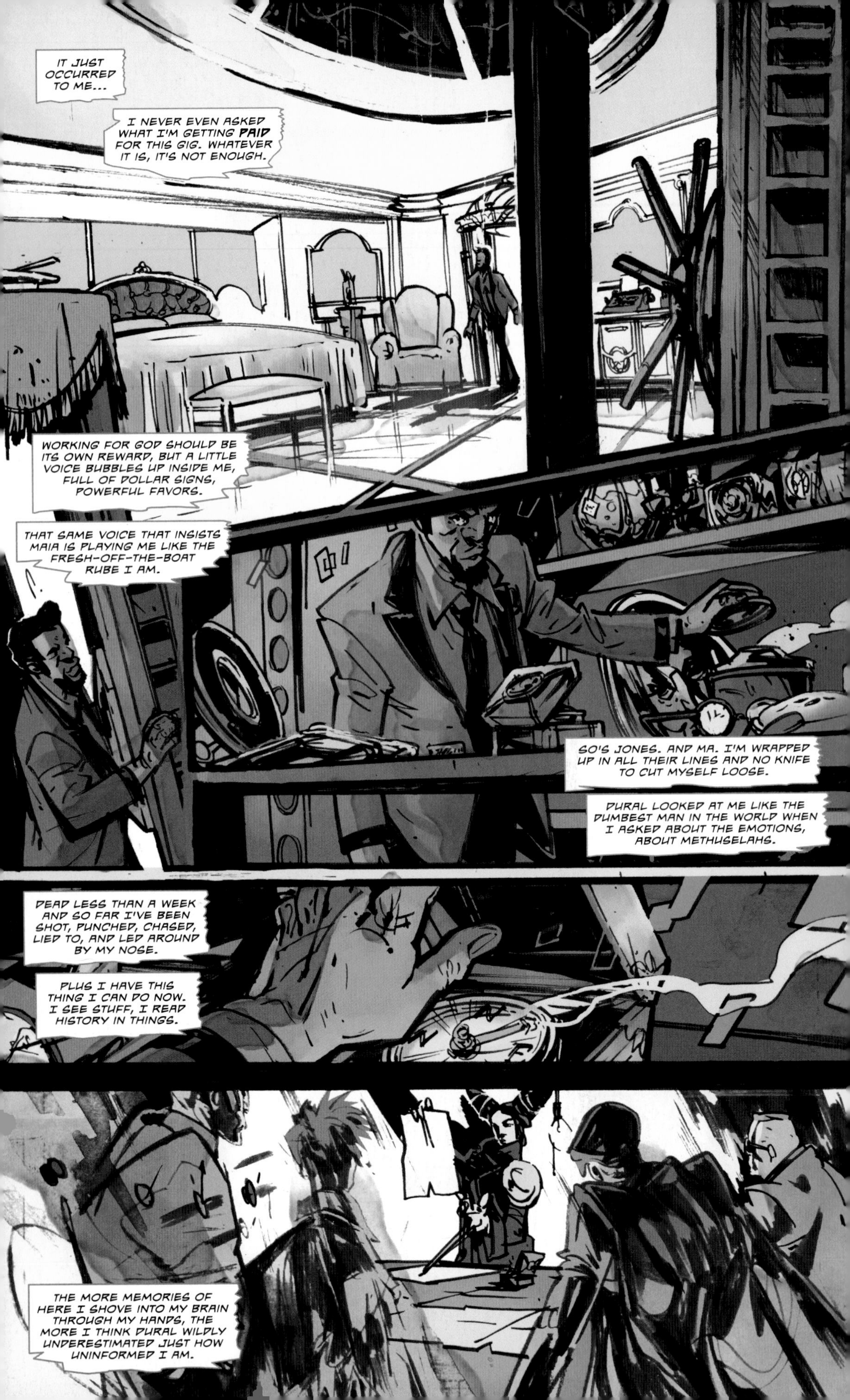

IT JUST OCCURRED TO ME...
I NEVER EVEN ASKED WHAT I'M GETTING **PAID** FOR THIS GIG. WHATEVER IT IS, IT'S NOT ENOUGH.
WORKING FOR GOD SHOULD BE ITS OWN REWARD, BUT A LITTLE VOICE BUBBLES UP INSIDE ME, FULL OF DOLLAR SIGNS, POWERFUL FAVORS.
THAT SAME VOICE THAT INSISTS MAIA IS PLAYING ME LIKE THE FRESH-OFF-THE-BOAT RUBE I AM.
SO'S JONES. AND MA. I'M WRAPPED UP IN ALL THEIR LINES AND NO KNIFE TO CUT MYSELF LOOSE.
DURAL LOOKED AT ME LIKE THE DUMBEST MAN IN THE WORLD WHEN I ASKED ABOUT THE EMOTIONS, ABOUT METHUSELAHS.
DEAD LESS THAN A WEEK AND SO FAR I'VE BEEN SHOT, PUNCHED, CHASED, LIED TO, AND LED AROUND BY MY NOSE.
PLUS I HAVE THIS THING I CAN DO NOW. I SEE STUFF, I READ HISTORY IN THINGS.
THE MORE MEMORIES OF HERE I SHOVE INTO MY BRAIN THROUGH MY HANDS, THE MORE I THINK DURAL WILDLY UNDERESTIMATED JUST HOW UNINFORMED I AM.

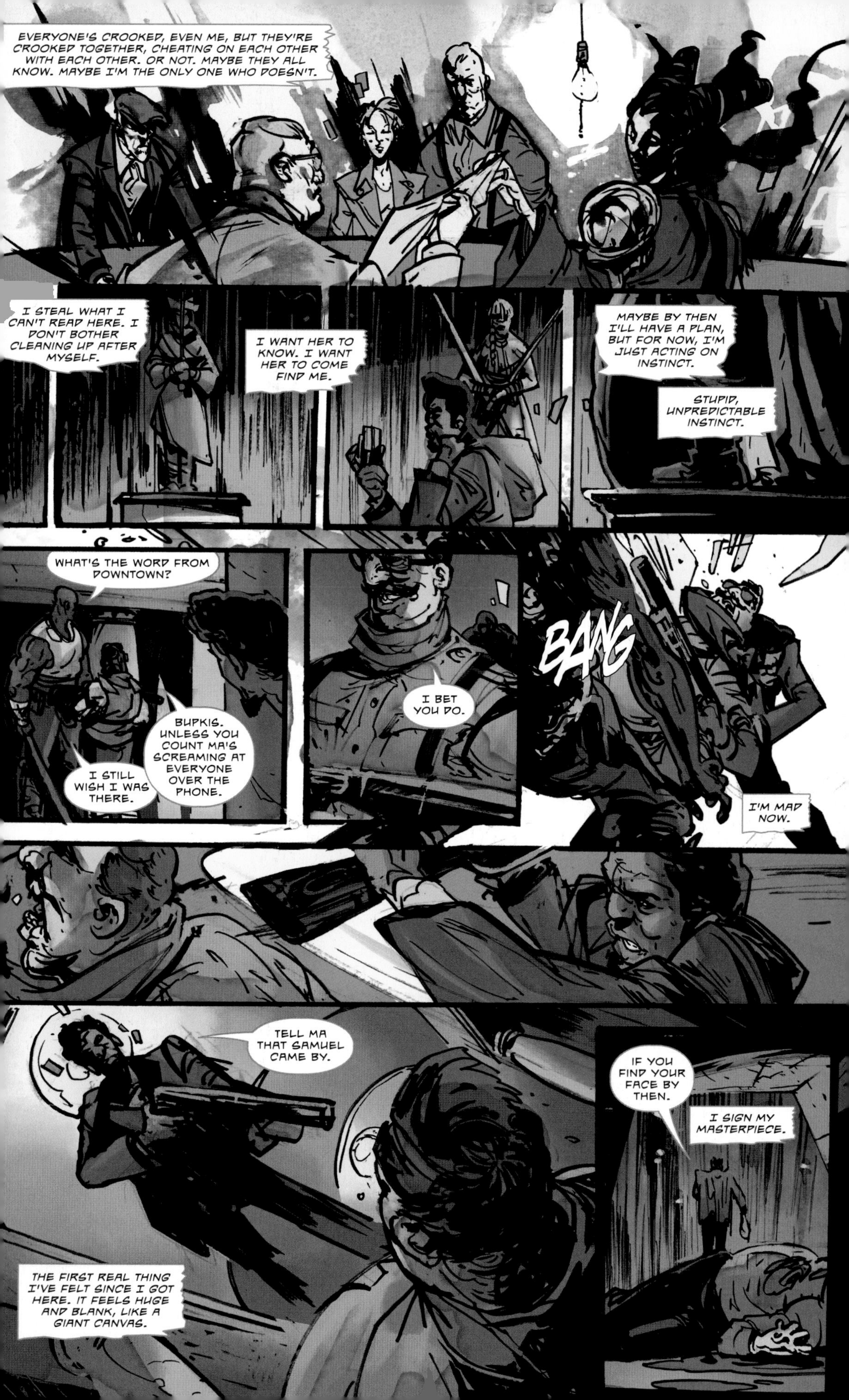
EVERYONE'S CROOKED, EVEN ME, BUT THEY'RE CROOKED TOGETHER, CHEATING ON EACH OTHER WITH EACH OTHER. OR NOT. MAYBE THEY ALL KNOW. MAYBE I'M THE ONLY ONE WHO DOESN'T.
I STEAL WHAT I CAN'T READ HERE. I DON'T BOTHER CLEANING UP AFTER MYSELF.
I WANT HER TO KNOW. I WANT HER TO COME FIND ME.
MAYBE BY THEN I'LL HAVE A PLAN, BUT FOR NOW, I'M JUST ACTING ON INSTINCT.
STUPID, UNPREDICTABLE INSTINCT.
WHAT'S THE WORD FROM DOWNTOWN?
BUPKIS. UNLESS YOU COUNT MA'S SCREAMING AT EVERYONE OVER THE PHONE.
I STILL WISH I WAS THERE.
I BET YOU DO.
BANG
I'M MAD NOW.
TELL MA THAT SAMUEL CAME BY.
IF YOU FIND YOUR FACE BY THEN.
I SIGN MY MASTERPIECE.
THE FIRST REAL THING I'VE FELT SINCE I GOT HERE. IT FEELS HUGE AND BLANK, LIKE A GIANT CANVAS.

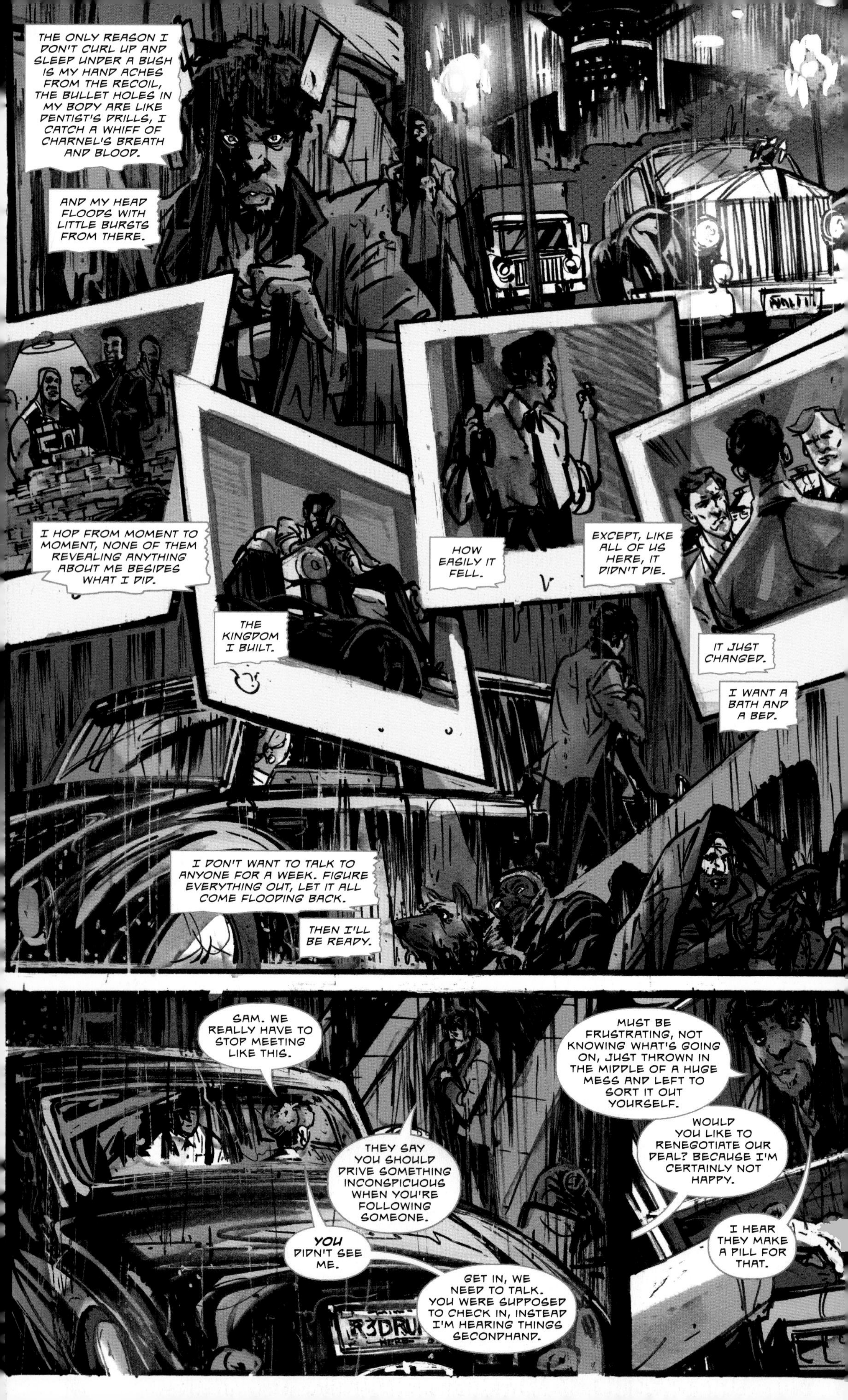
THE ONLY REASON I DON'T CURL UP AND SLEEP UNDER A BUSH IS MY HAND ACHES FROM THE RECOIL, THE BULLET HOLES IN MY BODY ARE LIKE DENTIST'S DRILLS, I CATCH A WHIFF OF CHARNEL'S BREATH AND BLOOD.
AND MY HEAD FLOODS WITH LITTLE BURSTS FROM THERE.
I HOP FROM MOMENT TO MOMENT, NONE OF THEM REVEALING ANYTHING ABOUT ME BESIDES WHAT I DID.
THE KINGDOM I BUILT.
HOW EASILY IT FELL.
EXCEPT, LIKE ALL OF US HERE, IT DIDN'T DIE.
IT JUST CHANGED.
I WANT A BATH AND A BED.
I DON'T WANT TO TALK TO ANYONE FOR A WEEK. FIGURE EVERYTHING OUT, LET IT ALL COME FLOODING BACK.
THEN I'LL BE READY.
SAM. WE REALLY HAVE TO STOP MEETING LIKE THIS.
THEY SAY YOU SHOULD DRIVE SOMETHING INCONSPICUOUS WHEN YOU'RE FOLLOWING SOMEONE.
YOU DIDN'T SEE ME.
GET IN, WE NEED TO TALK. YOU WERE SUPPOSED TO CHECK IN, INSTEAD I'M HEARING THINGS SECONDHAND.
MUST BE FRUSTRATING, NOT KNOWING WHAT'S GOING ON, JUST THROWN IN THE MIDDLE OF A HUGE MESS AND LEFT TO SORT IT OUT YOURSELF.
WOULD YOU LIKE TO RENEGOTIATE OUR DEAL? BECAUSE I'M CERTAINLY NOT HAPPY.
I HEAR THEY MAKE A PILL FOR THAT.

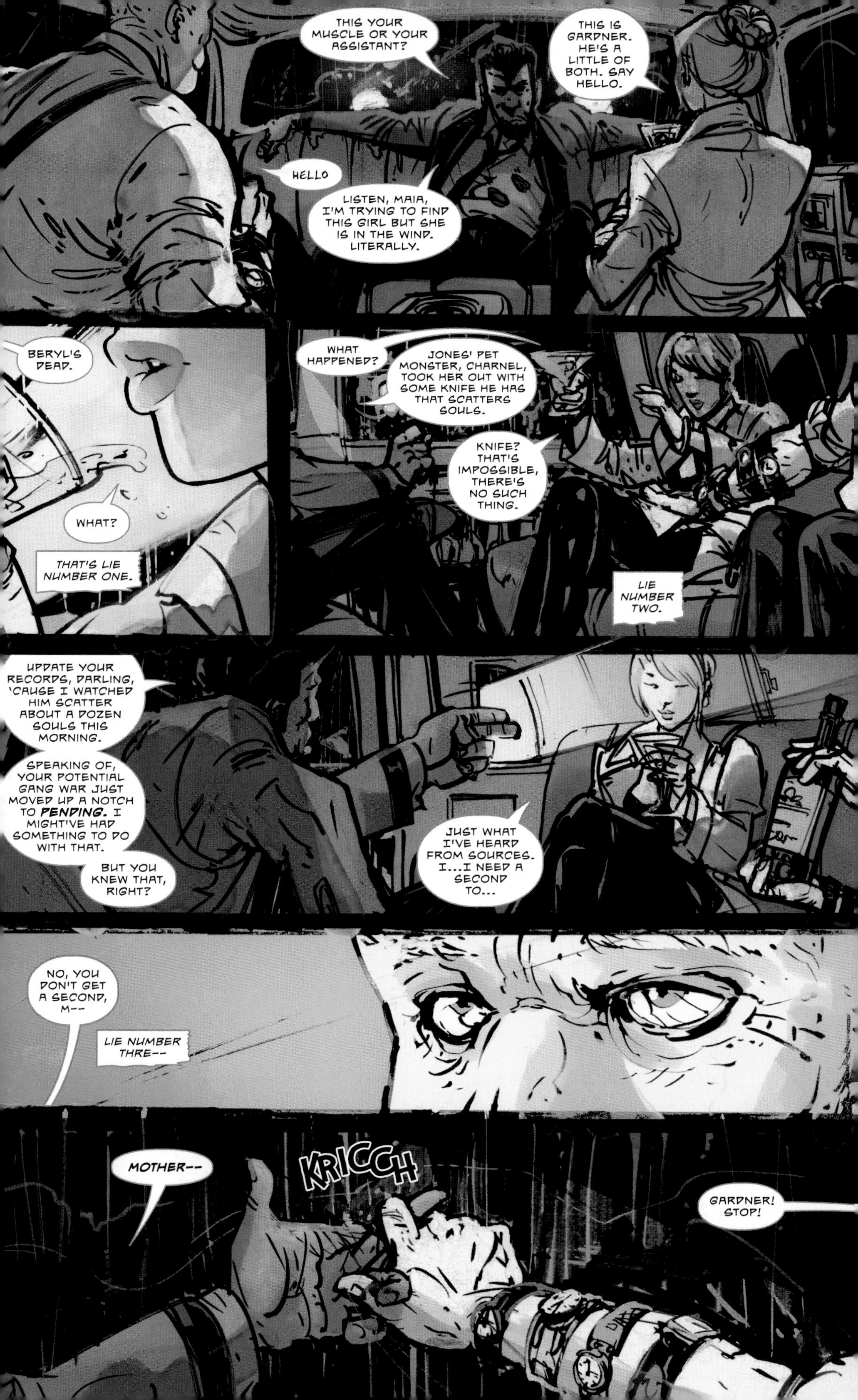
THIS YOUR MUSCLE OR YOUR ASSISTANT?
THIS IS GARDNER. HE'S A LITTLE OF BOTH. SAY HELLO.
HELLO
LISTEN, MAIA, I'M TRYING TO FIND THIS GIRL BUT SHE IS IN THE WIND. LITERALLY.
BERYL'S DEAD.
WHAT?
THAT'S LIE NUMBER ONE.
WHAT HAPPENED?
JONES' PET MONSTER, CHARNEL, TOOK HER OUT WITH SOME KNIFE HE HAS THAT SCATTERS SOULS.
KNIFE? THAT'S IMPOSSIBLE, THERE'S NO SUCH THING.
LIE NUMBER TWO.
UPDATE YOUR RECORDS, DARLING, 'CAUSE I WATCHED HIM SCATTER ABOUT A DOZEN SOULS THIS MORNING.
SPEAKING OF, YOUR POTENTIAL GANG WAR JUST MOVED UP A NOTCH TO **PENDING**. I MIGHT'VE HAD SOMETHING TO DO WITH THAT.
BUT YOU KNEW THAT, RIGHT?
JUST WHAT I'VE HEARD FROM SOURCES. I...I NEED A SECOND TO...
NO, YOU DON'T GET A SECOND, M--
LIE NUMBER THRE--
MOTHER--
KRICCH
GARDNER! STOP!

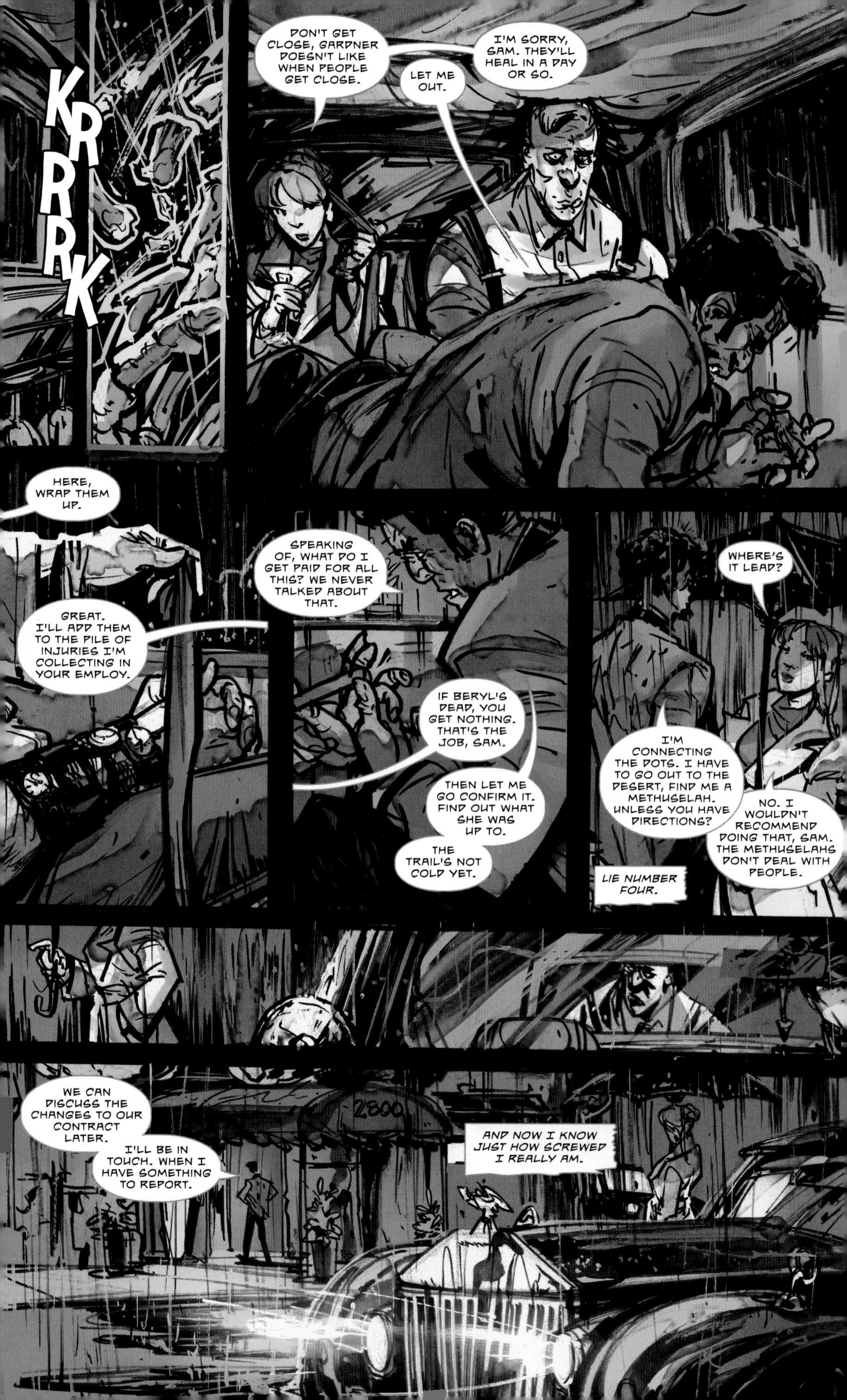
KRRRK
DON'T GET CLOSE, GARDNER DOESN'T LIKE WHEN PEOPLE GET CLOSE.
I'M SORRY, SAM. THEY'LL HEAL IN A DAY OR SO.
LET ME OUT.
HERE, WRAP THEM UP.
GREAT. I'LL ADD THEM TO THE PILE OF INJURIES I'M COLLECTING IN YOUR EMPLOY.
SPEAKING OF, WHAT DO I GET PAID FOR ALL THIS? WE NEVER TALKED ABOUT THAT.
IF BERYL'S DEAD, YOU GET NOTHING. THAT'S THE JOB, SAM.
THEN LET ME GO CONFIRM IT. FIND OUT WHAT SHE WAS UP TO.
THE TRAIL'S NOT COLD YET.
WHERE'S IT LEAD?
I'M CONNECTING THE DOTS. I HAVE TO GO OUT TO THE DESERT, FIND ME A METHUSELAH. UNLESS YOU HAVE DIRECTIONS?
NO. I WOULDN'T RECOMMEND DOING THAT, SAM. THE METHUSELAHS DON'T DEAL WITH PEOPLE.
LIE NUMBER FOUR.
WE CAN DISCUSS THE CHANGES TO OUR CONTRACT LATER.
I'LL BE IN TOUCH. WHEN I HAVE SOMETHING TO REPORT.
2800
AND NOW I KNOW JUST HOW SCREWED I REALLY AM.

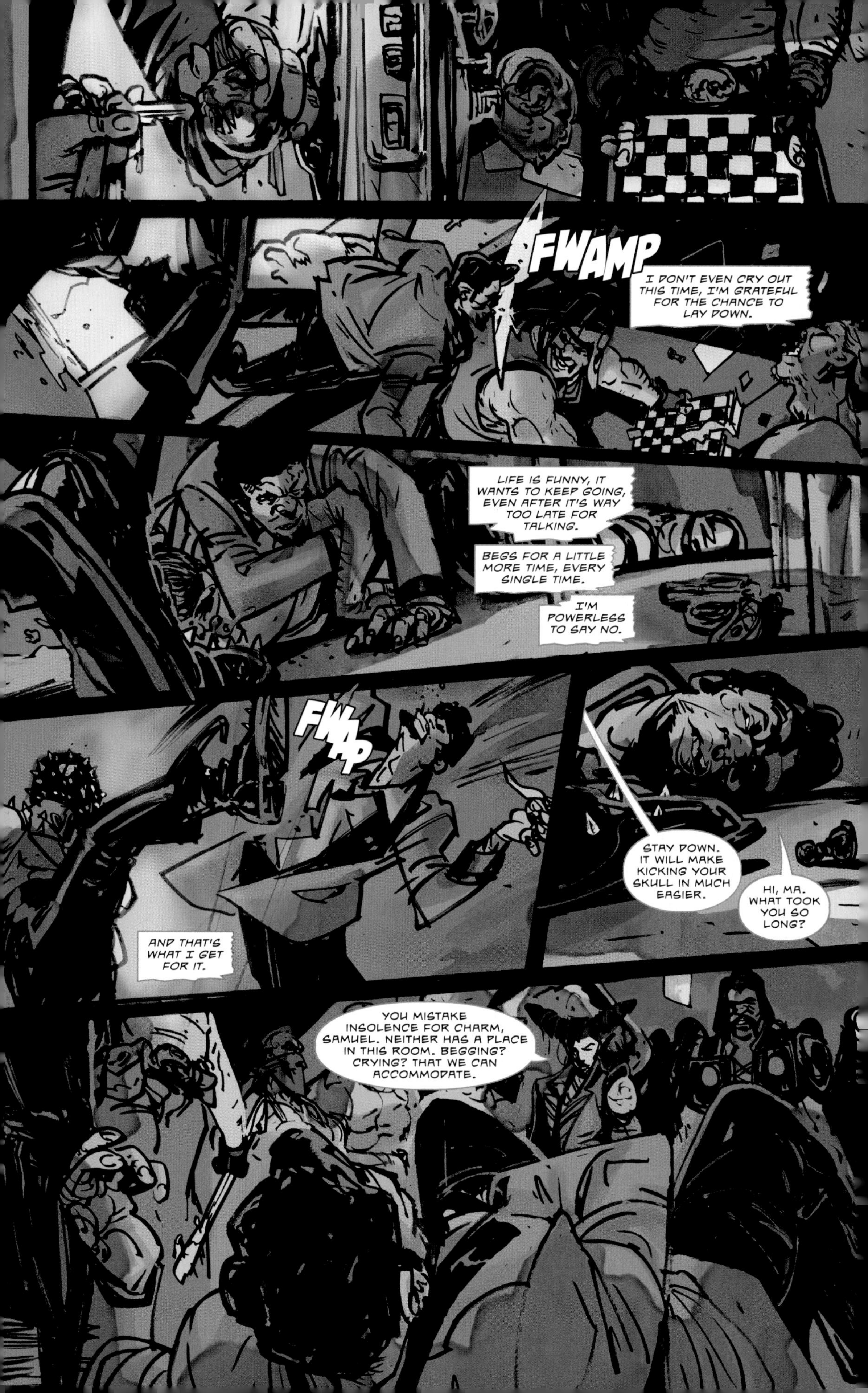
FWAMP
I DON'T EVEN CRY OUT THIS TIME, I'M GRATEFUL FOR THE CHANCE TO LAY DOWN.
LIFE IS FUNNY, IT WANTS TO KEEP GOING, EVEN AFTER IT'S WAY TOO LATE FOR TALKING.
BEGS FOR A LITTLE MORE TIME, EVERY SINGLE TIME.
I'M POWERLESS TO SAY NO.
FWAP
AND THAT'S WHAT I GET FOR IT.
STAY DOWN. IT WILL MAKE KICKING YOUR SKULL IN MUCH EASIER.
HI, MA. WHAT TOOK YOU SO LONG?
YOU MISTAKE INSOLENCE FOR CHARM, SAMUEL. NEITHER HAS A PLACE IN THIS ROOM. BEGGING? CRYING? THAT WE CAN ACCOMMODATE.

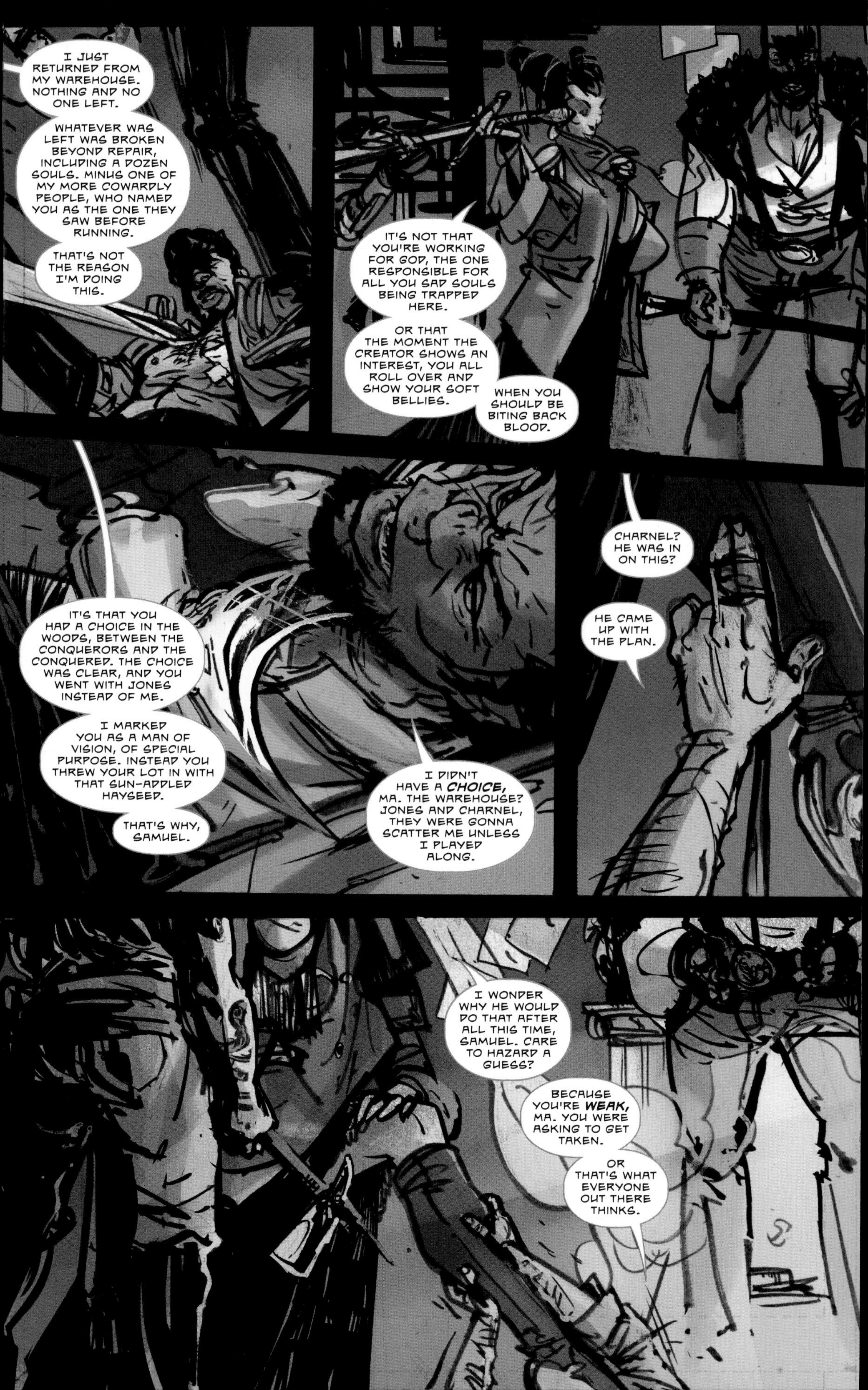
I JUST RETURNED FROM MY WAREHOUSE. NOTHING AND NO ONE LEFT.
WHATEVER WAS LEFT WAS BROKEN BEYOND REPAIR, INCLUDING A DOZEN SOULS. MINUS ONE OF MY MORE COWARDLY PEOPLE, WHO NAMED YOU AS THE ONE THEY SAW BEFORE RUNNING.
THAT'S NOT THE REASON I'M DOING THIS.
IT'S NOT THAT YOU'RE WORKING FOR GOD, THE ONE RESPONSIBLE FOR ALL YOU SAD SOULS BEING TRAPPED HERE.
OR THAT THE MOMENT THE CREATOR SHOWS AN INTEREST, YOU ALL ROLL OVER AND SHOW YOUR SOFT BELLIES.
WHEN YOU SHOULD BE BITING BACK BLOOD.
IT'S THAT YOU HAD A CHOICE IN THE WOODS, BETWEEN THE CONQUERORS AND THE CONQUERED. THE CHOICE WAS CLEAR, AND YOU WENT WITH JONES INSTEAD OF ME.
I MARKED YOU AS A MAN OF VISION, OF SPECIAL PURPOSE. INSTEAD YOU THREW YOUR LOT IN WITH THAT SUN-ADDLED HAYSEED.
THAT'S WHY, SAMUEL.
I DIDN'T HAVE A **CHOICE,** MA. THE WAREHOUSE? JONES AND CHARNEL, THEY WERE GONNA SCATTER ME UNLESS I PLAYED ALONG.
CHARNEL? HE WAS IN ON THIS?
HE CAME UP WITH THE PLAN.
I WONDER WHY HE WOULD DO THAT AFTER ALL THIS TIME, SAMUEL. CARE TO HAZARD A GUESS?
BECAUSE YOU'RE **WEAK,** MA. YOU WERE ASKING TO GET TAKEN.
OR THAT'S WHAT EVERYONE OUT THERE THINKS.

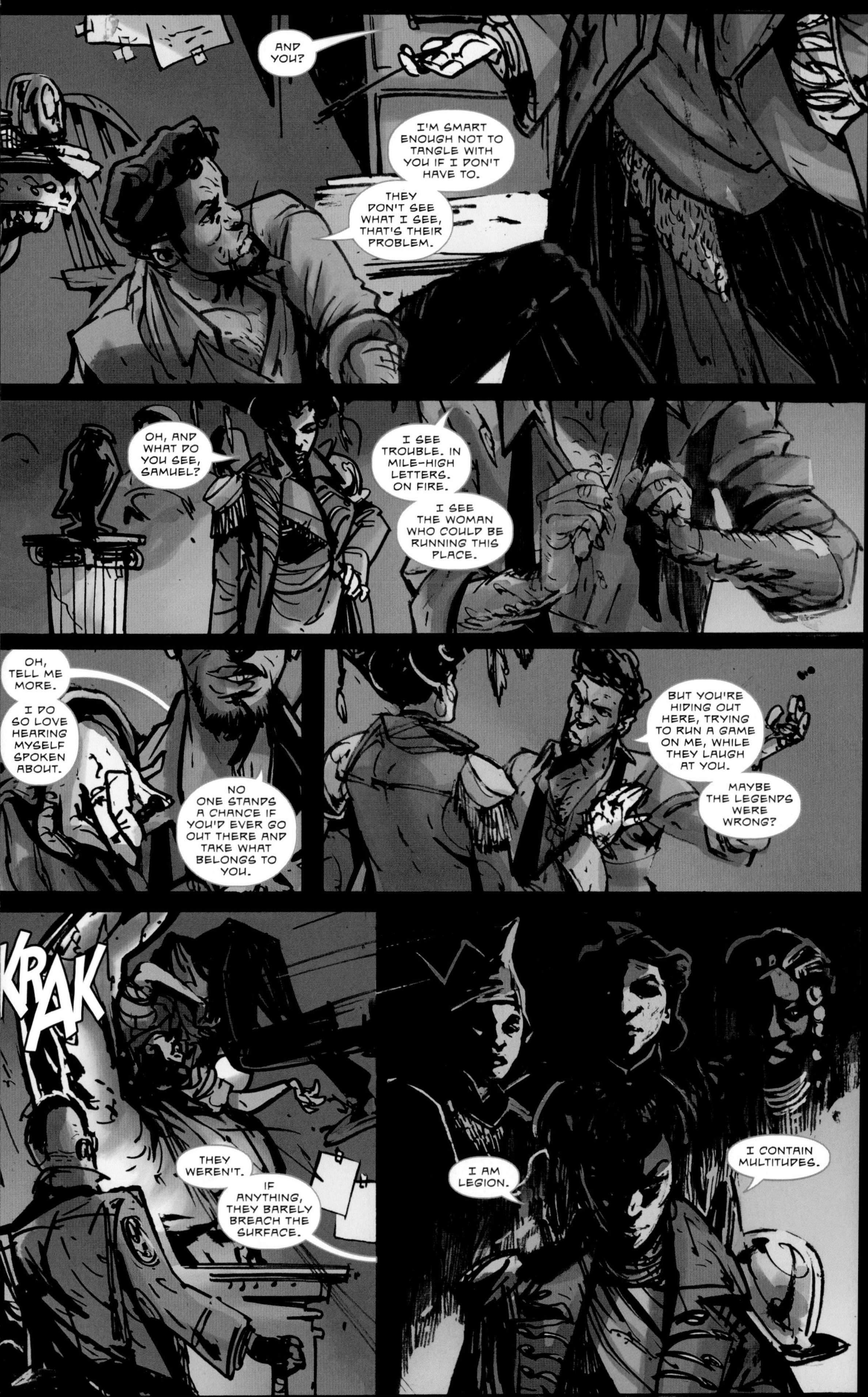
AND YOU?
I'M SMART ENOUGH NOT TO TANGLE WITH YOU IF I DON'T HAVE TO.
THEY DON'T SEE WHAT I SEE, THAT'S THEIR PROBLEM.
OH, AND WHAT DO YOU SEE, SAMUEL?
I SEE TROUBLE. IN MILE-HIGH LETTERS. ON FIRE.
I SEE THE WOMAN WHO COULD BE RUNNING THIS PLACE.
OH, TELL ME MORE.
I DO SO LOVE HEARING MYSELF SPOKEN ABOUT.
NO ONE STANDS A CHANCE IF YOU'D EVER GO OUT THERE AND TAKE WHAT BELONGS TO YOU.
BUT YOU'RE HIDING OUT HERE, TRYING TO RUN A GAME ON ME, WHILE THEY LAUGH AT YOU.
MAYBE THE LEGENDS WERE WRONG?
KRAK
THEY WEREN'T.
IF ANYTHING, THEY BARELY BREACH THE SURFACE.
I AM LEGION.
I CONTAIN MULTITUDES.

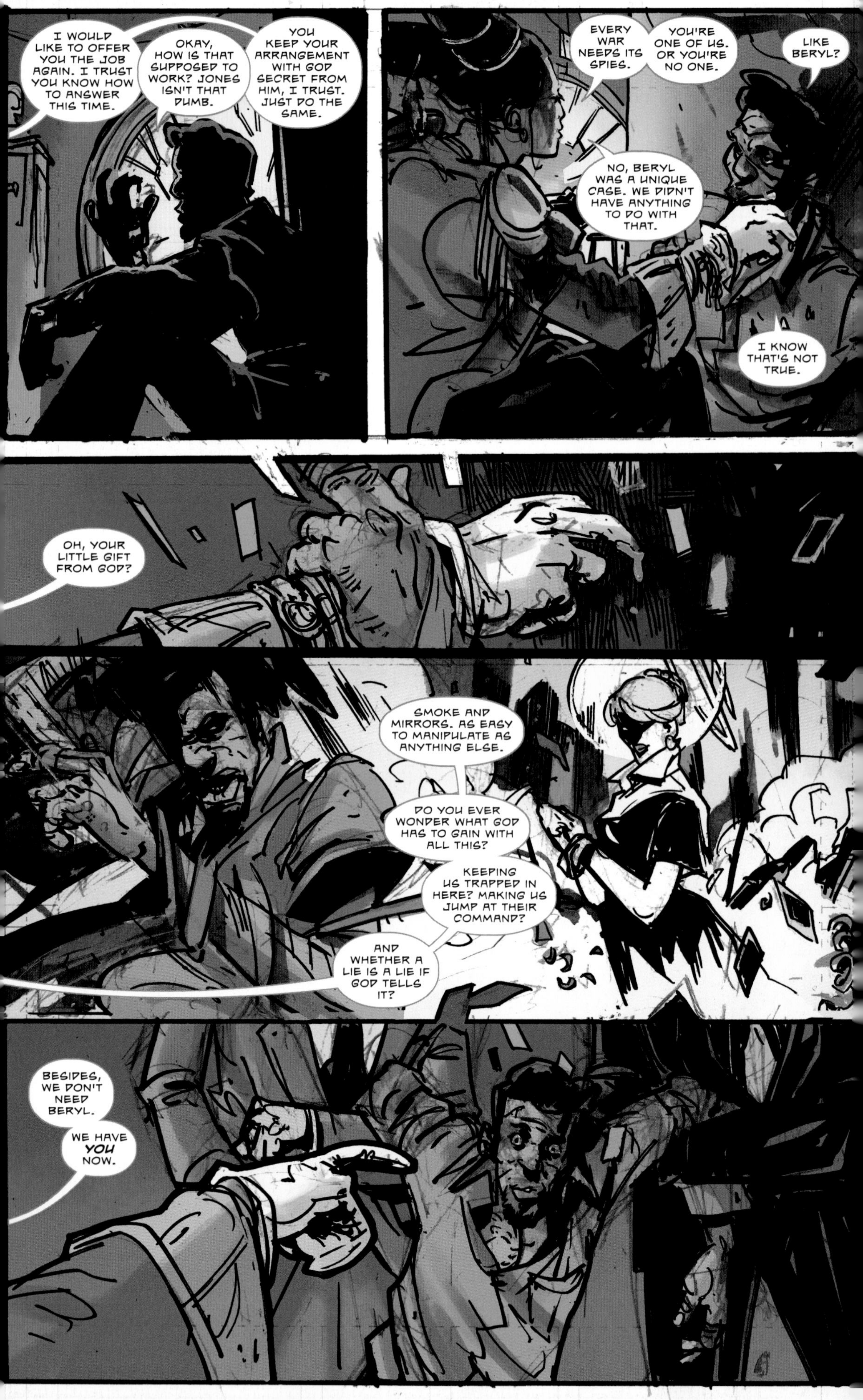
I WOULD LIKE TO OFFER YOU THE JOB AGAIN. I TRUST YOU KNOW HOW TO ANSWER THIS TIME.
OKAY, HOW IS THAT SUPPOSED TO WORK? JONES ISN'T THAT DUMB.
YOU KEEP YOUR ARRANGEMENT WITH GOD SECRET FROM HIM, I TRUST. JUST DO THE SAME.
EVERY WAR NEEDS ITS SPIES.
YOU'RE ONE OF US. OR YOU'RE NO ONE.
LIKE BERYL?
NO, BERYL WAS A UNIQUE CASE. WE DIDN'T HAVE ANYTHING TO DO WITH THAT.
I KNOW THAT'S NOT TRUE.
OH, YOUR LITTLE GIFT FROM GOD?
SMOKE AND MIRRORS. AS EASY TO MANIPULATE AS ANYTHING ELSE.
DO YOU EVER WONDER WHAT GOD HAS TO GAIN WITH ALL THIS?
KEEPING US TRAPPED IN HERE? MAKING US JUMP AT THEIR COMMAND?
AND WHETHER A LIE IS A LIE IF GOD TELLS IT?
BESIDES, WE DON'T NEED BERYL.
WE HAVE *YOU* NOW.

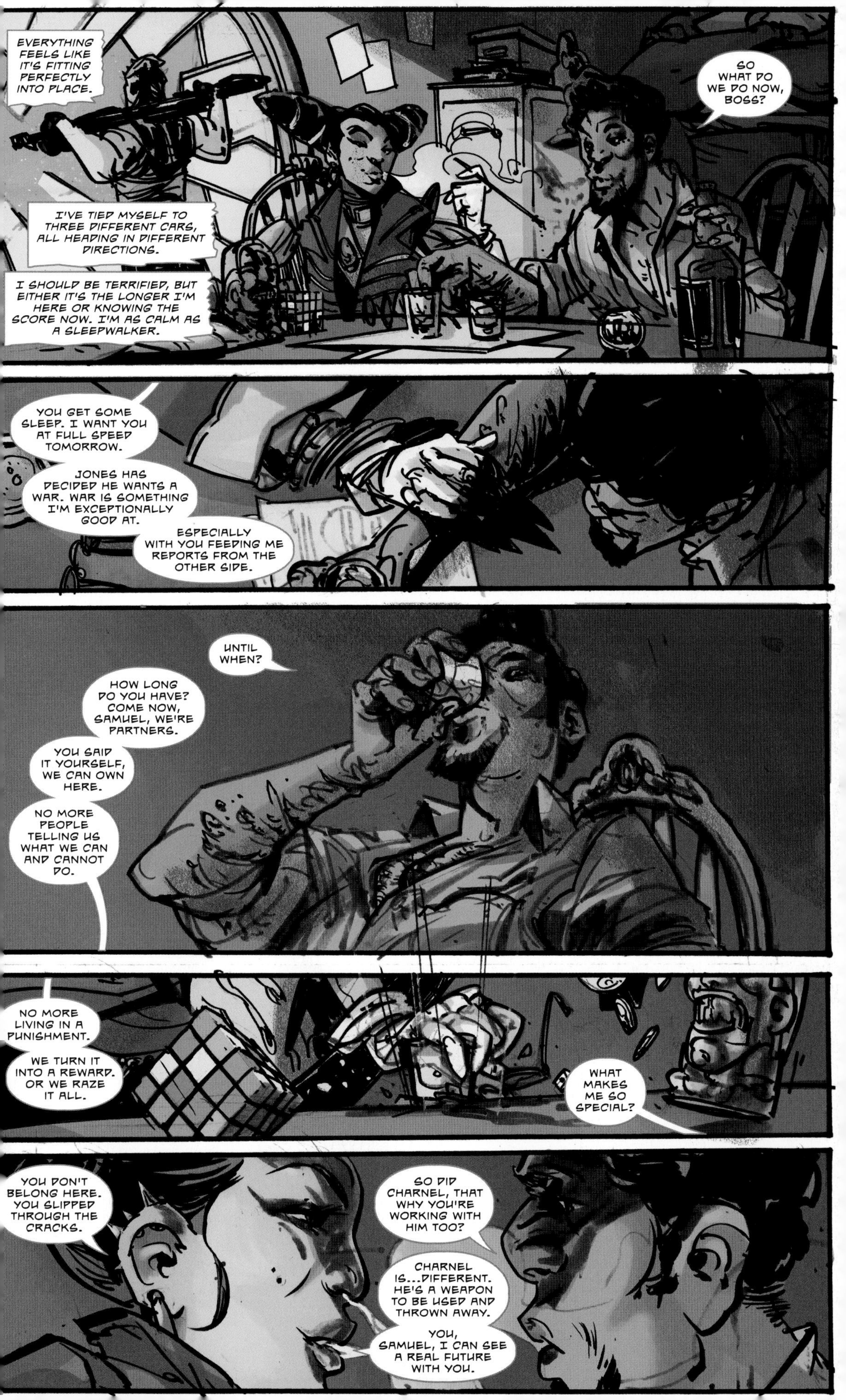
EVERYTHING FEELS LIKE IT'S FITTING PERFECTLY INTO PLACE.
SO WHAT DO WE DO NOW, BOSS?
I'VE TIED MYSELF TO THREE DIFFERENT CARS, ALL HEADING IN DIFFERENT DIRECTIONS.
I SHOULD BE TERRIFIED, BUT EITHER IT'S THE LONGER I'M HERE OR KNOWING THE SCORE NOW. I'M AS CALM AS A SLEEPWALKER.
YOU GET SOME SLEEP. I WANT YOU AT FULL SPEED TOMORROW.
JONES HAS DECIDED HE WANTS A WAR. WAR IS SOMETHING I'M EXCEPTIONALLY GOOD AT.
ESPECIALLY WITH YOU FEEDING ME REPORTS FROM THE OTHER SIDE.
UNTIL WHEN?
HOW LONG DO YOU HAVE? COME NOW, SAMUEL, WE'RE PARTNERS.
YOU SAID IT YOURSELF, WE CAN OWN HERE.
NO MORE PEOPLE TELLING US WHAT WE CAN AND CANNOT DO.
NO MORE LIVING IN A PUNISHMENT.
WE TURN IT INTO A REWARD. OR WE RAZE IT ALL.
WHAT MAKES ME SO SPECIAL?
YOU DON'T BELONG HERE. YOU SLIPPED THROUGH THE CRACKS.
SO DID CHARNEL, THAT WHY YOU'RE WORKING WITH HIM TOO?
CHARNEL IS...DIFFERENT. HE'S A WEAPON TO BE USED AND THROWN AWAY.
YOU, SAMUEL, I CAN SEE A REAL FUTURE WITH YOU.

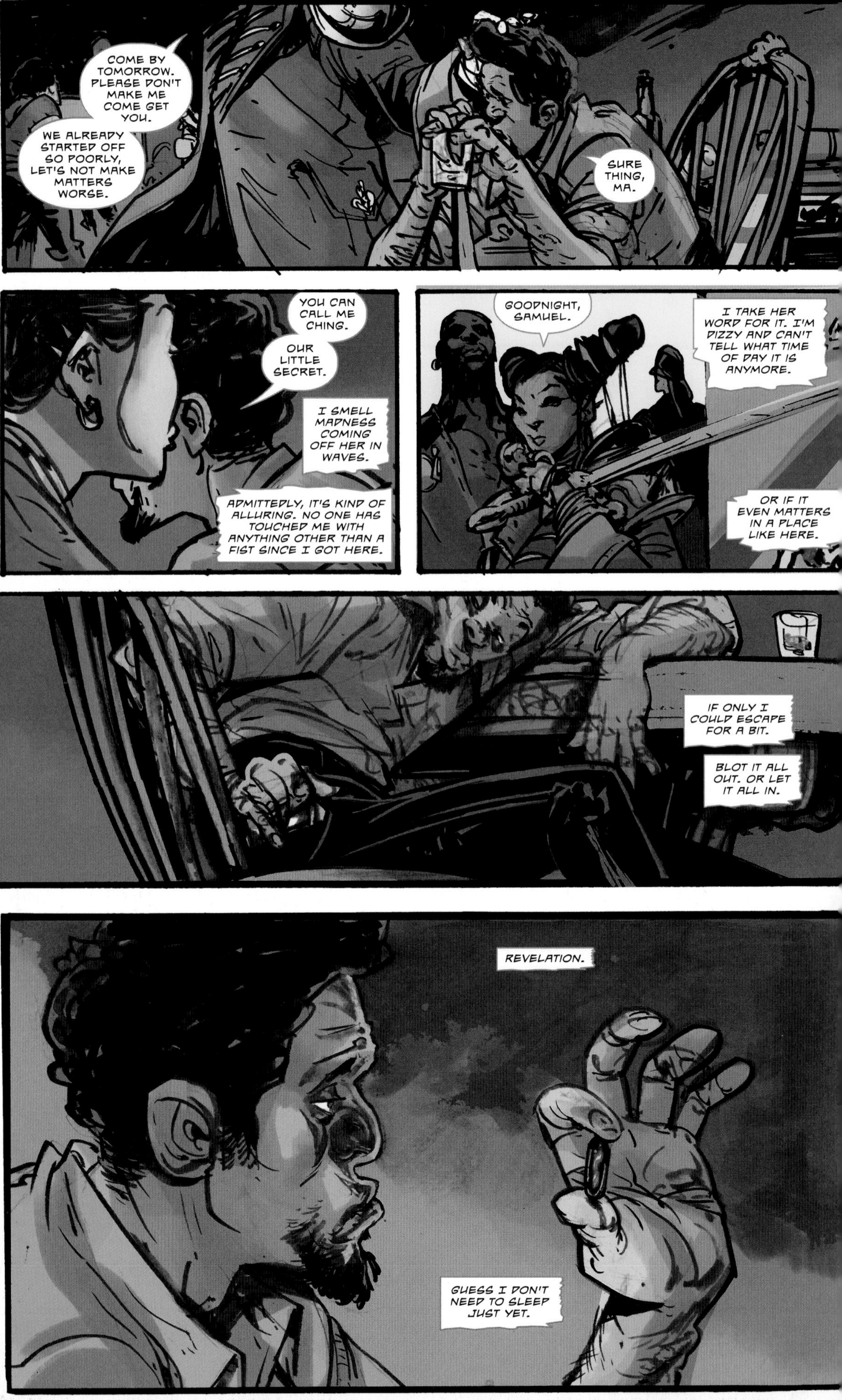
COME BY TOMORROW. PLEASE DON'T MAKE ME COME GET YOU.
WE ALREADY STARTED OFF SO POORLY, LET'S NOT MAKE MATTERS WORSE.
SURE THING, MA.
YOU CAN CALL ME CHING.
OUR LITTLE SECRET.
I SMELL MADNESS COMING OFF HER IN WAVES.
ADMITTEDLY, IT'S KIND OF ALLURING. NO ONE HAS TOUCHED ME WITH ANYTHING OTHER THAN A FIST SINCE I GOT HERE.
GOODNIGHT, SAMUEL.
I TAKE HER WORD FOR IT. I'M DIZZY AND CAN'T TELL WHAT TIME OF DAY IT IS ANYMORE.
OR IF IT EVEN MATTERS IN A PLACE LIKE HERE.
IF ONLY I COULD ESCAPE FOR A BIT.
BLOT IT ALL OUT. OR LET IT ALL IN.
REVELATION.
GUESS I DON'T NEED TO SLEEP JUST YET.

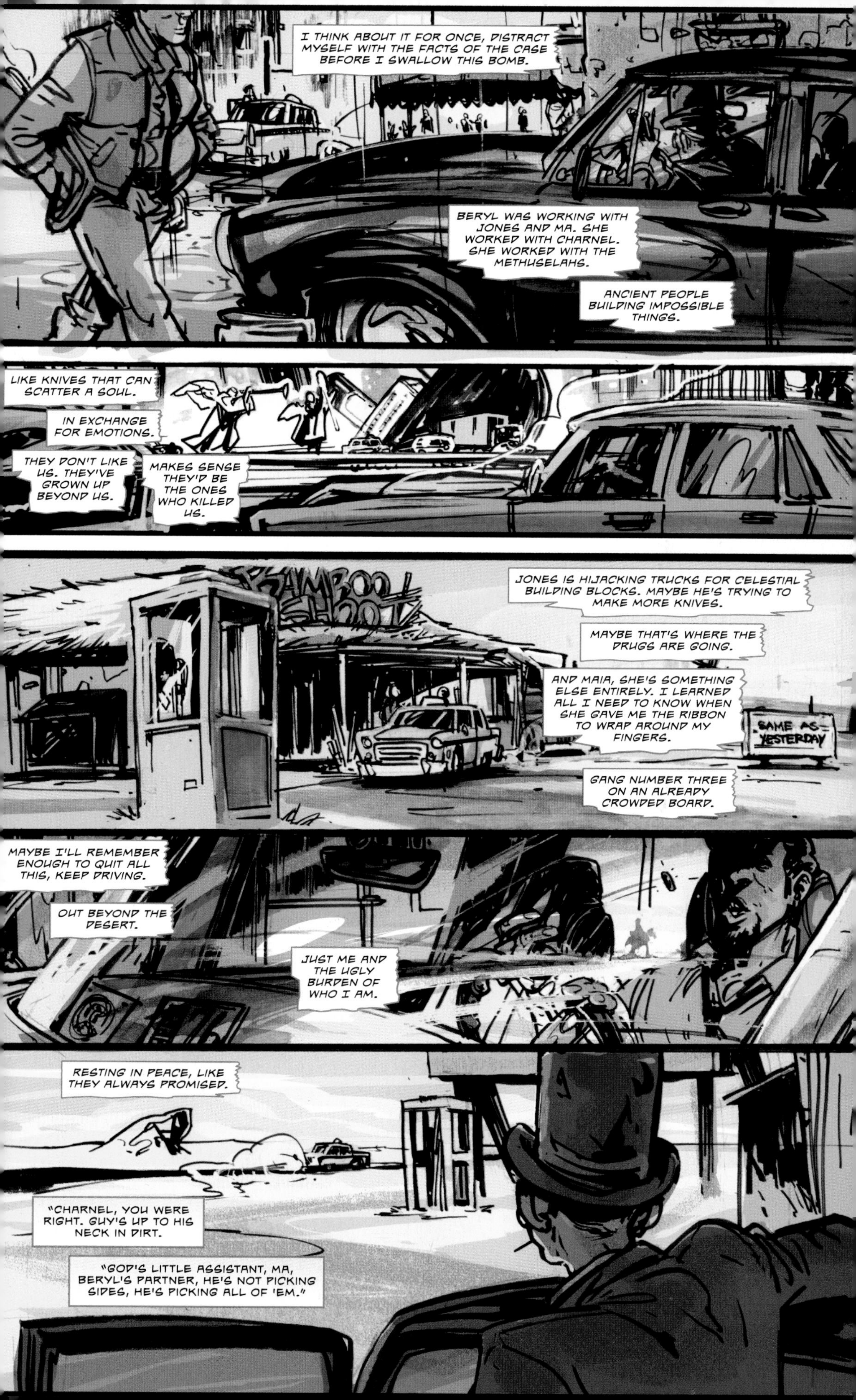
I THINK ABOUT IT FOR ONCE, DISTRACT MYSELF WITH THE FACTS OF THE CASE BEFORE I SWALLOW THIS BOMB.
BERYL WAS WORKING WITH JONES AND MA. SHE WORKED WITH CHARNEL. SHE WORKED WITH THE METHUSELAHS.
ANCIENT PEOPLE BUILDING IMPOSSIBLE THINGS.
LIKE KNIVES THAT CAN SCATTER A SOUL.
IN EXCHANGE FOR EMOTIONS.
THEY DON'T LIKE US. THEY'VE GROWN UP BEYOND US.
MAKES SENSE THEY'D BE THE ONES WHO KILLED US.
BAMBOO SHOOT
JONES IS HIJACKING TRUCKS FOR CELESTIAL BUILDING BLOCKS. MAYBE HE'S TRYING TO MAKE MORE KNIVES.
MAYBE THAT'S WHERE THE DRUGS ARE GOING.
AND MAIA, SHE'S SOMETHING ELSE ENTIRELY. I LEARNED ALL I NEED TO KNOW WHEN SHE GAVE ME THE RIBBON TO WRAP AROUND MY FINGERS.
SAME AS YESTERDAY
GANG NUMBER THREE ON AN ALREADY CROWDED BOARD.
MAYBE I'LL REMEMBER ENOUGH TO QUIT ALL THIS, KEEP DRIVING.
OUT BEYOND THE DESERT.
JUST ME AND THE UGLY BURDEN OF WHO I AM.
RESTING IN PEACE, LIKE THEY ALWAYS PROMISED.
"CHARNEL, YOU WERE RIGHT. GUY'S UP TO HIS NECK IN DIRT.
"GOD'S LITTLE ASSISTANT, MA, BERYL'S PARTNER, HE'S NOT PICKING SIDES, HE'S PICKING ALL OF 'EM."

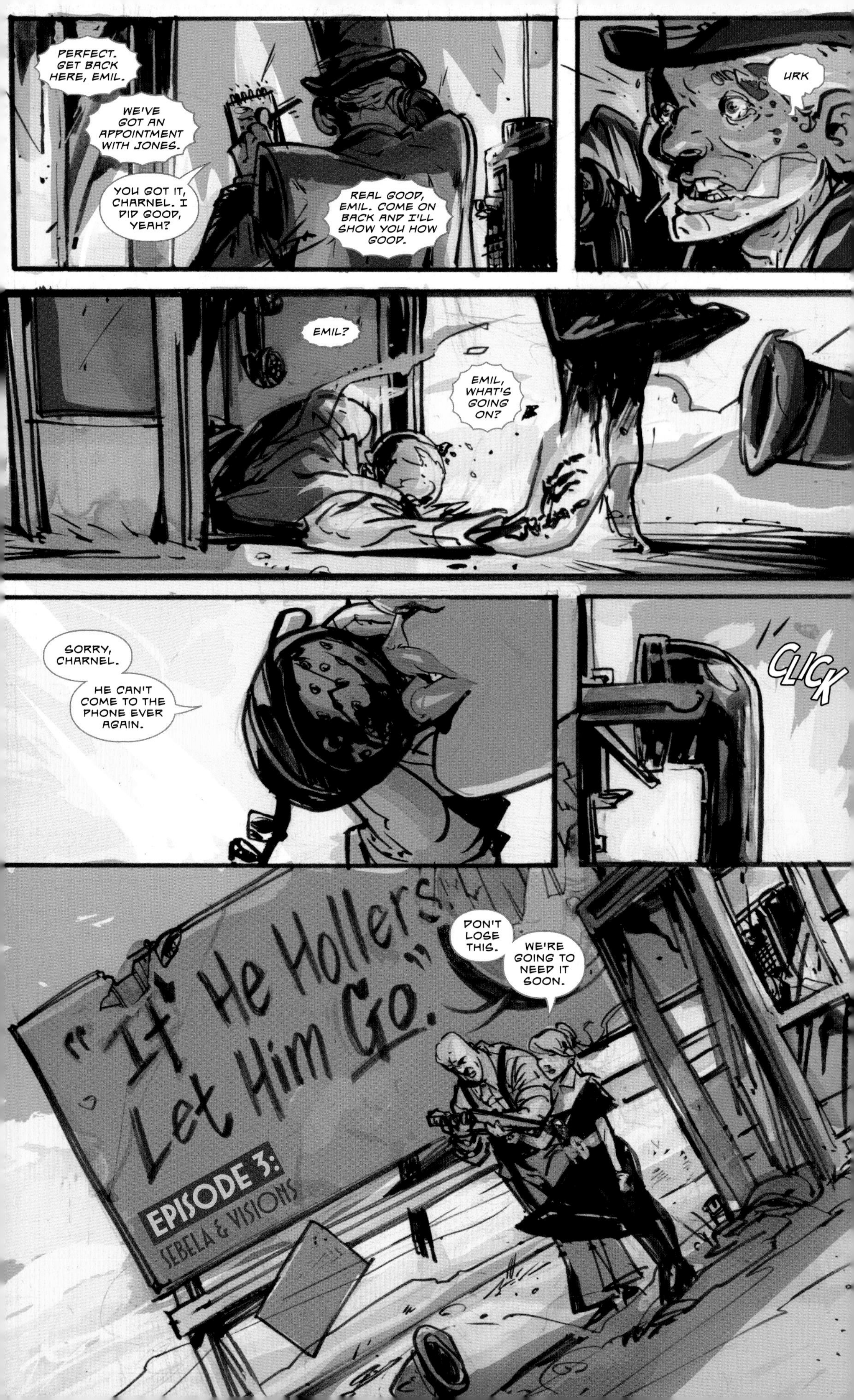
PERFECT. GET BACK HERE, EMIL.
WE'VE GOT AN APPOINTMENT WITH JONES.
YOU GOT IT, CHARNEL. I DID GOOD, YEAH?
REAL GOOD, EMIL. COME ON BACK AND I'LL SHOW YOU HOW GOOD.
URK
EMIL?
EMIL, WHAT'S GOING ON?
SORRY, CHARNEL.
HE CAN'T COME TO THE PHONE EVER AGAIN.
CLICK
"If He Hollers, Let Him Go."
EPISODE 3:
SEBELA & VISIONS
DON'T LOSE THIS.
WE'RE GOING TO NEED IT SOON.

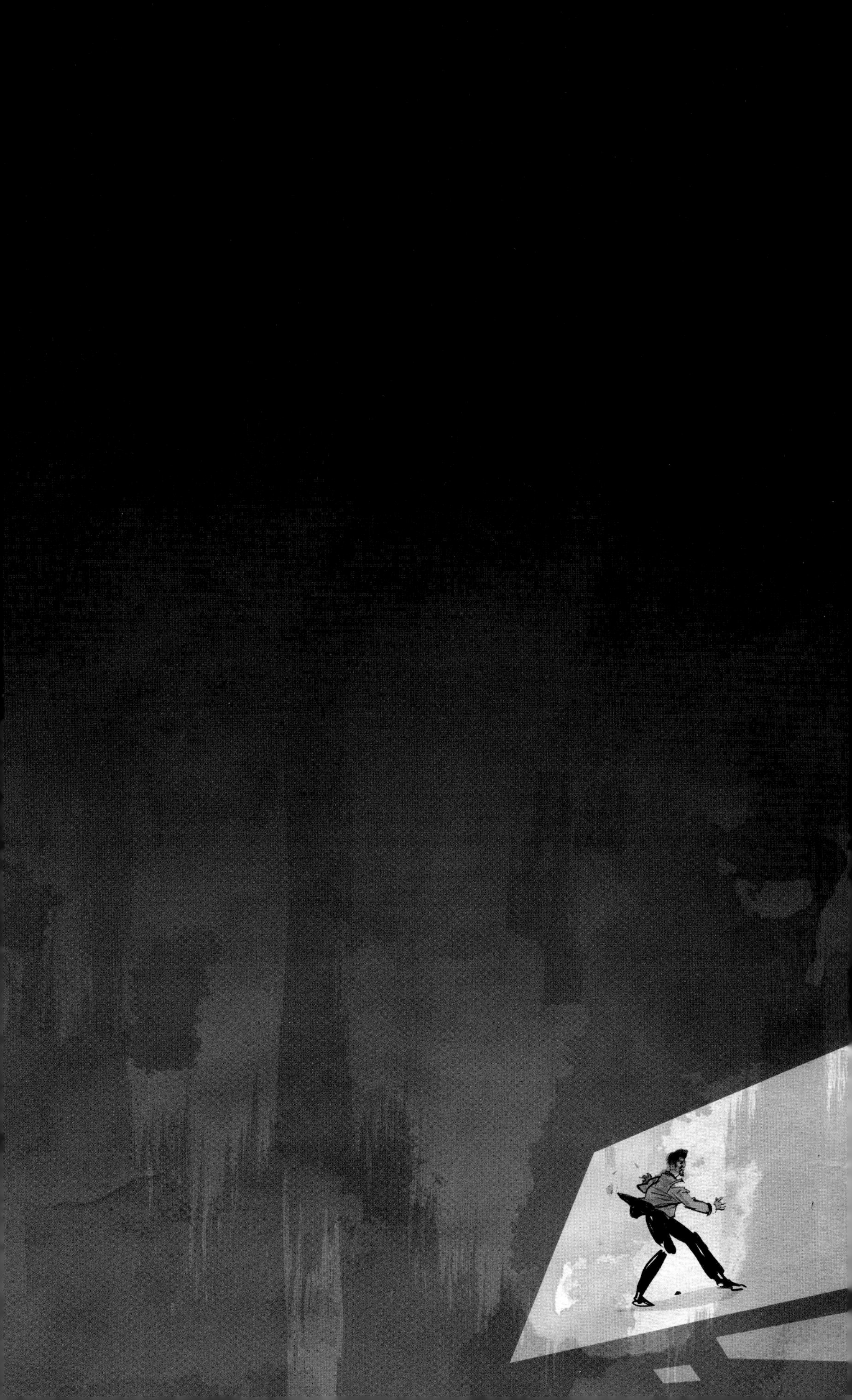

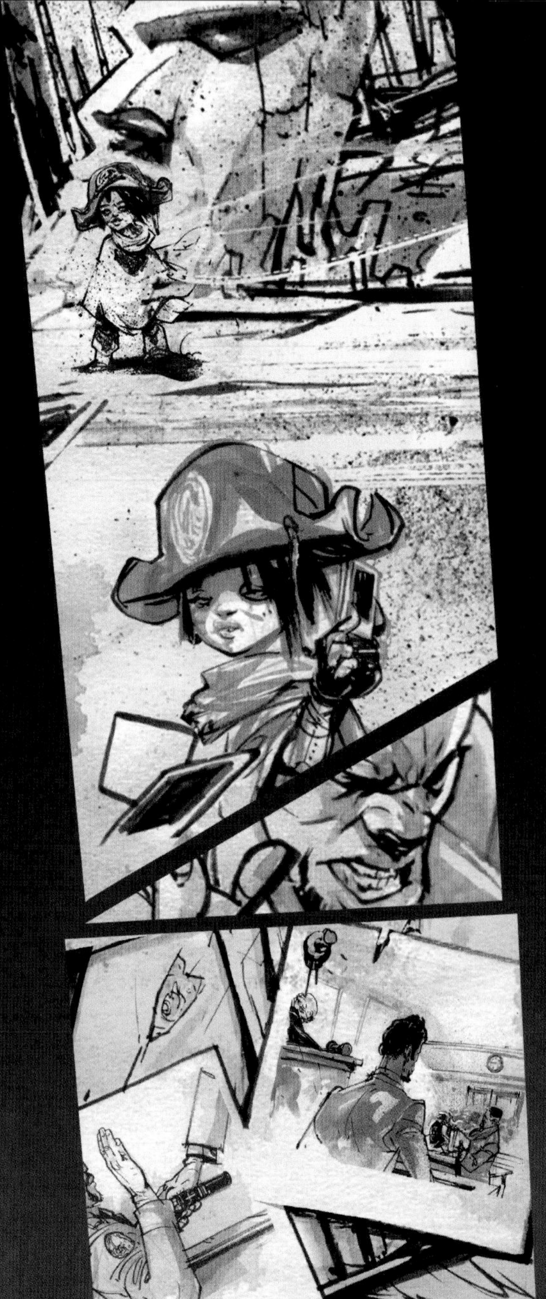

EPISODE FOUR

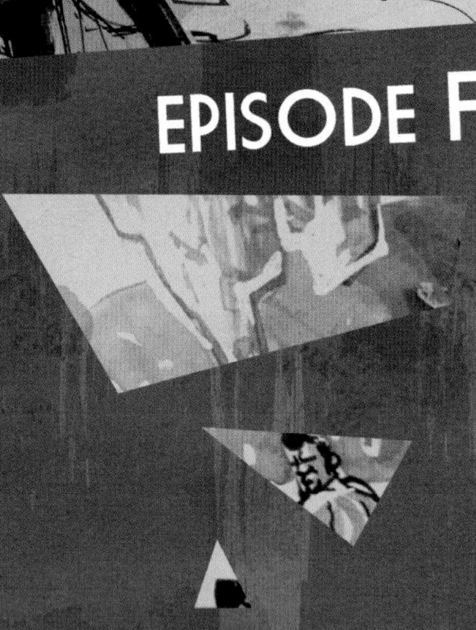

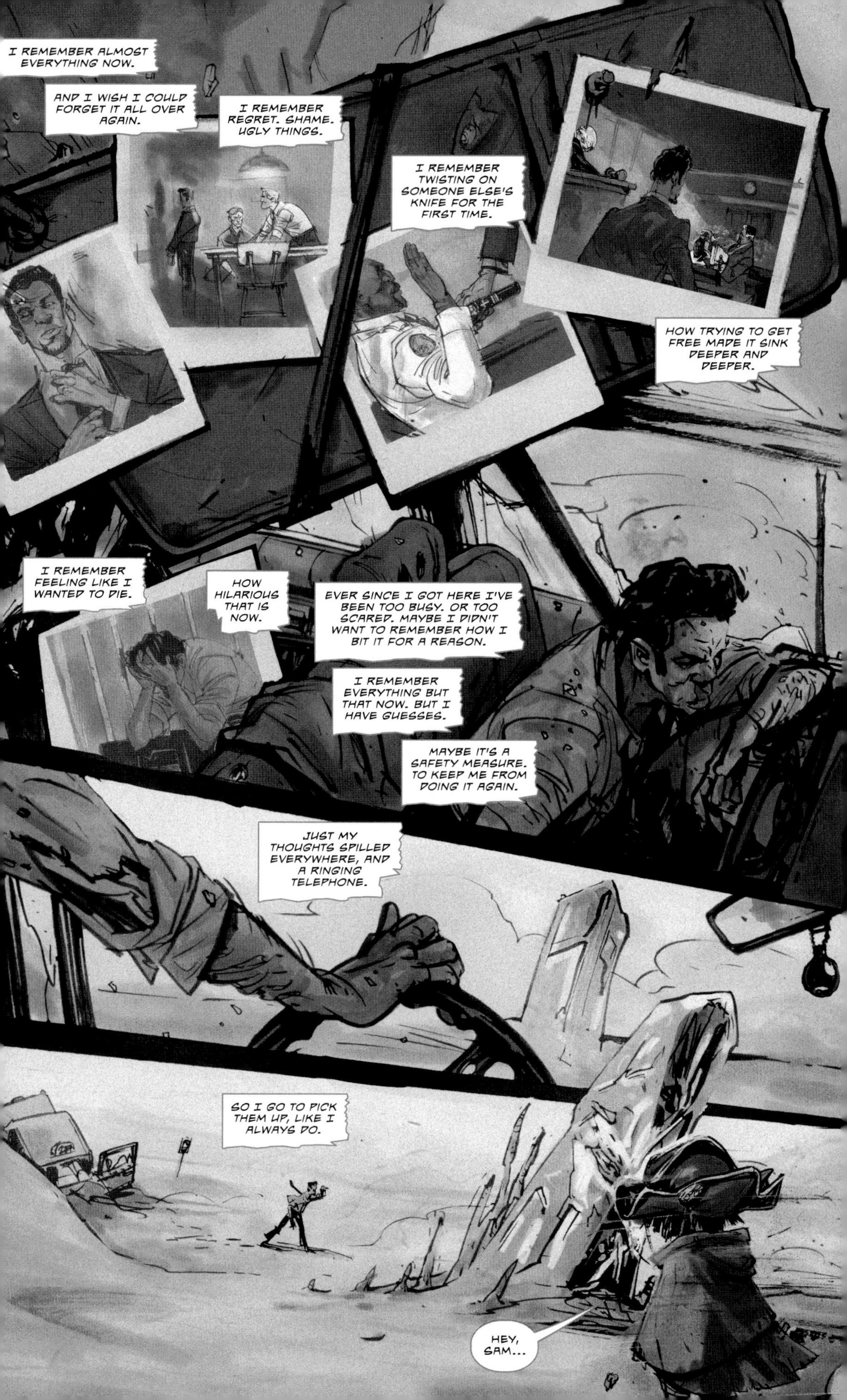
I REMEMBER ALMOST EVERYTHING NOW.
AND I WISH I COULD FORGET IT ALL OVER AGAIN.
I REMEMBER REGRET. SHAME. UGLY THINGS.
I REMEMBER TWISTING ON SOMEONE ELSE'S KNIFE FOR THE FIRST TIME.
HOW TRYING TO GET FREE MADE IT SINK DEEPER AND DEEPER.
I REMEMBER FEELING LIKE I WANTED TO DIE.
HOW HILARIOUS THAT IS NOW.
EVER SINCE I GOT HERE I'VE BEEN TOO BUSY. OR TOO SCARED. MAYBE I DIDN'T WANT TO REMEMBER HOW I BIT IT FOR A REASON.
I REMEMBER EVERYTHING BUT THAT NOW. BUT I HAVE GUESSES.
MAYBE IT'S A SAFETY MEASURE. TO KEEP ME FROM DOING IT AGAIN.
JUST MY THOUGHTS SPILLED EVERYWHERE, AND A RINGING TELEPHONE.
SO I GO TO PICK THEM UP, LIKE I ALWAYS DO.
HEY, SAM...

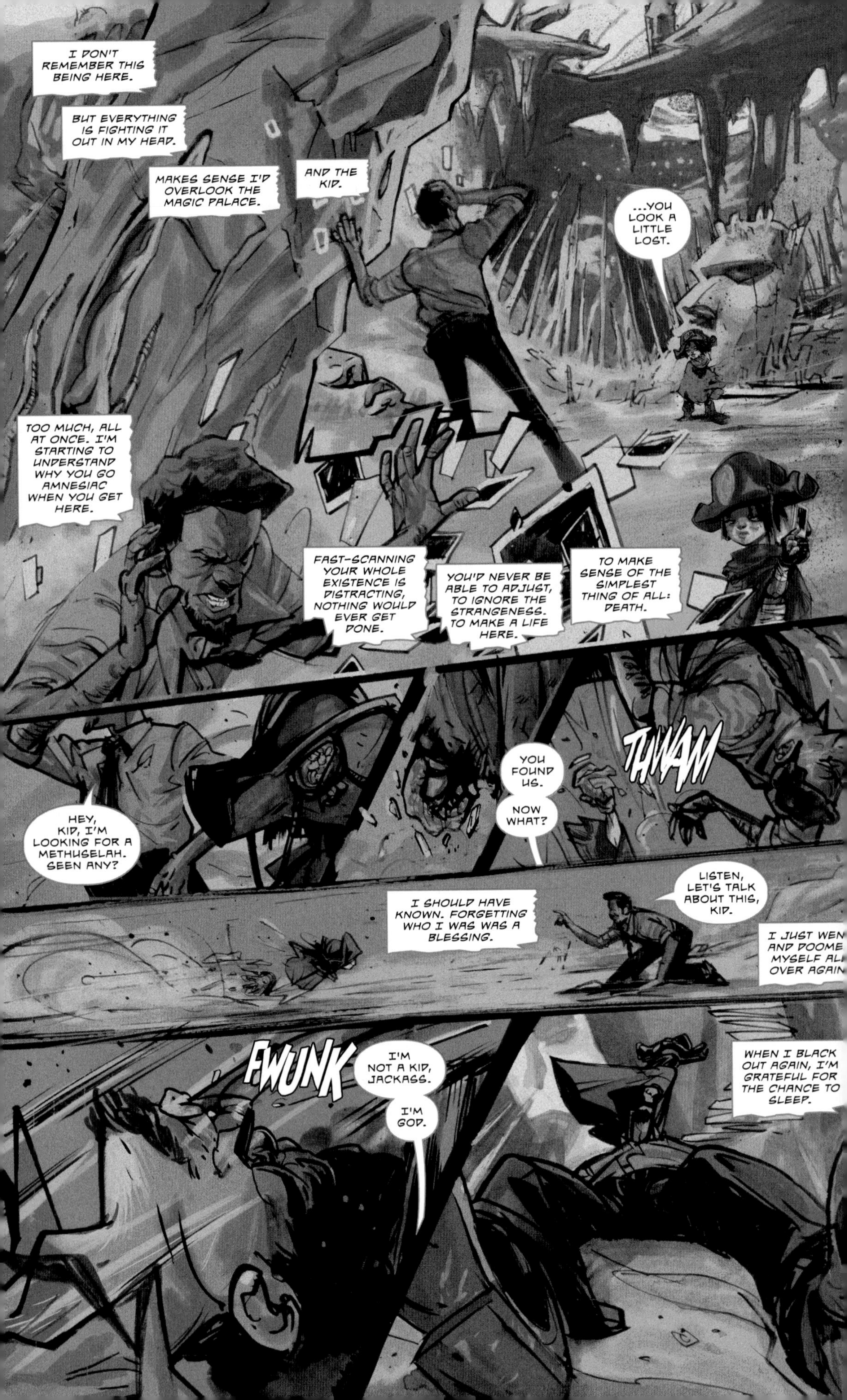
I DON'T REMEMBER THIS BEING HERE.
BUT EVERYTHING IS FIGHTING IT OUT IN MY HEAD.
MAKES SENSE I'D OVERLOOK THE MAGIC PALACE.
AND THE KID.
...YOU LOOK A LITTLE LOST.
TOO MUCH, ALL AT ONCE. I'M STARTING TO UNDERSTAND WHY YOU GO AMNESIAC WHEN YOU GET HERE.
FAST-SCANNING YOUR WHOLE EXISTENCE IS DISTRACTING, NOTHING WOULD EVER GET DONE.
YOU'D NEVER BE ABLE TO ADJUST, TO IGNORE THE STRANGENESS. TO MAKE A LIFE HERE.
TO MAKE SENSE OF THE SIMPLEST THING OF ALL: DEATH.
HEY, KID, I'M LOOKING FOR A METHUSELAH. SEEN ANY?
YOU FOUND US.
NOW WHAT?
THWAM
I SHOULD HAVE KNOWN. FORGETTING WHO I WAS WAS A BLESSING.
LISTEN, LET'S TALK ABOUT THIS, KID.
I JUST WEN AND DOOME MYSELF AL OVER AGAIN
FWUNK
I'M NOT A KID, JACKASS.
I'M GOD.
WHEN I BLACK OUT AGAIN, I'M GRATEFUL FOR THE CHANCE TO SLEEP.

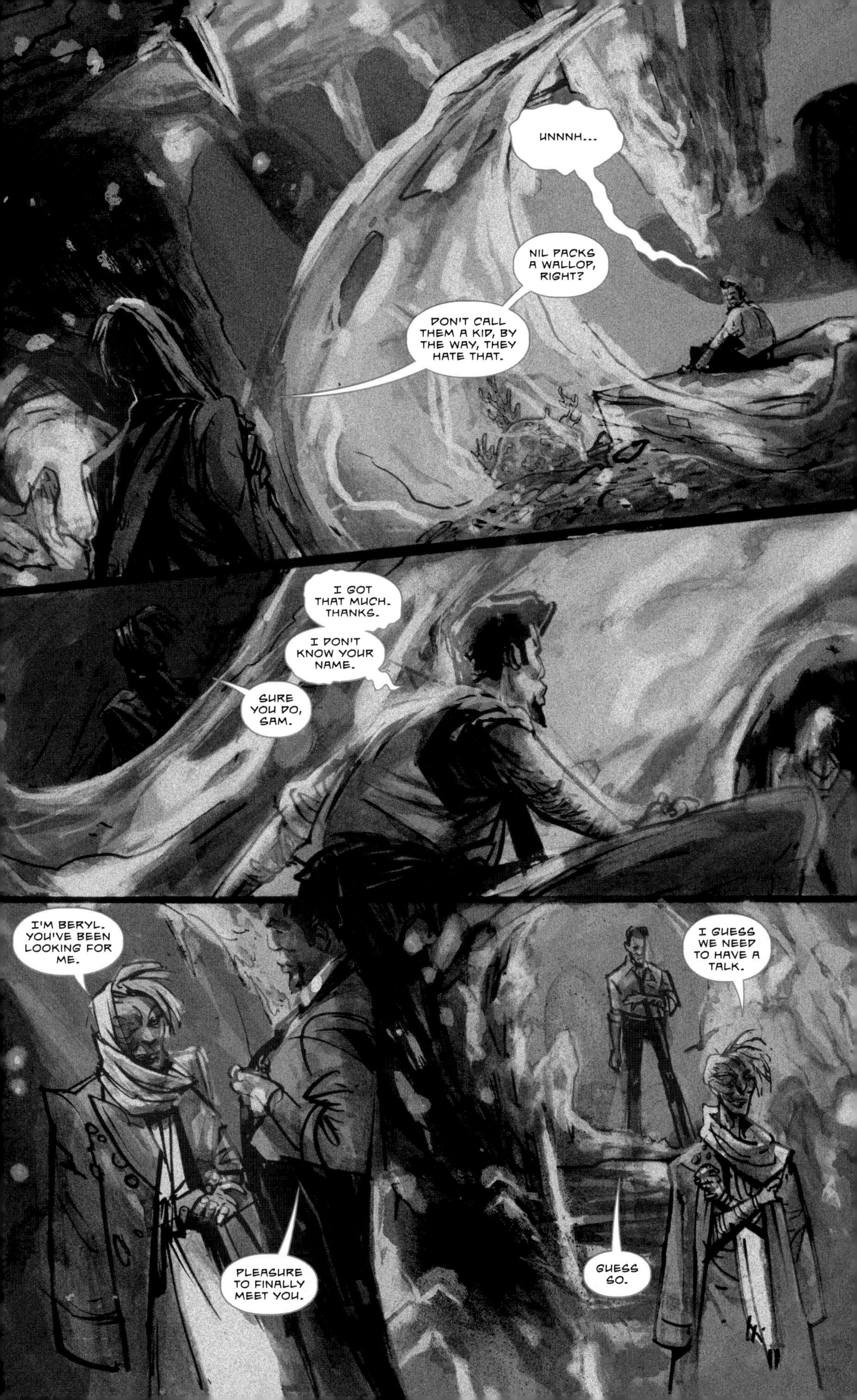
UNNNH...
NIL PACKS A WALLOP, RIGHT?
DON'T CALL THEM A KID, BY THE WAY, THEY HATE THAT.
I GOT THAT MUCH. THANKS.
I DON'T KNOW YOUR NAME.
SURE YOU DO, SAM.
I'M BERYL. YOU'VE BEEN LOOKING FOR ME.
PLEASURE TO FINALLY MEET YOU.
I GUESS WE NEED TO HAVE A TALK.
GUESS SO.

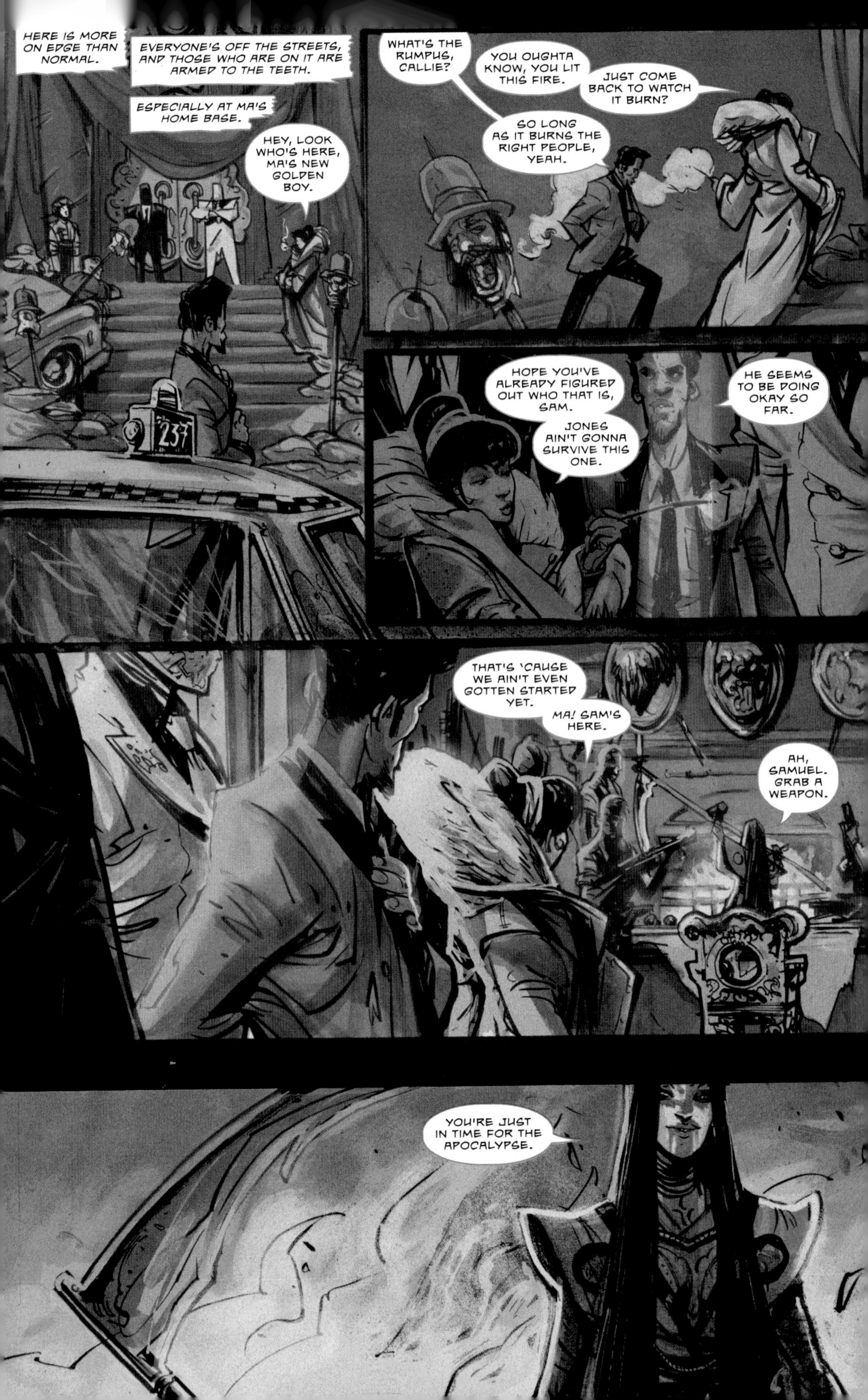
HERE IS MORE ON EDGE THAN NORMAL.
EVERYONE'S OFF THE STREETS, AND THOSE WHO ARE ON IT ARE ARMED TO THE TEETH.
ESPECIALLY AT MA'S HOME BASE.
HEY, LOOK WHO'S HERE, MA'S NEW GOLDEN BOY.
237
WHAT'S THE RUMPUS, CALLIE?
YOU OUGHTA KNOW, YOU LIT THIS FIRE.
JUST COME BACK TO WATCH IT BURN?
SO LONG AS IT BURNS THE RIGHT PEOPLE, YEAH.
HOPE YOU'VE ALREADY FIGURED OUT WHO THAT IS, SAM.
JONES AIN'T GONNA SURVIVE THIS ONE.
HE SEEMS TO BE DOING OKAY SO FAR.
THAT'S 'CAUSE WE AIN'T EVEN GOTTEN STARTED YET.
MA! SAM'S HERE.
AH, SAMUEL. GRAB A WEAPON.
YOU'RE JUST IN TIME FOR THE APOCALYPSE.

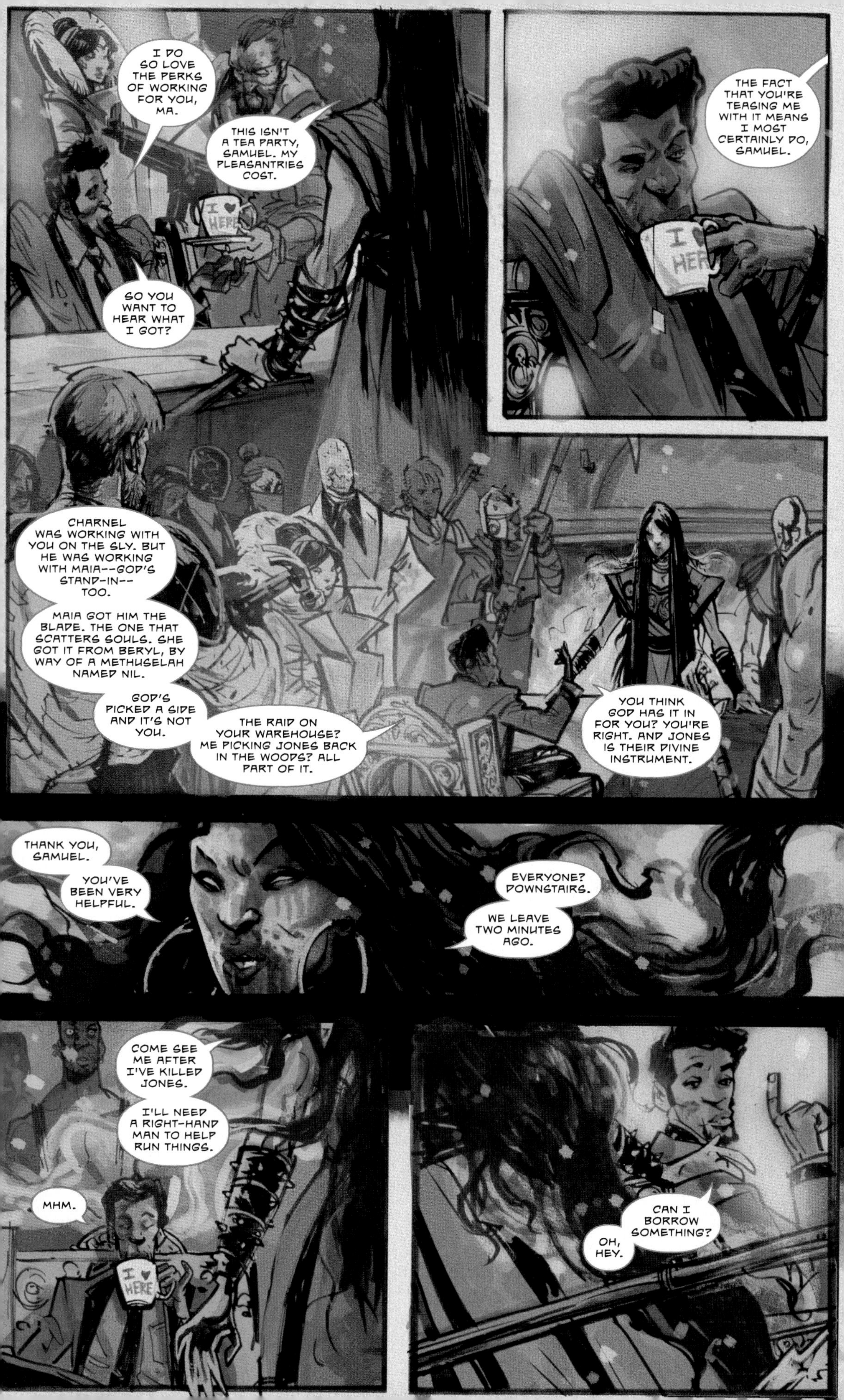
I DO SO LOVE THE PERKS OF WORKING FOR YOU, MA.
THIS ISN'T A TEA PARTY, SAMUEL. MY PLEASANTRIES COST.
SO YOU WANT TO HEAR WHAT I GOT?
THE FACT THAT YOU'RE TEASING ME WITH IT MEANS I MOST CERTAINLY DO, SAMUEL.
CHARNEL WAS WORKING WITH YOU ON THE SLY. BUT HE WAS WORKING WITH MAIA--GOD'S STAND-IN-- TOO.
MAIA GOT HIM THE BLADE. THE ONE THAT SCATTERS SOULS. SHE GOT IT FROM BERYL, BY WAY OF A METHUSELAH NAMED NIL.
GOD'S PICKED A SIDE AND IT'S NOT YOU.
THE RAID ON YOUR WAREHOUSE? ME PICKING JONES BACK IN THE WOODS? ALL PART OF IT.
YOU THINK GOD HAS IT IN FOR YOU? YOU'RE RIGHT. AND JONES IS THEIR DIVINE INSTRUMENT.
THANK YOU, SAMUEL.
YOU'VE BEEN VERY HELPFUL.
EVERYONE? DOWNSTAIRS.
WE LEAVE TWO MINUTES AGO.
COME SEE ME AFTER I'VE KILLED JONES.
I'LL NEED A RIGHT-HAND MAN TO HELP RUN THINGS.
MHM.
OH, HEY.
CAN I BORROW SOMETHING?

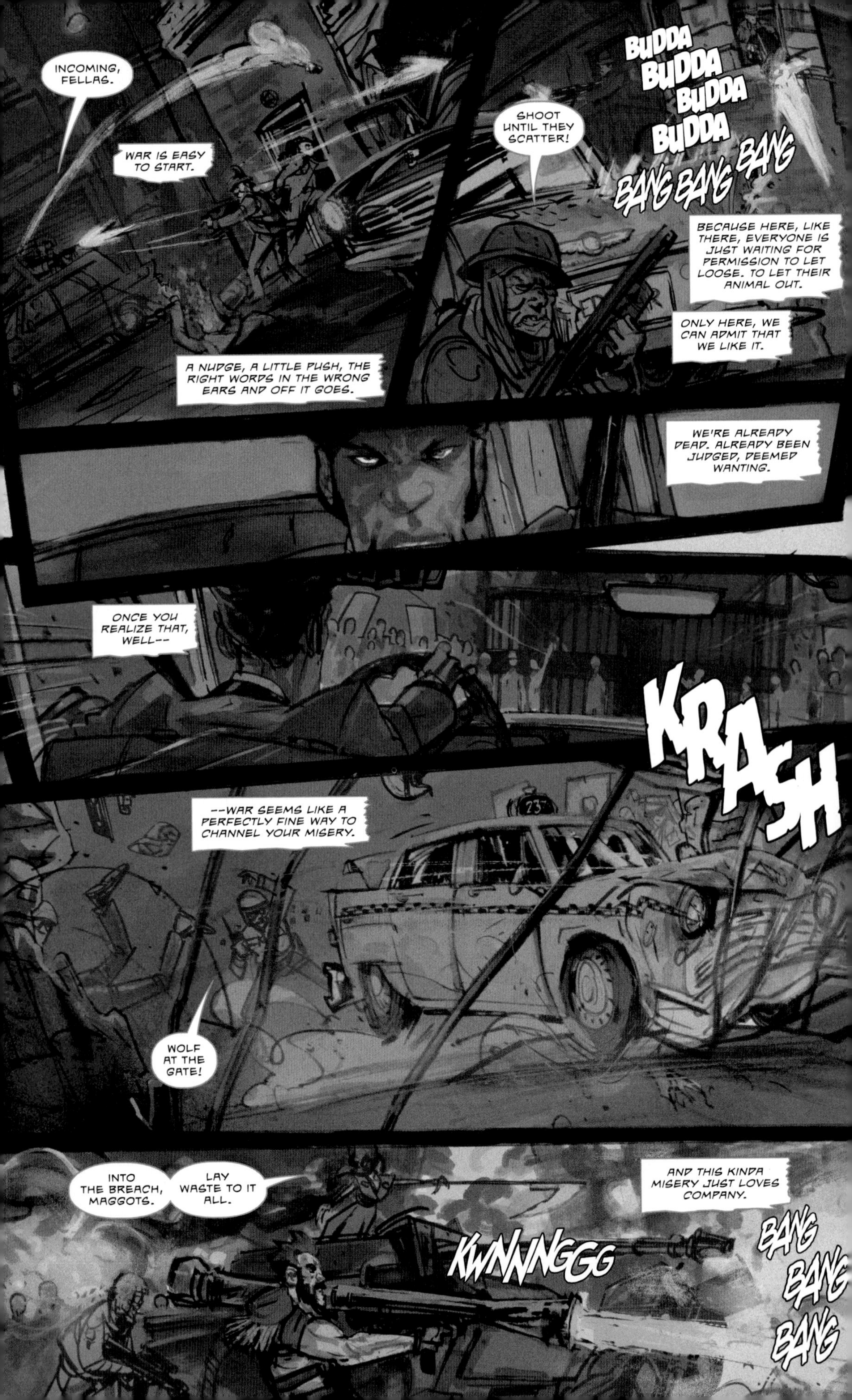
INCOMING, FELLAS.
WAR IS EASY TO START.
SHOOT UNTIL THEY SCATTER!
BUDDA BUDDA BUDDA BUDDA
BANG BANG BANG
BECAUSE HERE, LIKE THERE, EVERYONE IS JUST WAITING FOR PERMISSION TO LET LOOSE. TO LET THEIR ANIMAL OUT.
ONLY HERE, WE CAN ADMIT THAT WE LIKE IT.
A NUDGE, A LITTLE PUSH, THE RIGHT WORDS IN THE WRONG EARS AND OFF IT GOES.
WE'RE ALREADY DEAD. ALREADY BEEN JUDGED, DEEMED WANTING.
ONCE YOU REALIZE THAT, WELL--
KRASH
--WAR SEEMS LIKE A PERFECTLY FINE WAY TO CHANNEL YOUR MISERY.
WOLF AT THE GATE!
INTO THE BREACH, MAGGOTS.
LAY WASTE TO IT ALL.
AND THIS KINDA MISERY JUST LOVES COMPANY.
KWNNNGGG
BANG BANG BANG

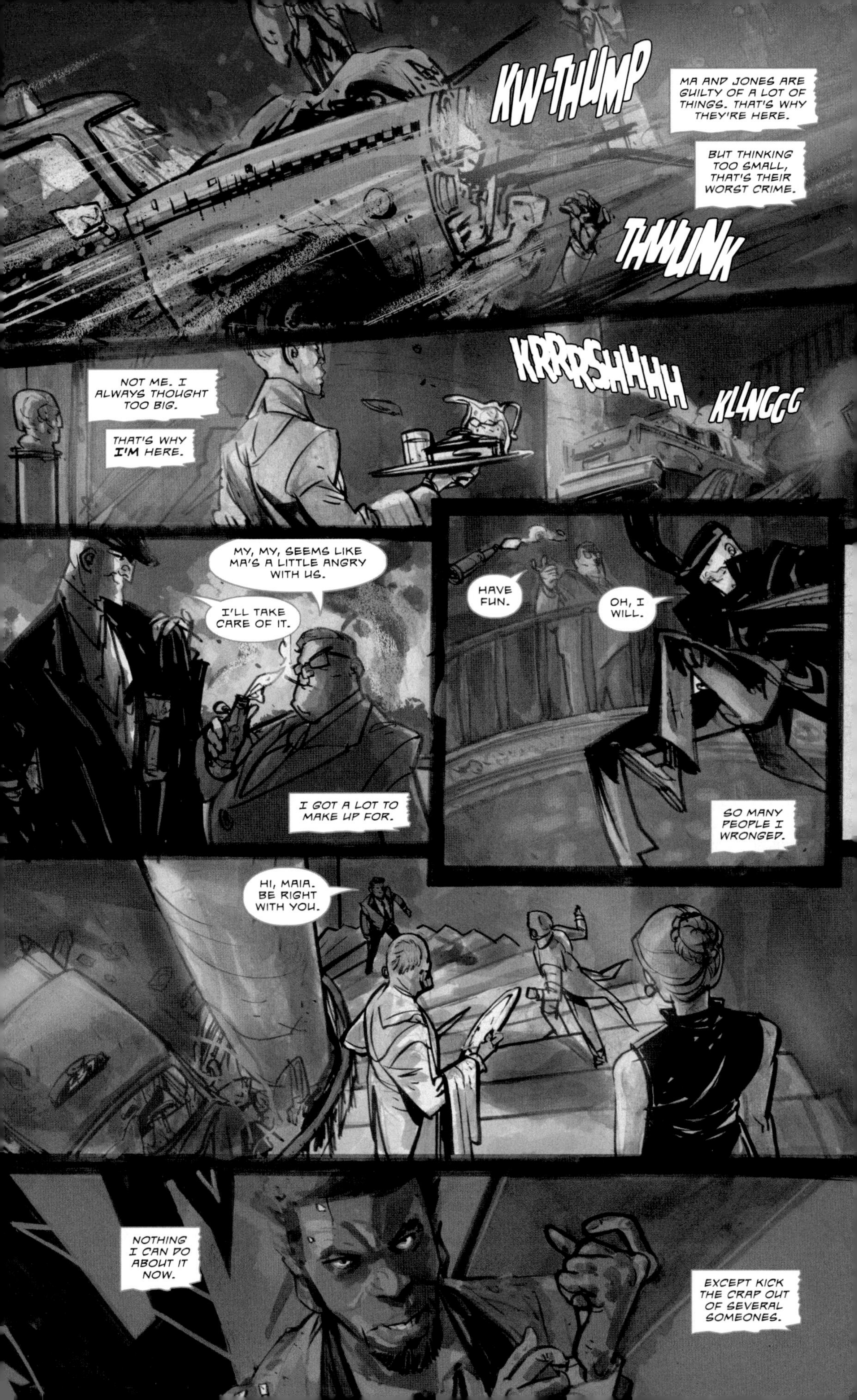
KW-THUMP
MA AND JONES ARE GUILTY OF A LOT OF THINGS. THAT'S WHY THEY'RE HERE.
BUT THINKING TOO SMALL, THAT'S THEIR WORST CRIME.
THWUNK
KRRRSHHHH
KLLNGGG
NOT ME. I ALWAYS THOUGHT TOO BIG.
THAT'S WHY I'M HERE.
MY, MY, SEEMS LIKE MA'S A LITTLE ANGRY WITH US.
I'LL TAKE CARE OF IT.
I GOT A LOT TO MAKE UP FOR.
HAVE FUN.
OH, I WILL.
SO MANY PEOPLE I WRONGED.
HI, MAIA. BE RIGHT WITH YOU.
NOTHING I CAN DO ABOUT IT NOW.
EXCEPT KICK THE CRAP OUT OF SEVERAL SOMEONES.

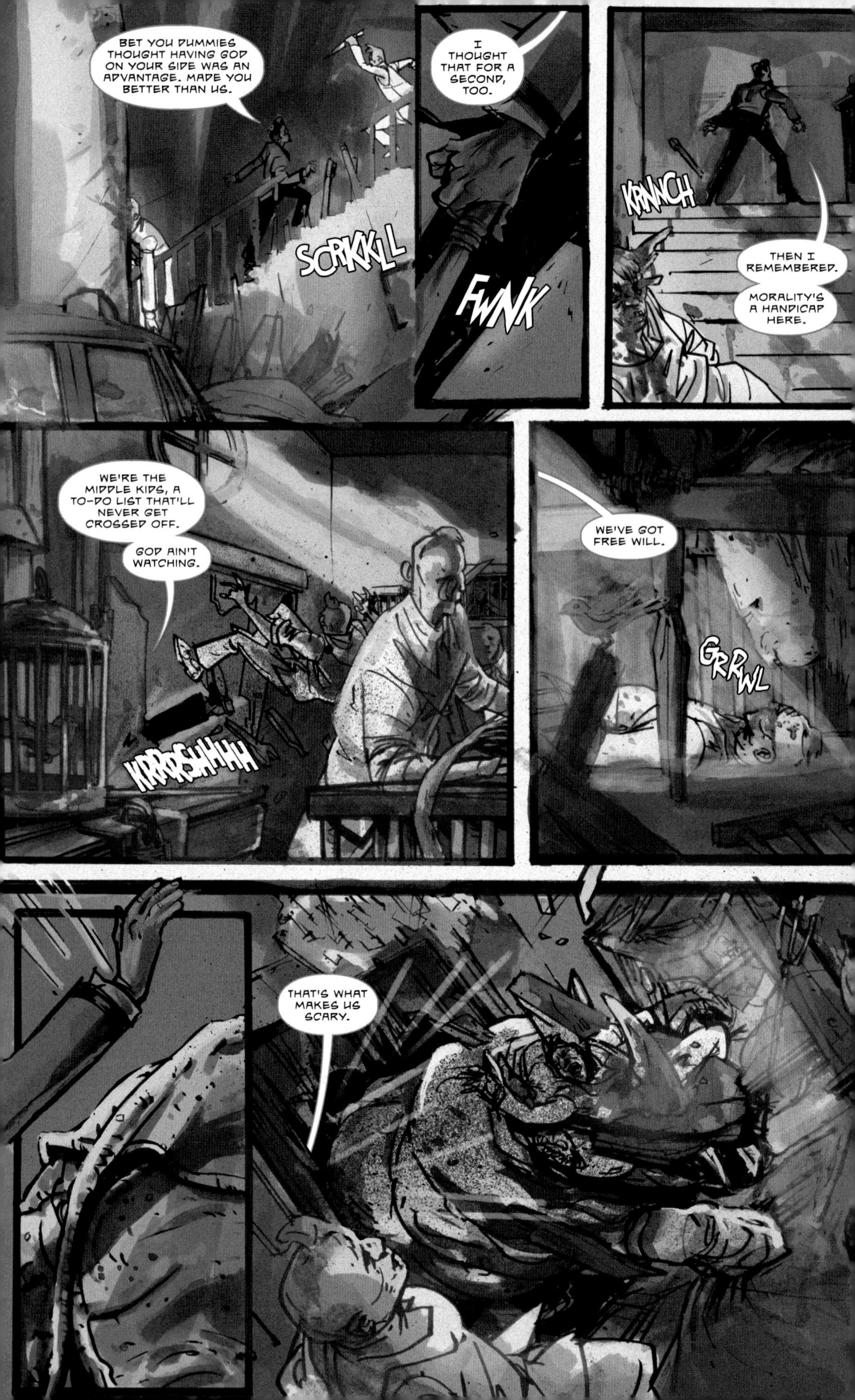
BET YOU DUMMIES THOUGHT HAVING GOD ON YOUR SIDE WAS AN ADVANTAGE. MADE YOU BETTER THAN US.
SCRKKLL
I THOUGHT THAT FOR A SECOND, TOO.
FWNK
KRNNCH
THEN I REMEMBERED.
MORALITY'S A HANDICAP HERE.
WE'RE THE MIDDLE KIDS, A TO-DO LIST THAT'LL NEVER GET CROSSED OFF.
GOD AIN'T WATCHING.
KRRRRSHHHH
WE'VE GOT FREE WILL.
GRRWL
THAT'S WHAT MAKES US SCARY.

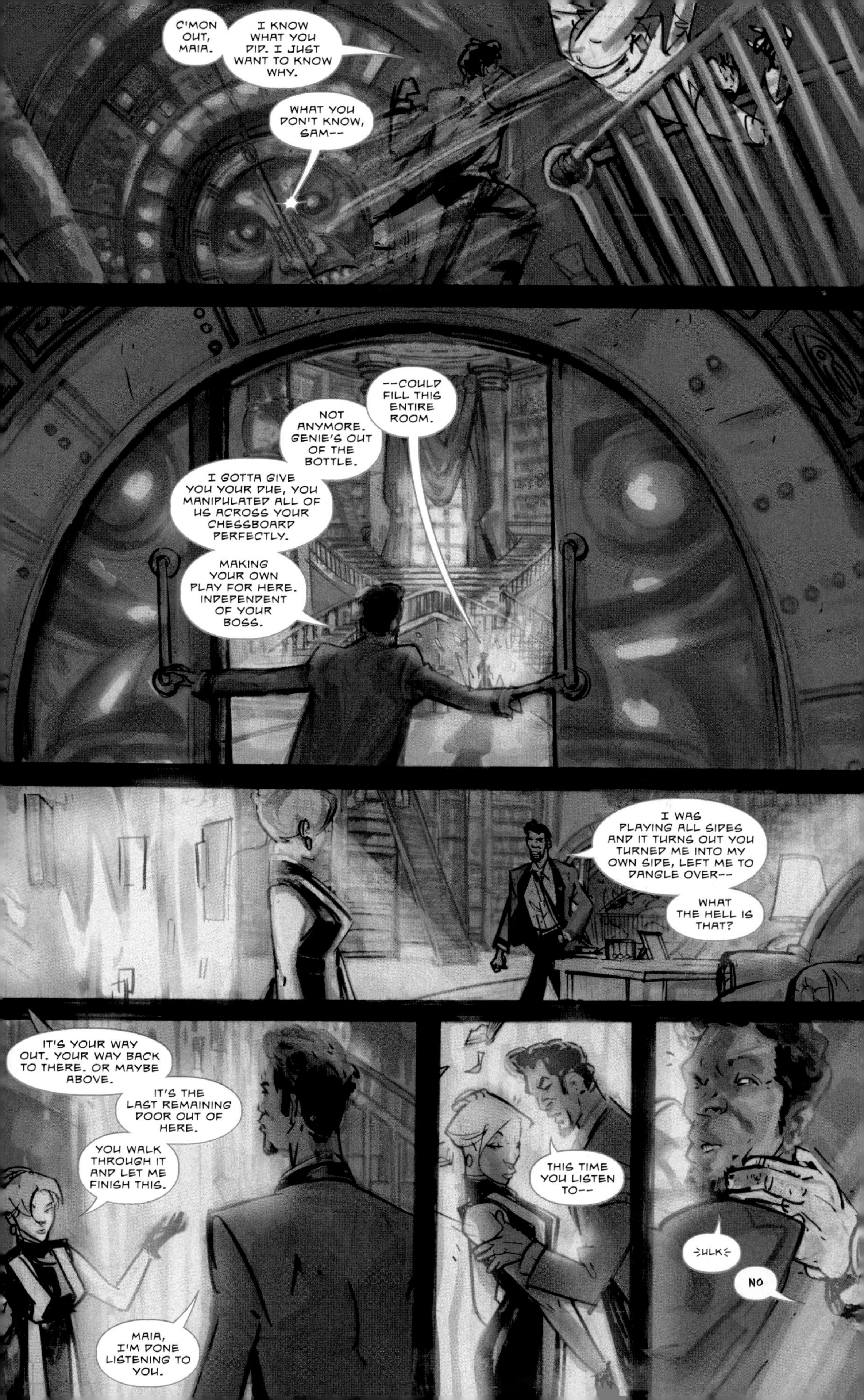
C'MON OUT, MAIA.
I KNOW WHAT YOU DID. I JUST WANT TO KNOW WHY.
WHAT YOU DON'T KNOW, SAM--
--COULD FILL THIS ENTIRE ROOM.
NOT ANYMORE. GENIE'S OUT OF THE BOTTLE.
I GOTTA GIVE YOU YOUR DUE, YOU MANIPULATED ALL OF US ACROSS YOUR CHESSBOARD PERFECTLY.
MAKING YOUR OWN PLAY FOR HERE. INDEPENDENT OF YOUR BOSS.
I WAS PLAYING ALL SIDES AND IT TURNS OUT YOU TURNED ME INTO MY OWN SIDE, LEFT ME TO DANGLE OVER--
WHAT THE HELL IS THAT?
IT'S YOUR WAY OUT. YOUR WAY BACK TO THERE. OR MAYBE ABOVE.
IT'S THE LAST REMAINING DOOR OUT OF HERE.
YOU WALK THROUGH IT AND LET ME FINISH THIS.
MAIA, I'M DONE LISTENING TO YOU.
THIS TIME YOU LISTEN TO--
ULK
NO

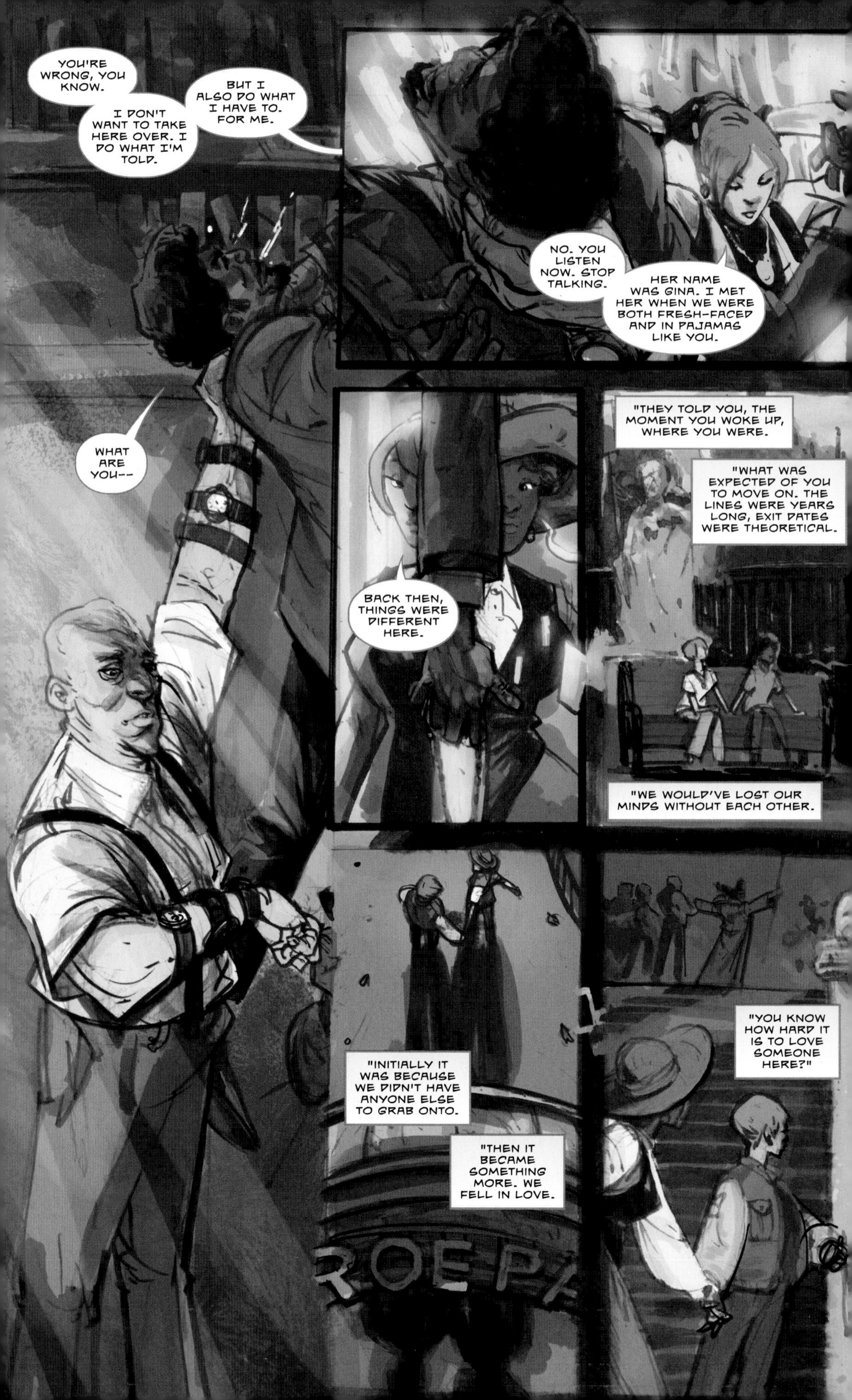
YOU'RE WRONG, YOU KNOW.
I DON'T WANT TO TAKE HERE OVER. I DO WHAT I'M TOLD.
BUT I ALSO DO WHAT I HAVE TO. FOR ME.
WHAT ARE YOU--
NO. YOU LISTEN NOW. STOP TALKING.
HER NAME WAS GINA. I MET HER WHEN WE WERE BOTH FRESH-FACED AND IN PAJAMAS LIKE YOU.
BACK THEN, THINGS WERE DIFFERENT HERE.
"THEY TOLD YOU, THE MOMENT YOU WOKE UP, WHERE YOU WERE.
"WHAT WAS EXPECTED OF YOU TO MOVE ON. THE LINES WERE YEARS LONG, EXIT DATES WERE THEORETICAL.
"WE WOULD'VE LOST OUR MINDS WITHOUT EACH OTHER.
"INITIALLY IT WAS BECAUSE WE DIDN'T HAVE ANYONE ELSE TO GRAB ONTO.
"THEN IT BECAME SOMETHING MORE. WE FELL IN LOVE.
"YOU KNOW HOW HARD IT IS TO LOVE SOMEONE HERE?"
ROE PA

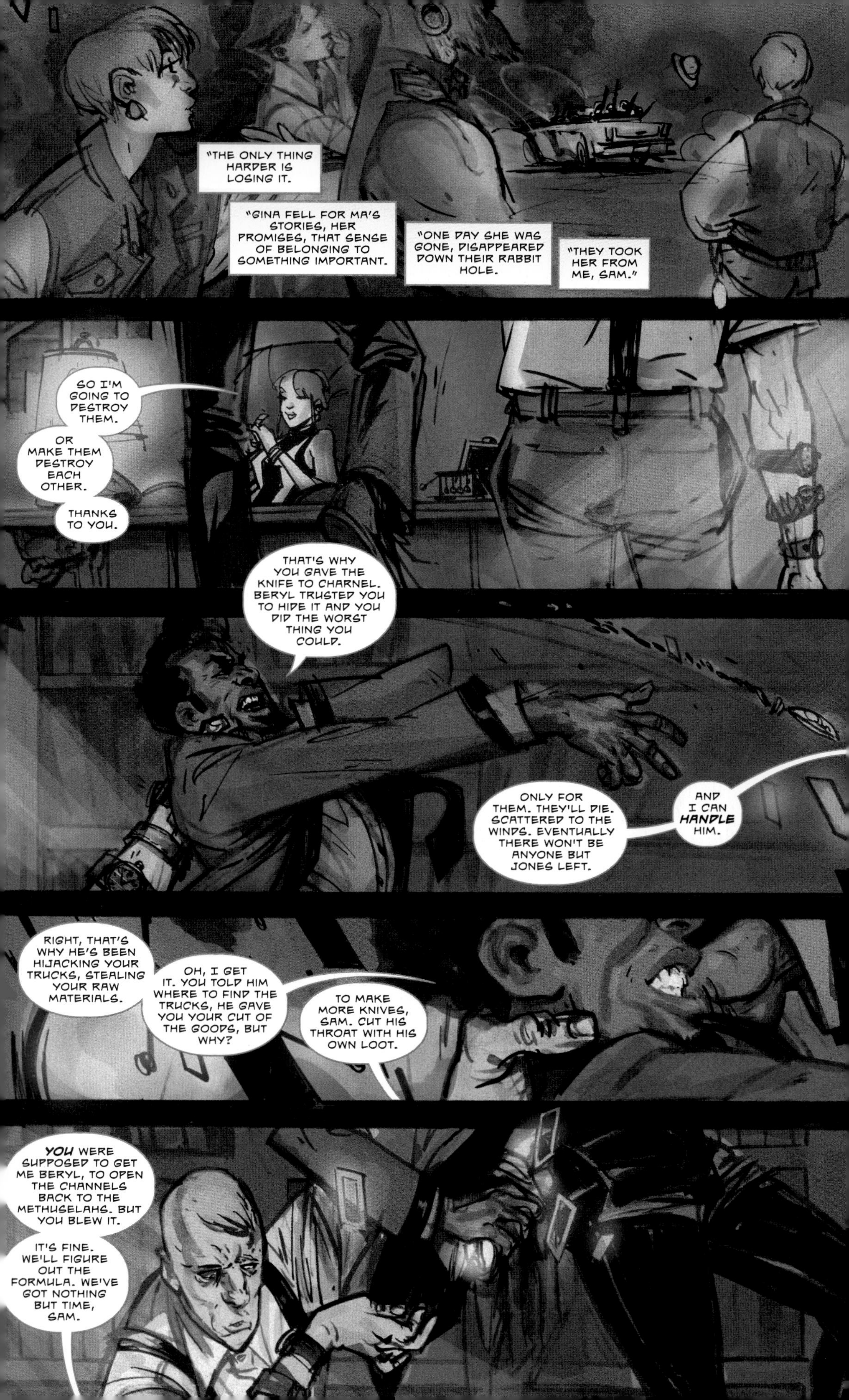
"THE ONLY THING HARDER IS LOSING IT.
"GINA FELL FOR MA'S STORIES, HER PROMISES, THAT SENSE OF BELONGING TO SOMETHING IMPORTANT.
"ONE DAY SHE WAS GONE, DISAPPEARED DOWN THEIR RABBIT HOLE.
"THEY TOOK HER FROM ME, SAM."
SO I'M GOING TO DESTROY THEM.
OR MAKE THEM DESTROY EACH OTHER.
THANKS TO YOU.
THAT'S WHY YOU GAVE THE KNIFE TO CHARNEL. BERYL TRUSTED YOU TO HIDE IT AND YOU DID THE WORST THING YOU COULD.
ONLY FOR THEM. THEY'LL DIE. SCATTERED TO THE WINDS. EVENTUALLY THERE WON'T BE ANYONE BUT JONES LEFT.
AND I CAN ***HANDLE*** HIM.
RIGHT, THAT'S WHY HE'S BEEN HIJACKING YOUR TRUCKS, STEALING YOUR RAW MATERIALS.
OH, I GET IT. YOU TOLD HIM WHERE TO FIND THE TRUCKS, HE GAVE YOU YOUR CUT OF THE GOODS, BUT WHY?
TO MAKE MORE KNIVES, SAM. CUT HIS THROAT WITH HIS OWN LOOT.
YOU WERE SUPPOSED TO GET ME BERYL, TO OPEN THE CHANNELS BACK TO THE METHUSELAHS. BUT YOU BLEW IT.
IT'S FINE. WE'LL FIGURE OUT THE FORMULA. WE'VE GOT NOTHING BUT TIME, SAM.

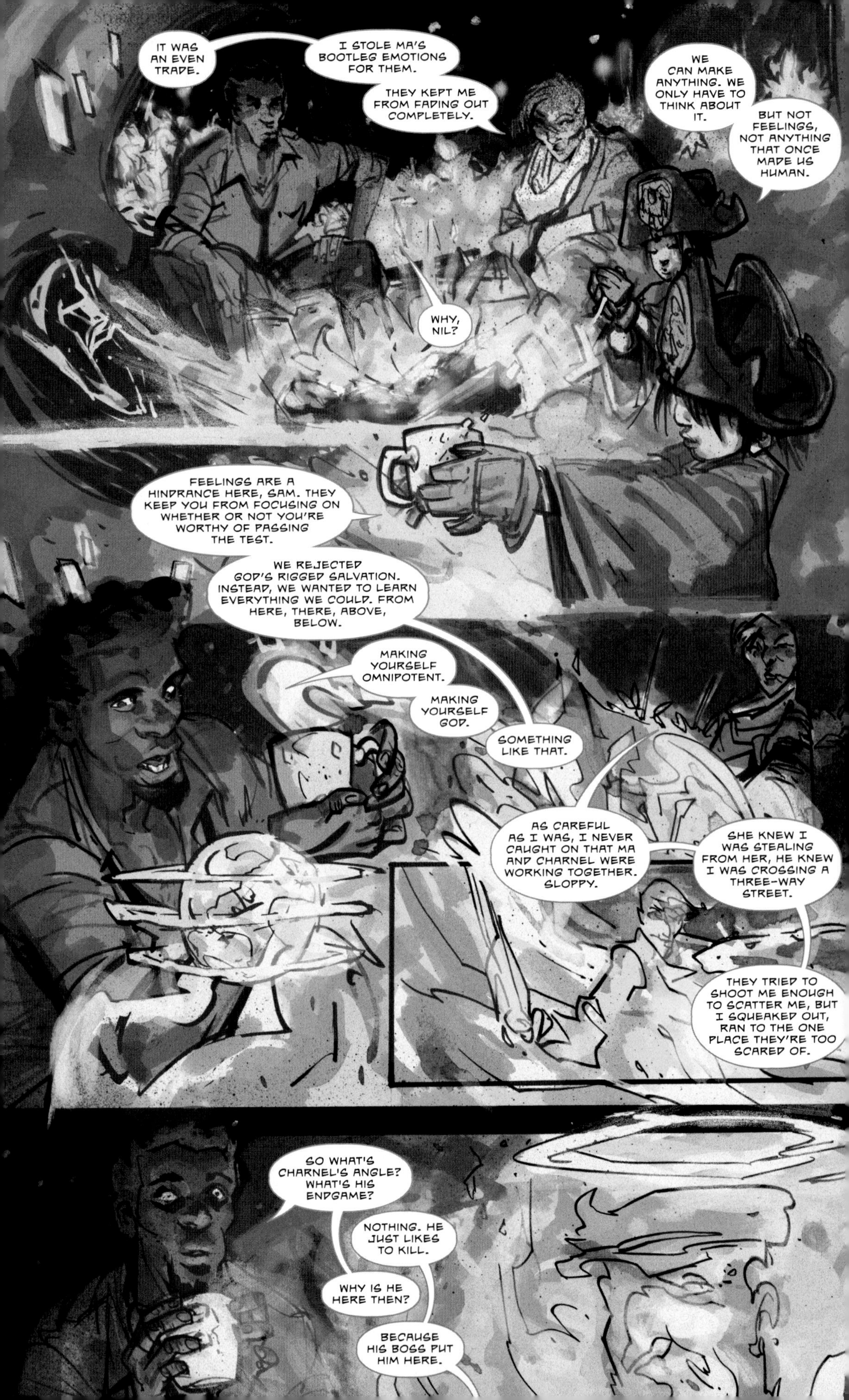

IT WAS AN EVEN TRADE.
I STOLE MA'S BOOTLEG EMOTIONS FOR THEM.
THEY KEPT ME FROM FADING OUT COMPLETELY.
WE CAN MAKE ANYTHING. WE ONLY HAVE TO THINK ABOUT IT.
BUT NOT FEELINGS, NOT ANYTHING THAT ONCE MADE US HUMAN.
WHY, NIL?
FEELINGS ARE A HINDRANCE HERE, SAM. THEY KEEP YOU FROM FOCUSING ON WHETHER OR NOT YOU'RE WORTHY OF PASSING THE TEST.
WE REJECTED GOD'S RIGGED SALVATION. INSTEAD, WE WANTED TO LEARN EVERYTHING WE COULD. FROM HERE, THERE, ABOVE, BELOW.
MAKING YOURSELF OMNIPOTENT.
MAKING YOURSELF GOD.
SOMETHING LIKE THAT.
AS CAREFUL AS I WAS, I NEVER CAUGHT ON THAT MA AND CHARNEL WERE WORKING TOGETHER. SLOPPY.
SHE KNEW I WAS STEALING FROM HER, HE KNEW I WAS CROSSING A THREE-WAY STREET.
THEY TRIED TO SHOOT ME ENOUGH TO SCATTER ME, BUT I SQUEAKED OUT, RAN TO THE ONE PLACE THEY'RE TOO SCARED OF.
SO WHAT'S CHARNEL'S ANGLE? WHAT'S HIS ENDGAME?
NOTHING. HE JUST LIKES TO KILL.
WHY IS HE HERE THEN?
BECAUSE HIS BOSS PUT HIM HERE.

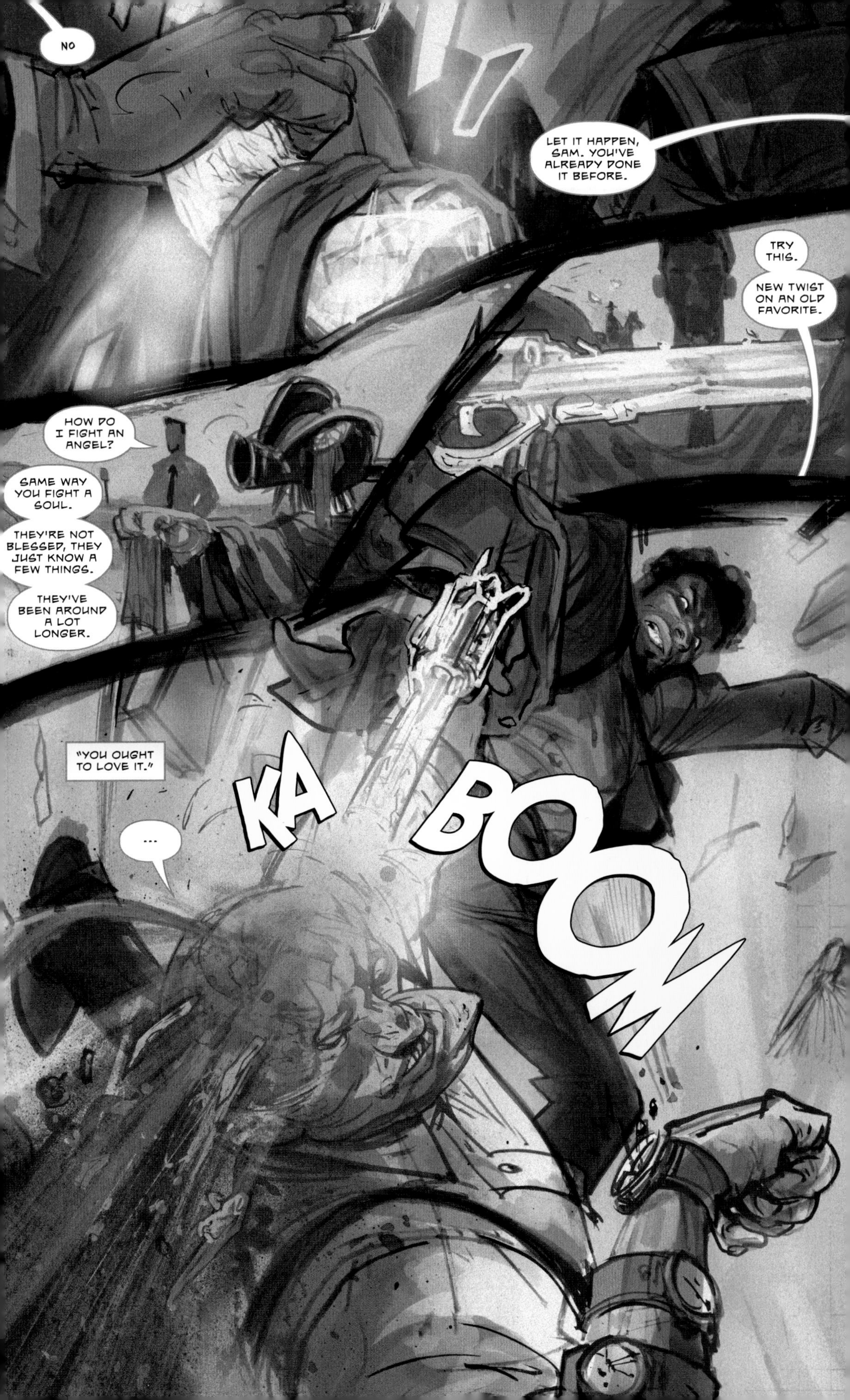
NO
LET IT HAPPEN, SAM. YOU'VE ALREADY DONE IT BEFORE.
TRY THIS.
NEW TWIST ON AN OLD FAVORITE.
HOW DO I FIGHT AN ANGEL?
SAME WAY YOU FIGHT A SOUL.
THEY'RE NOT BLESSED, THEY JUST KNOW A FEW THINGS.
THEY'VE BEEN AROUND A LOT LONGER.
"YOU OUGHT TO LOVE IT."
...
KA BOOM

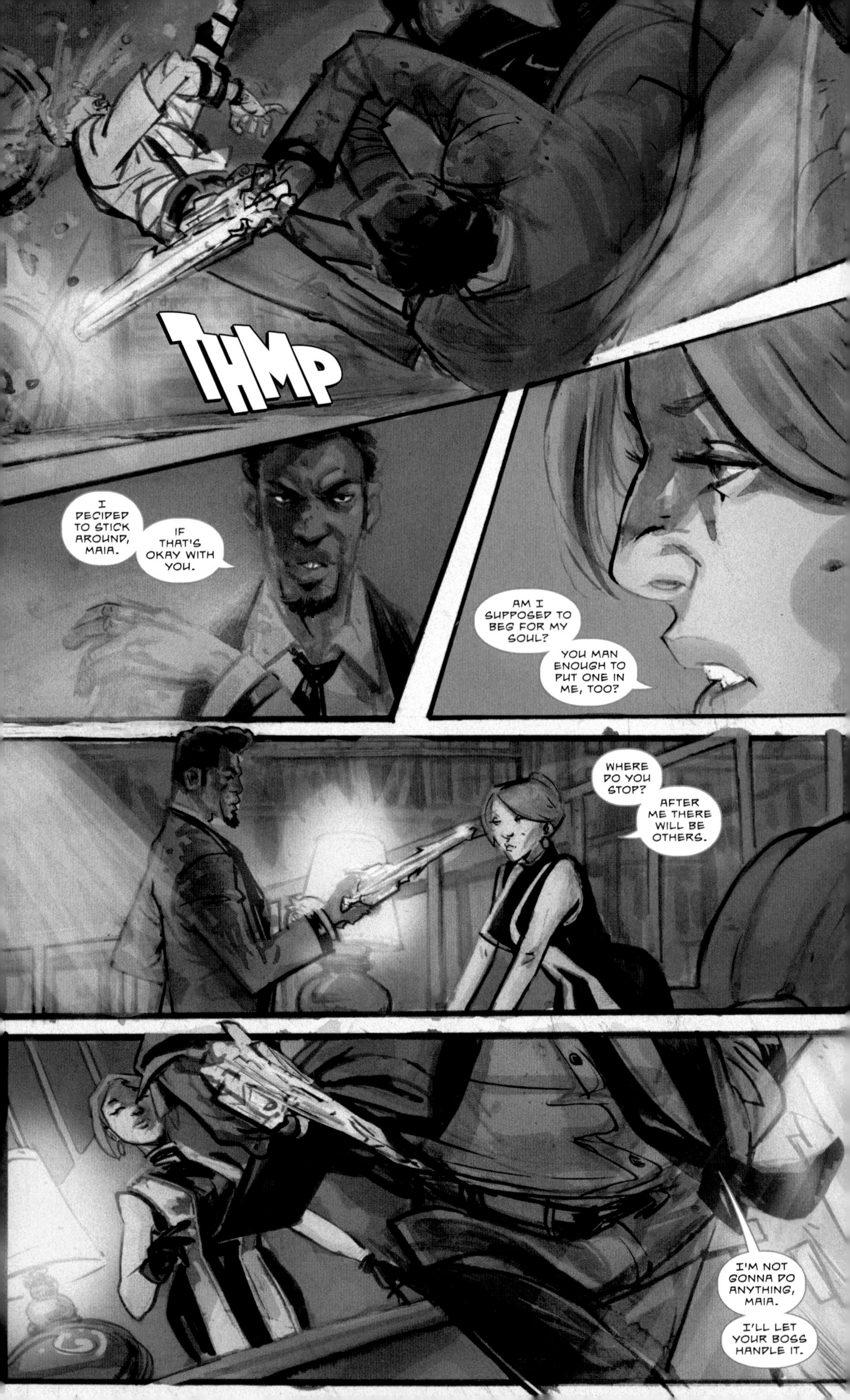
THMP
I DECIDED TO STICK AROUND, MAIA.
IF THAT'S OKAY WITH YOU.
AM I SUPPOSED TO BEG FOR MY SOUL?
YOU MAN ENOUGH TO PUT ONE IN ME, TOO?
WHERE DO YOU STOP?
AFTER ME THERE WILL BE OTHERS.
I'M NOT GONNA DO ANYTHING, MAIA.
I'LL LET YOUR BOSS HANDLE IT.

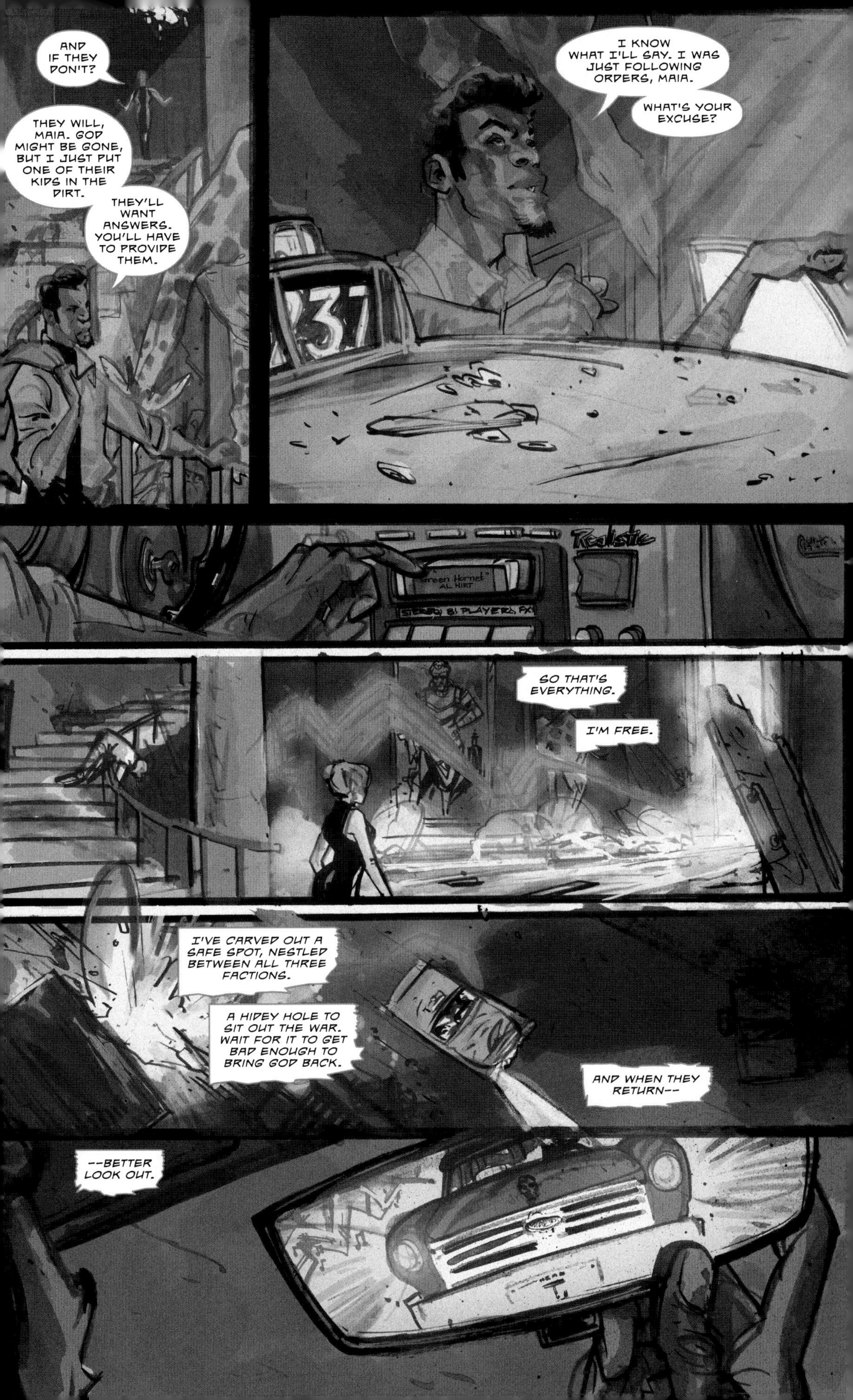
AND IF THEY DON'T?
THEY WILL, MAIA. GOD MIGHT BE GONE, BUT I JUST PUT ONE OF THEIR KIDS IN THE DIRT.
THEY'LL WANT ANSWERS. YOU'LL HAVE TO PROVIDE THEM.
I KNOW WHAT I'LL SAY. I WAS JUST FOLLOWING ORDERS, MAIA.
WHAT'S YOUR EXCUSE?
Realistic
"Green Hornet" AL HIRT
SO THAT'S EVERYTHING.
I'M FREE.
I'VE CARVED OUT A SAFE SPOT, NESTLED BETWEEN ALL THREE FACTIONS.
A HIDEY HOLE TO SIT OUT THE WAR. WAIT FOR IT TO GET BAD ENOUGH TO BRING GOD BACK.
AND WHEN THEY RETURN--
--BETTER LOOK OUT.

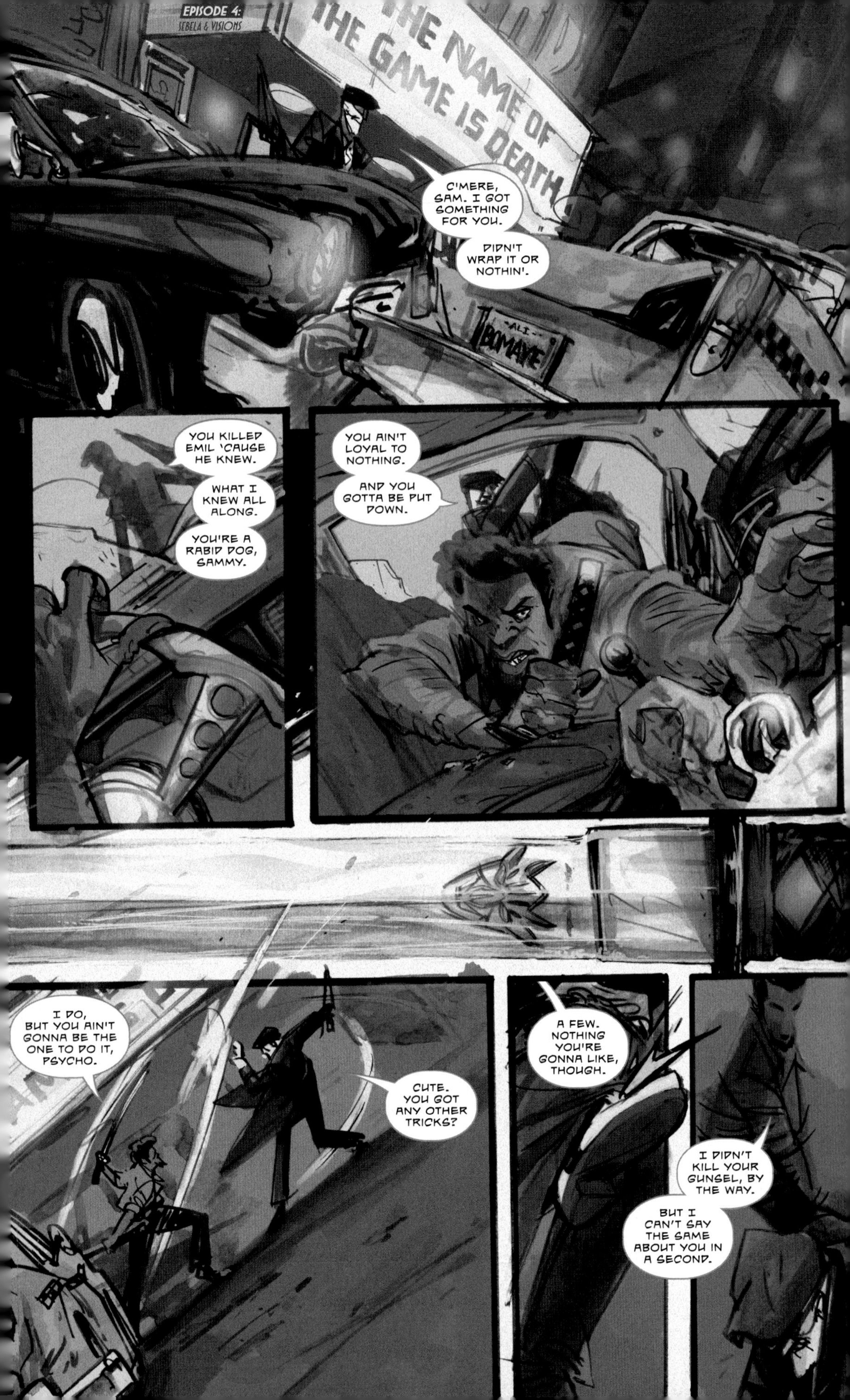
EPISODE 4:
SEBELA & VISIONS
THE NAME OF THE GAME IS DEATH
C'MERE, SAM. I GOT SOMETHING FOR YOU.
DIDN'T WRAP IT OR NOTHIN'.
ALI BOMAYE
YOU KILLED EMIL 'CAUSE HE KNEW.
WHAT I KNEW ALL ALONG.
YOU'RE A RABID DOG, SAMMY.
YOU AIN'T LOYAL TO NOTHING.
AND YOU GOTTA BE PUT DOWN.
I DO, BUT YOU AIN'T GONNA BE THE ONE TO DO IT, PSYCHO.
CUTE. YOU GOT ANY OTHER TRICKS?
A FEW. NOTHING YOU'RE GONNA LIKE, THOUGH.
I DIDN'T KILL YOUR GUNSEL, BY THE WAY.
BUT I CAN'T SAY THE SAME ABOUT YOU IN A SECOND.

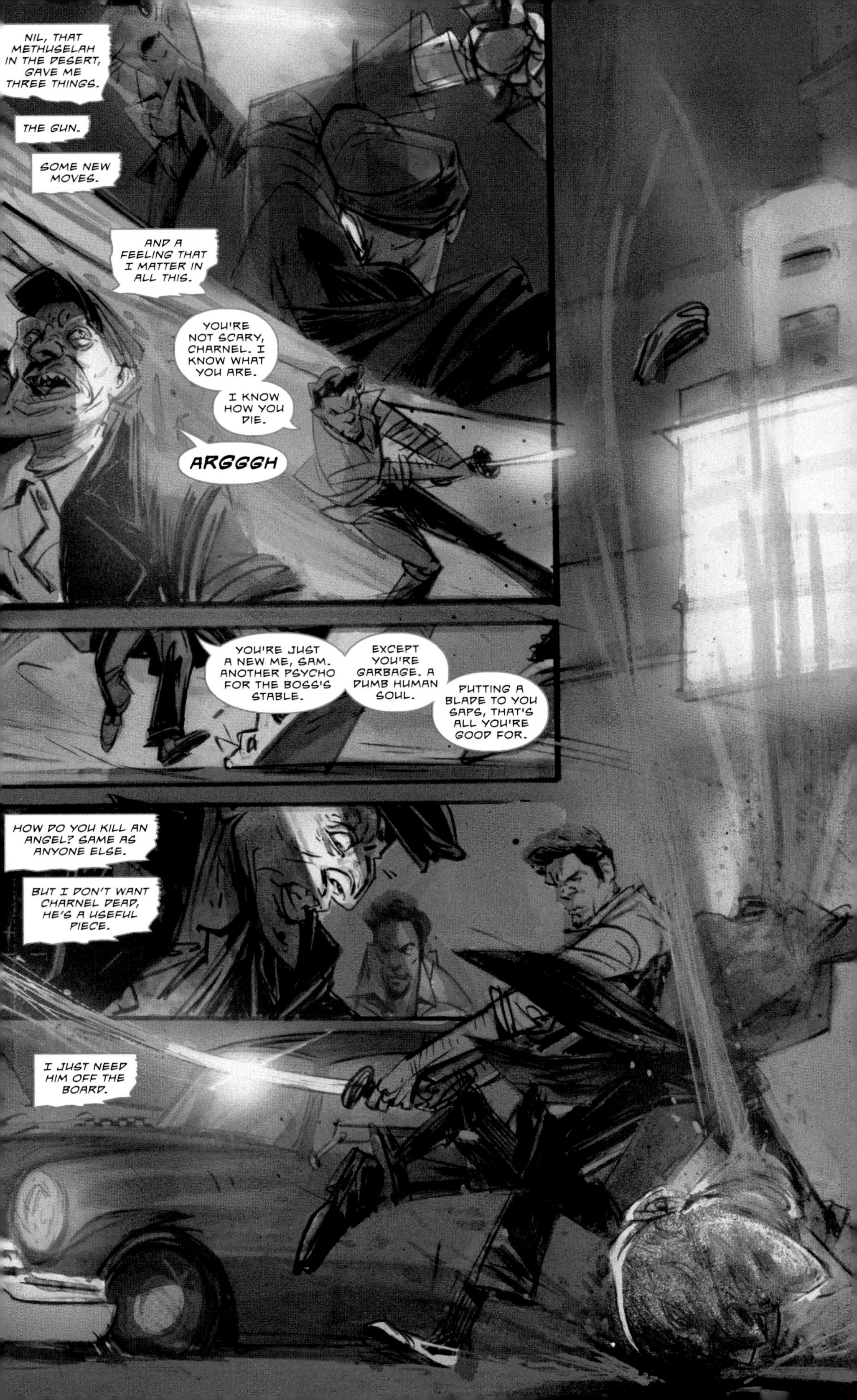
NIL, THAT METHUSELAH IN THE DESERT, GAVE ME THREE THINGS.
THE GUN.
SOME NEW MOVES.
AND A FEELING THAT I MATTER IN ALL THIS.
YOU'RE NOT SCARY, CHARNEL. I KNOW WHAT YOU ARE.
I KNOW HOW YOU DIE.
ARGGGH
YOU'RE JUST A NEW ME, SAM. ANOTHER PSYCHO FOR THE BOSS'S STABLE.
EXCEPT YOU'RE GARBAGE. A DUMB HUMAN SOUL.
PUTTING A BLADE TO YOU SAPS, THAT'S ALL YOU'RE GOOD FOR.
HOW DO YOU KILL AN ANGEL? SAME AS ANYONE ELSE.
BUT I DON'T WANT CHARNEL DEAD, HE'S A USEFUL PIECE.
I JUST NEED HIM OFF THE BOARD.

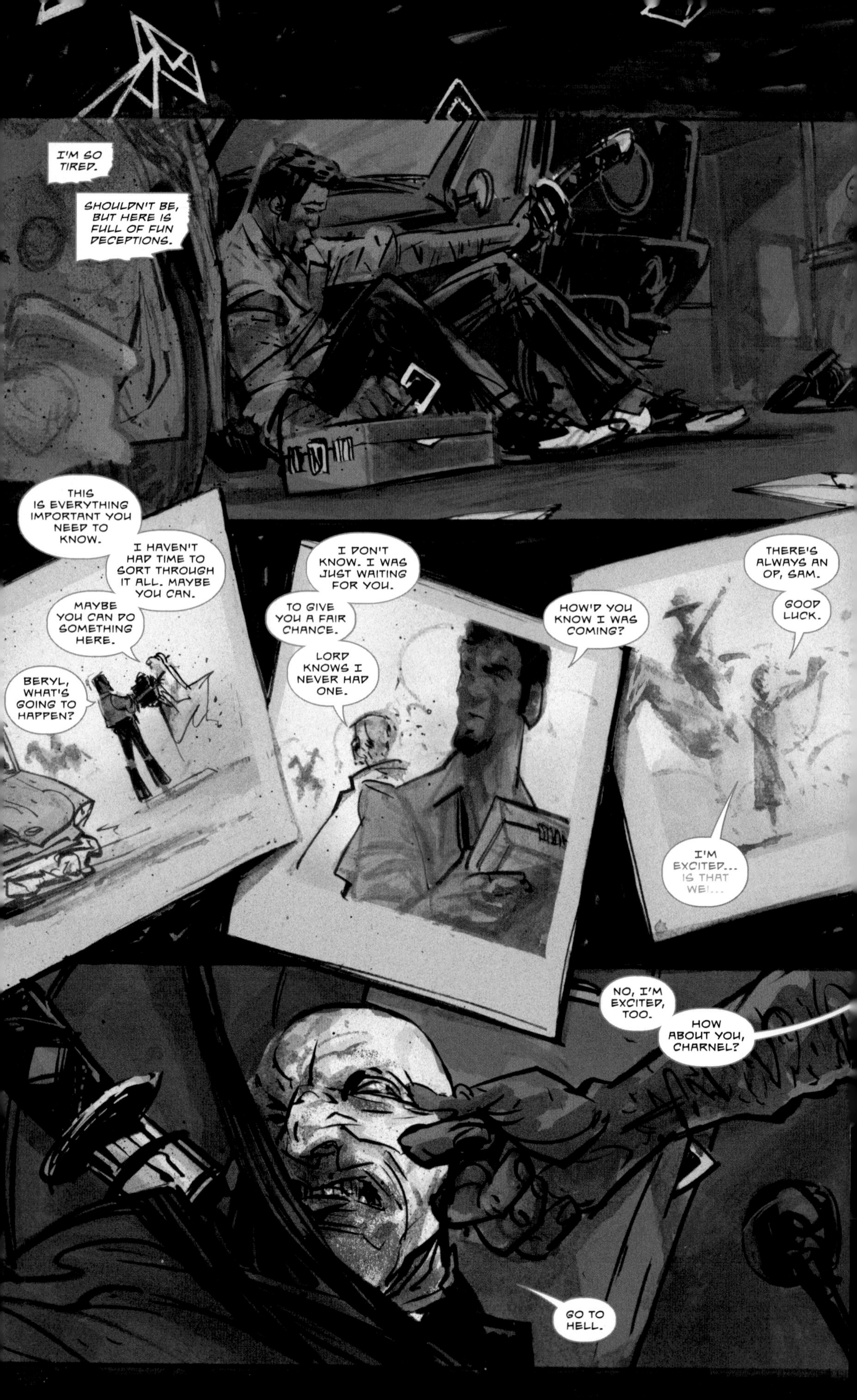
I'M SO TIRED.
SHOULDN'T BE, BUT HERE IS FULL OF FUN DECEPTIONS.
THIS IS EVERYTHING IMPORTANT YOU NEED TO KNOW.
I HAVEN'T HAD TIME TO SORT THROUGH IT ALL. MAYBE YOU CAN.
MAYBE YOU CAN DO SOMETHING HERE.
BERYL, WHAT'S GOING TO HAPPEN?
I DON'T KNOW. I WAS JUST WAITING FOR YOU.
TO GIVE YOU A FAIR CHANCE.
LORD KNOWS I NEVER HAD ONE.
HOW'D YOU KNOW I WAS COMING?
THERE'S ALWAYS AN OP, SAM.
GOOD LUCK.
I'M EXCITED... IS THAT WE!...
NO, I'M EXCITED, TOO.
HOW ABOUT YOU, CHARNEL?
GO TO HELL.

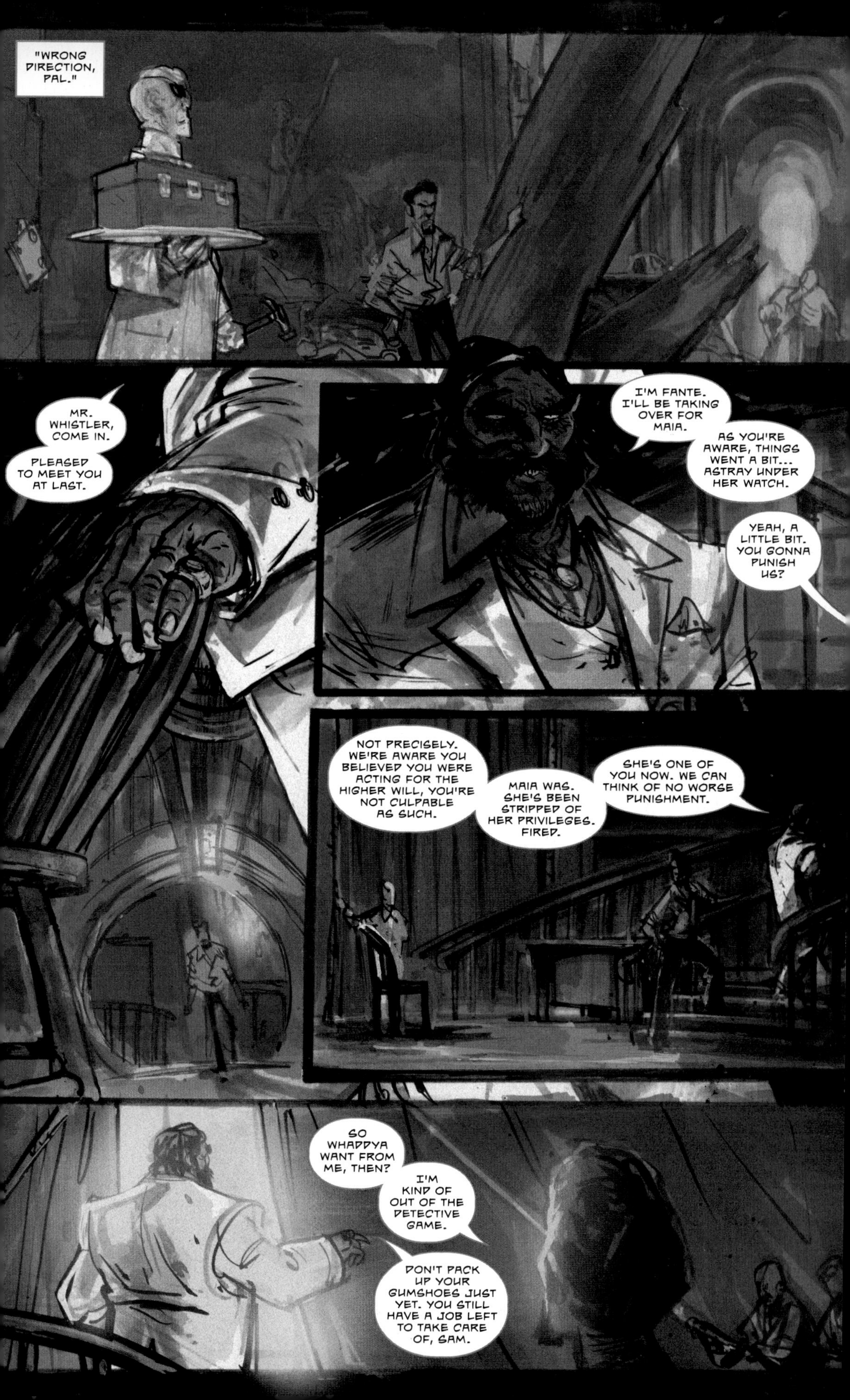
"WRONG DIRECTION, PAL."
MR. WHISTLER, COME IN.
PLEASED TO MEET YOU AT LAST.
I'M FANTE. I'LL BE TAKING OVER FOR MAIA.
AS YOU'RE AWARE, THINGS WENT A BIT... ASTRAY UNDER HER WATCH.
YEAH, A LITTLE BIT. YOU GONNA PUNISH US?
NOT PRECISELY. WE'RE AWARE YOU BELIEVED YOU WERE ACTING FOR THE HIGHER WILL, YOU'RE NOT CULPABLE AS SUCH.
MAIA WAS. SHE'S BEEN STRIPPED OF HER PRIVILEGES. FIRED.
SHE'S ONE OF YOU NOW. WE CAN THINK OF NO WORSE PUNISHMENT.
SO WHADDYA WANT FROM ME, THEN?
I'M KIND OF OUT OF THE DETECTIVE GAME.
DON'T PACK UP YOUR GUMSHOES JUST YET. YOU STILL HAVE A JOB LEFT TO TAKE CARE OF, SAM.

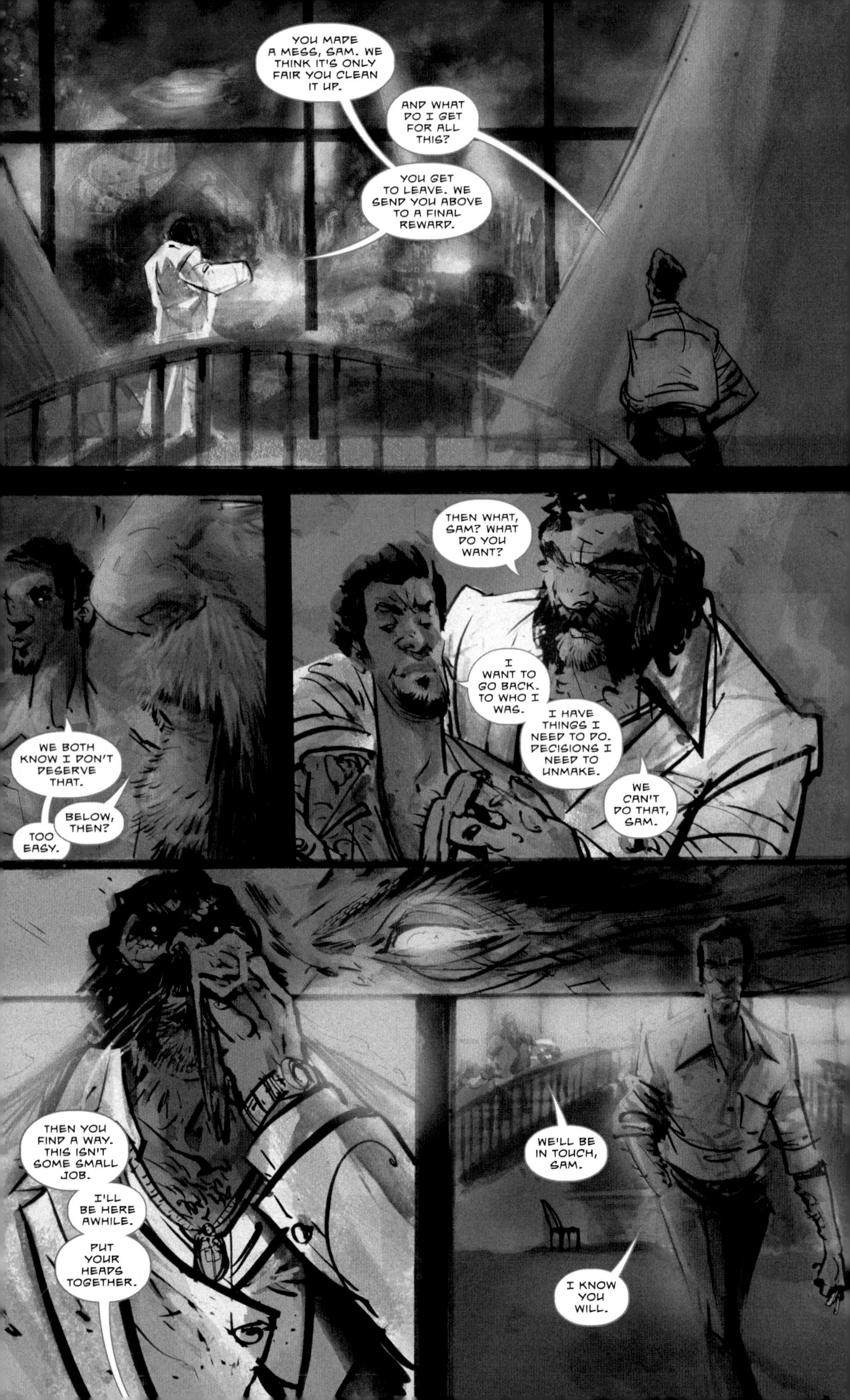
YOU MADE A MESS, SAM. WE THINK IT'S ONLY FAIR YOU CLEAN IT UP.
AND WHAT DO I GET FOR ALL THIS?
YOU GET TO LEAVE. WE SEND YOU ABOVE TO A FINAL REWARD.
WE BOTH KNOW I DON'T DESERVE THAT.
BELOW, THEN?
TOO EASY.
THEN WHAT, SAM? WHAT DO YOU WANT?
I WANT TO GO BACK. TO WHO I WAS.
I HAVE THINGS I NEED TO DO. DECISIONS I NEED TO UNMAKE.
WE CAN'T DO THAT, SAM.
THEN YOU FIND A WAY. THIS ISN'T SOME SMALL JOB.
I'LL BE HERE AWHILE.
PUT YOUR HEADS TOGETHER.
WE'LL BE IN TOUCH, SAM.
I KNOW YOU WILL.

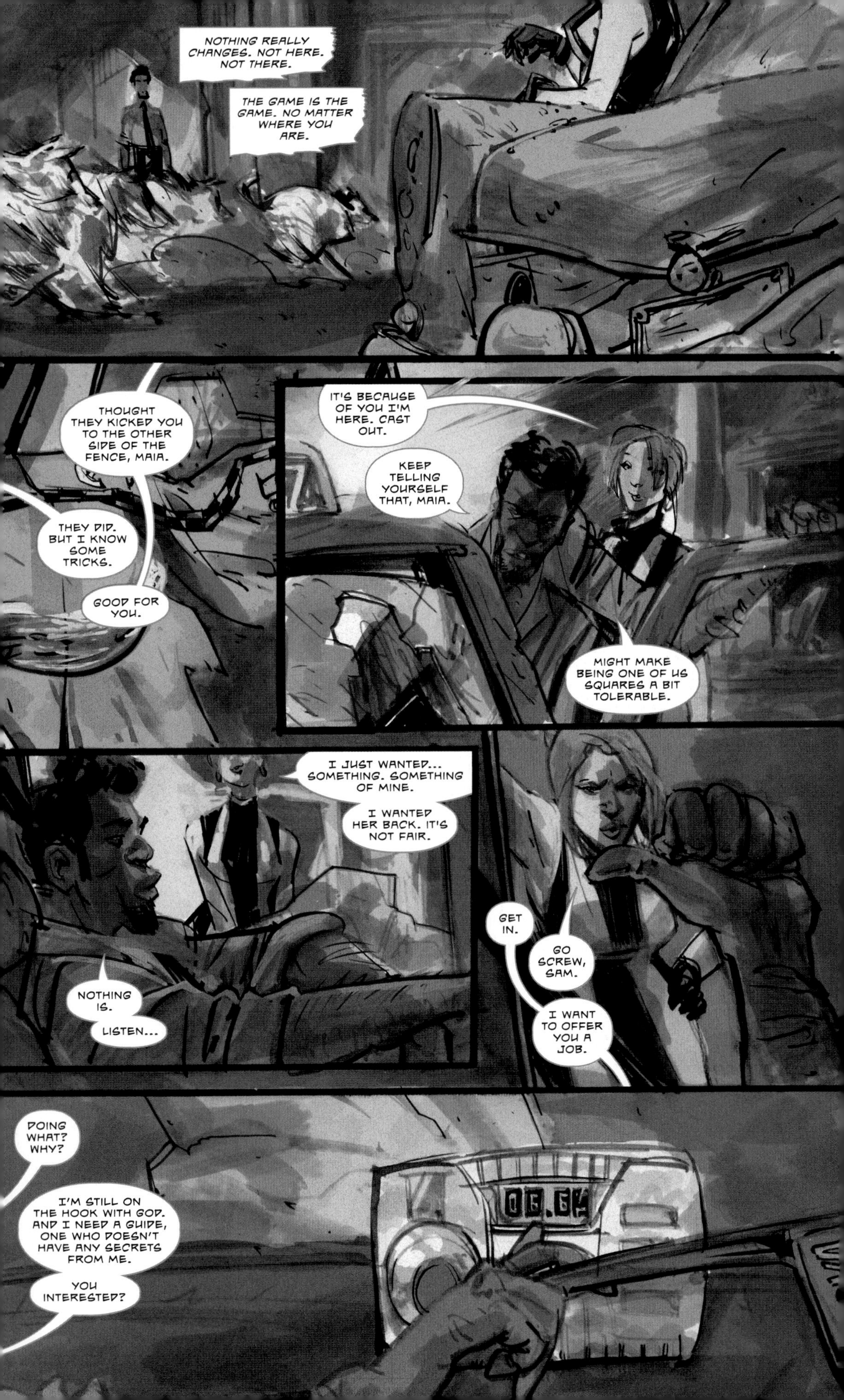

NOTHING REALLY CHANGES. NOT HERE. NOT THERE.
THE GAME IS THE GAME. NO MATTER WHERE YOU ARE.
THOUGHT THEY KICKED YOU TO THE OTHER SIDE OF THE FENCE, MAIA.
THEY DID. BUT I KNOW SOME TRICKS.
GOOD FOR YOU.
IT'S BECAUSE OF YOU I'M HERE. CAST OUT.
KEEP TELLING YOURSELF THAT, MAIA.
MIGHT MAKE BEING ONE OF US SQUARES A BIT TOLERABLE.
I JUST WANTED... SOMETHING. SOMETHING OF MINE.
I WANTED HER BACK. IT'S NOT FAIR.
NOTHING IS.
LISTEN...
GET IN.
GO SCREW, SAM.
I WANT TO OFFER YOU A JOB.
DOING WHAT? WHY?
I'M STILL ON THE HOOK WITH GOD. AND I NEED A GUIDE, ONE WHO DOESN'T HAVE ANY SECRETS FROM ME.
YOU INTERESTED?

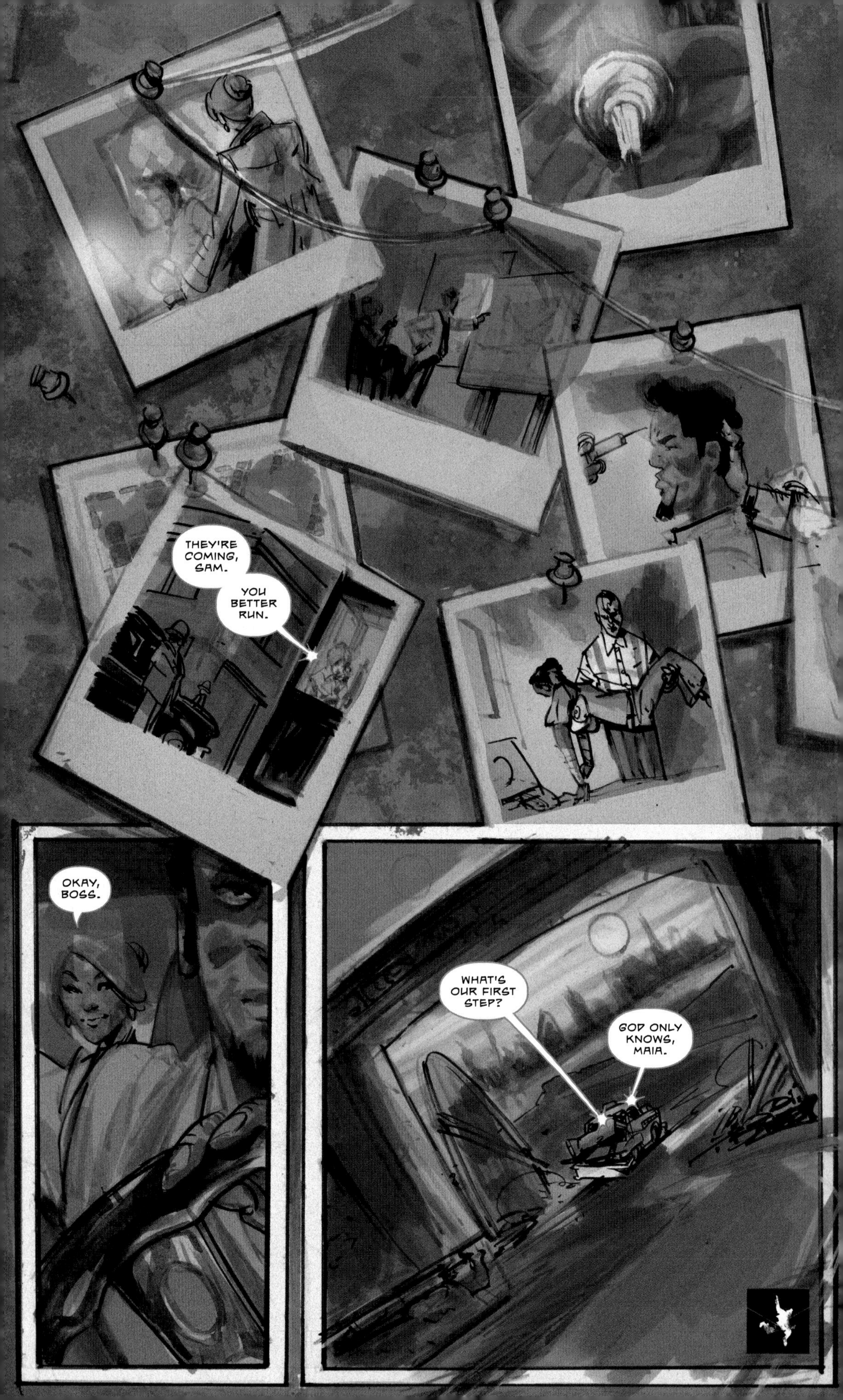
THEY'RE COMING, SAM.
YOU BETTER RUN.
OKAY, BOSS.
WHAT'S OUR FIRST STEP?
GOD ONLY KNOWS, MAIA.

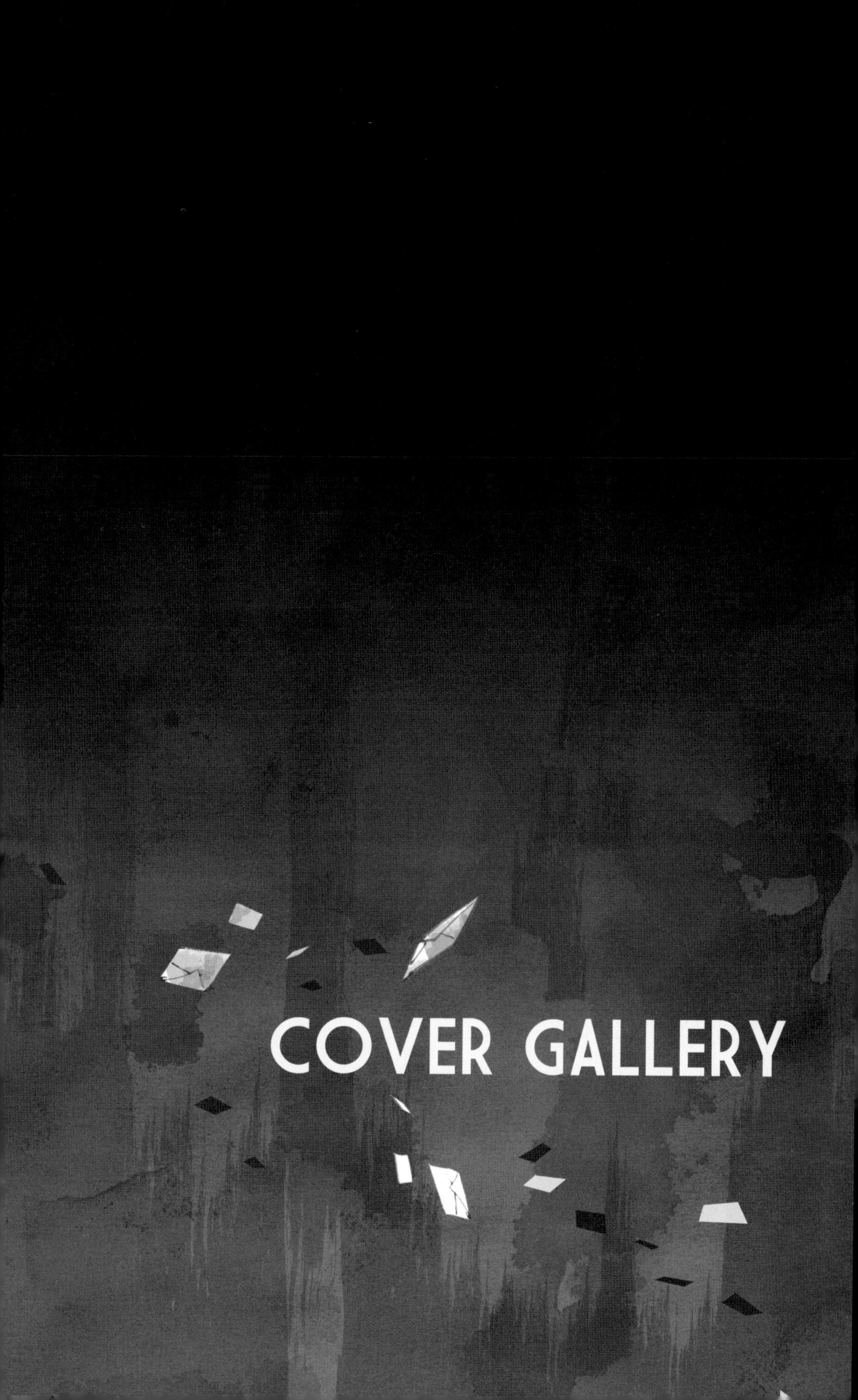
COVER GALLERY

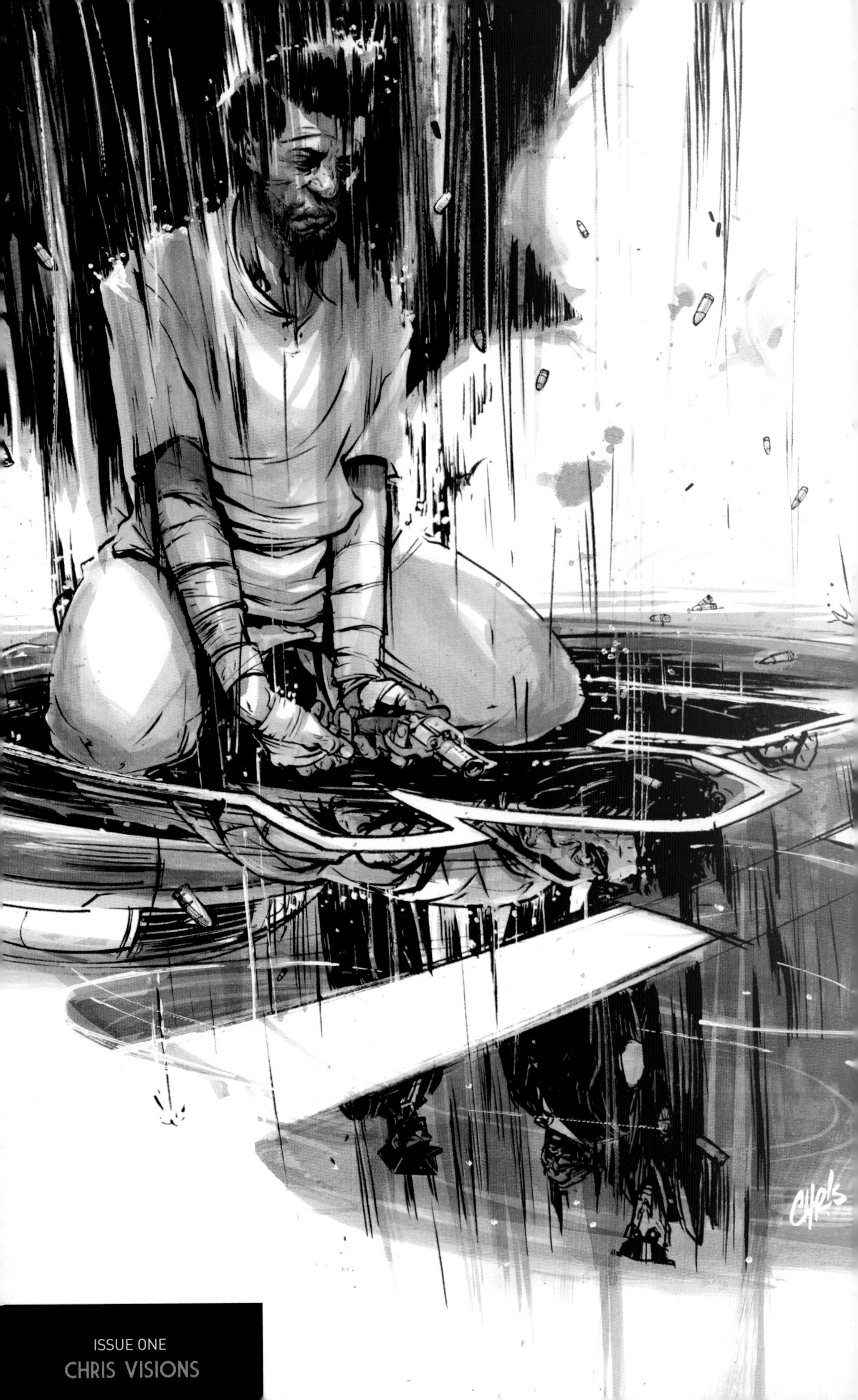
CHRIS

ISSUE ONE
CHRIS VISIONS

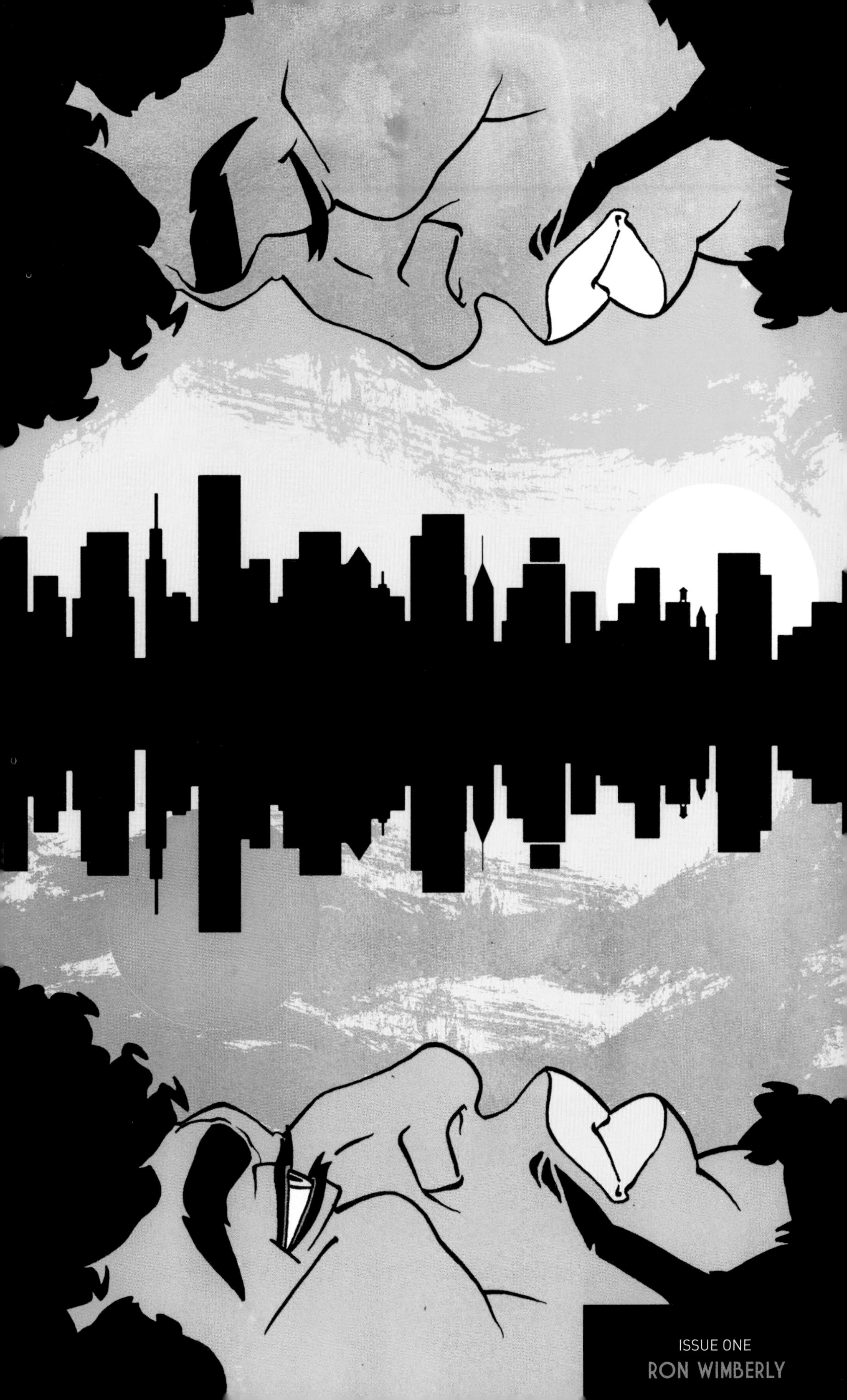

ISSUE ONE
RON WIMBERLY

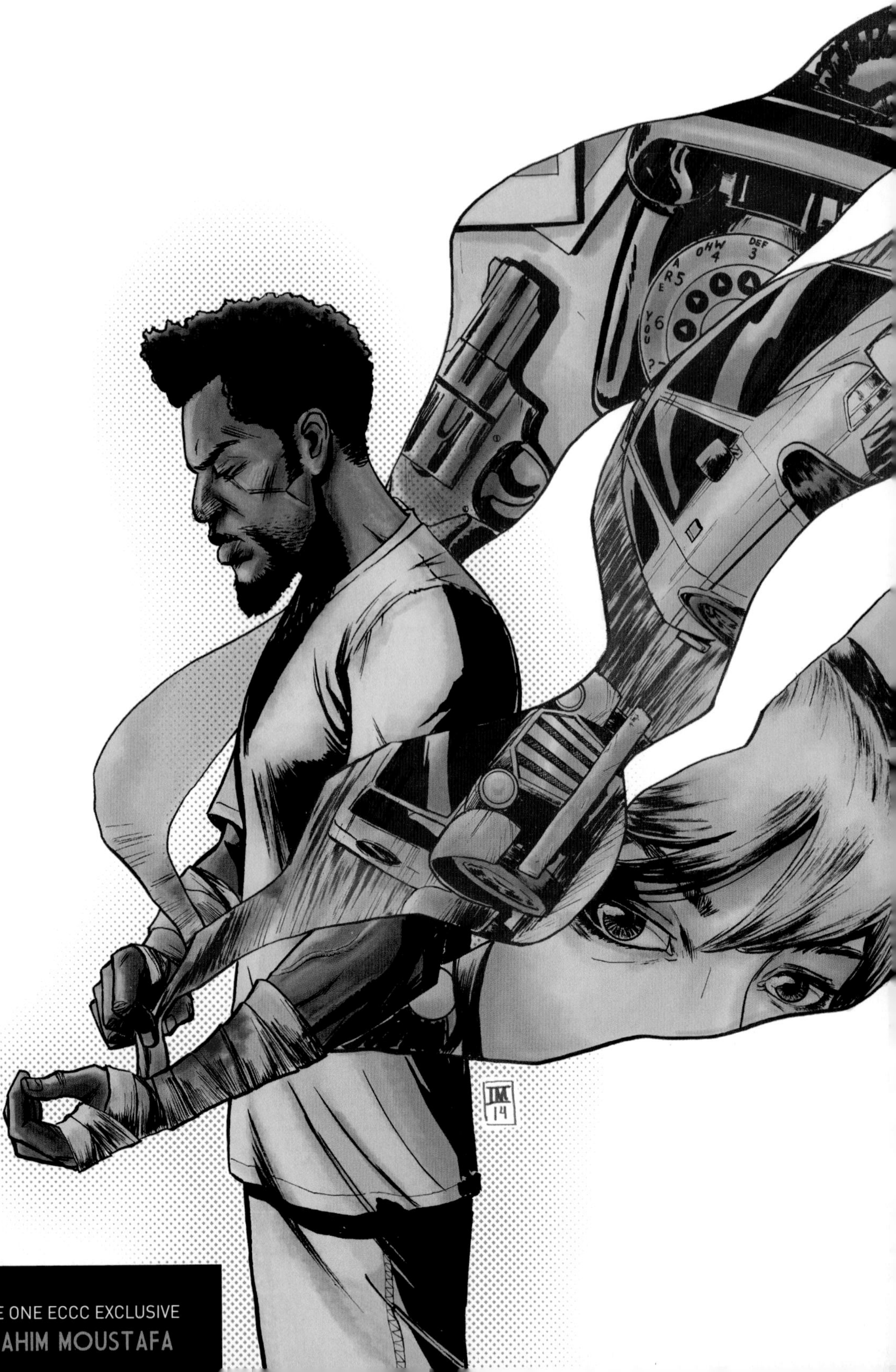

ISSUE ONE ECCC EXCLUSIVE
IBRAHIM MOUSTAFA

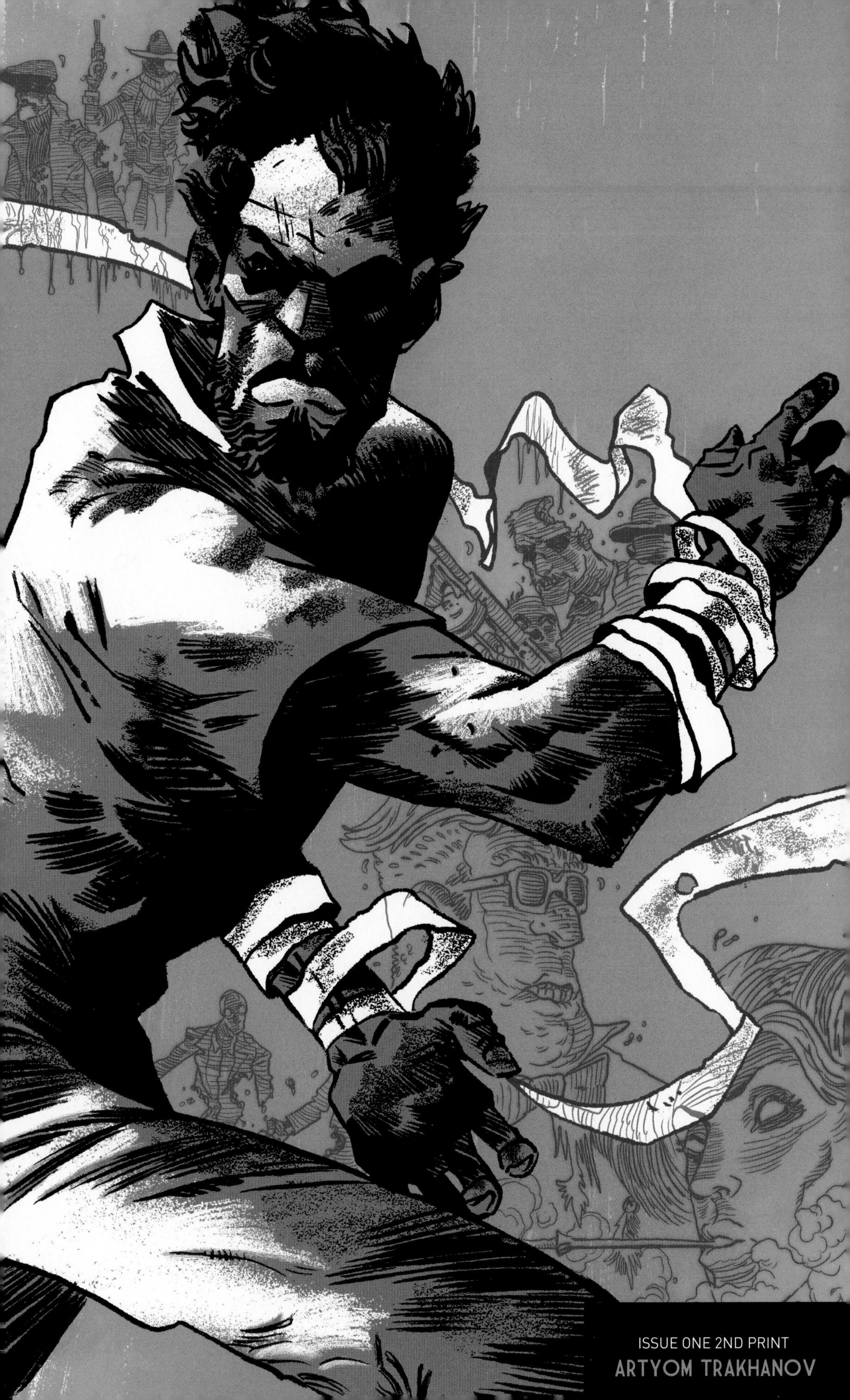

ISSUE ONE 2ND PRINT
ARTYOM TRAKHANOV

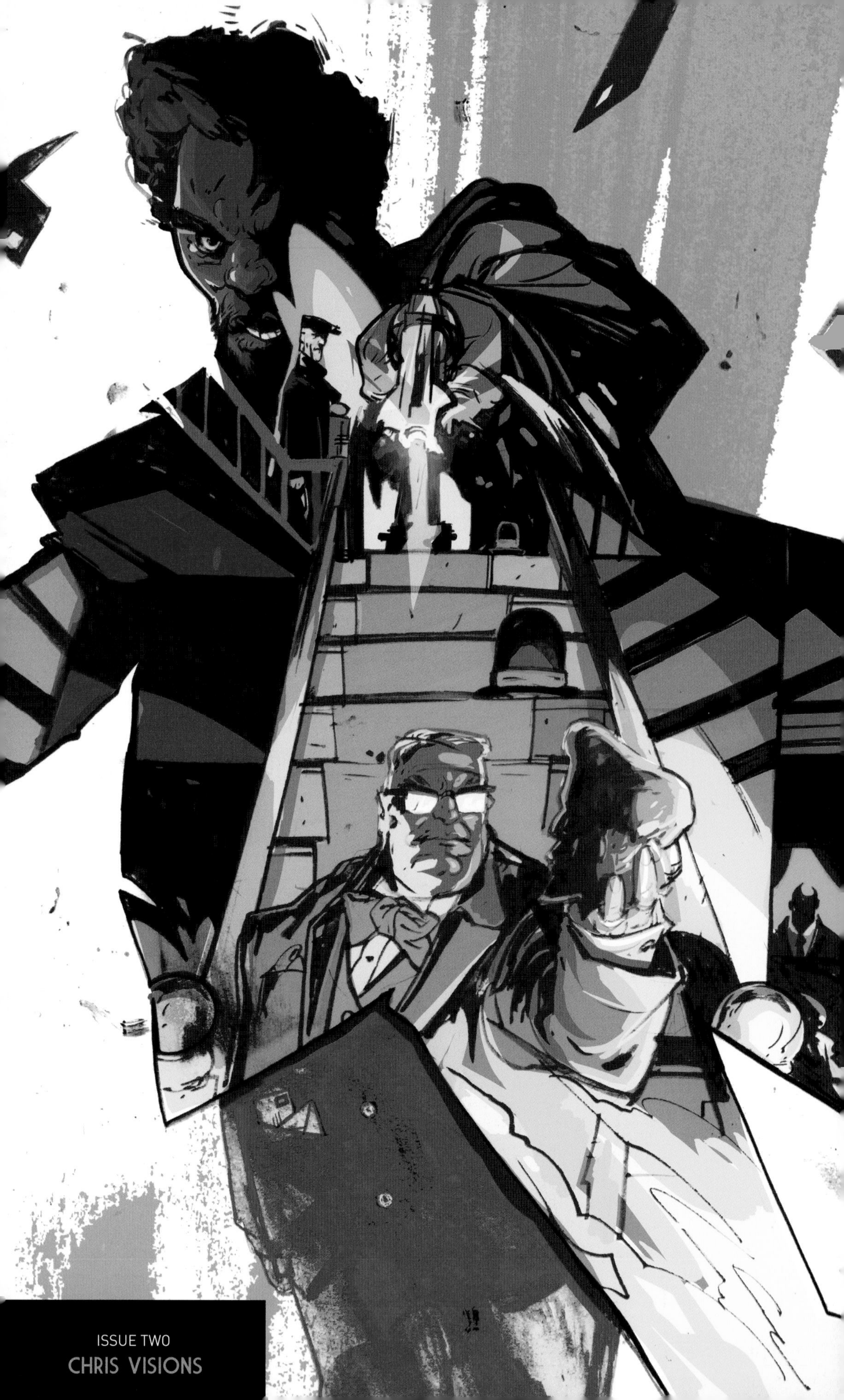

ISSUE TWO
CHRIS VISIONS

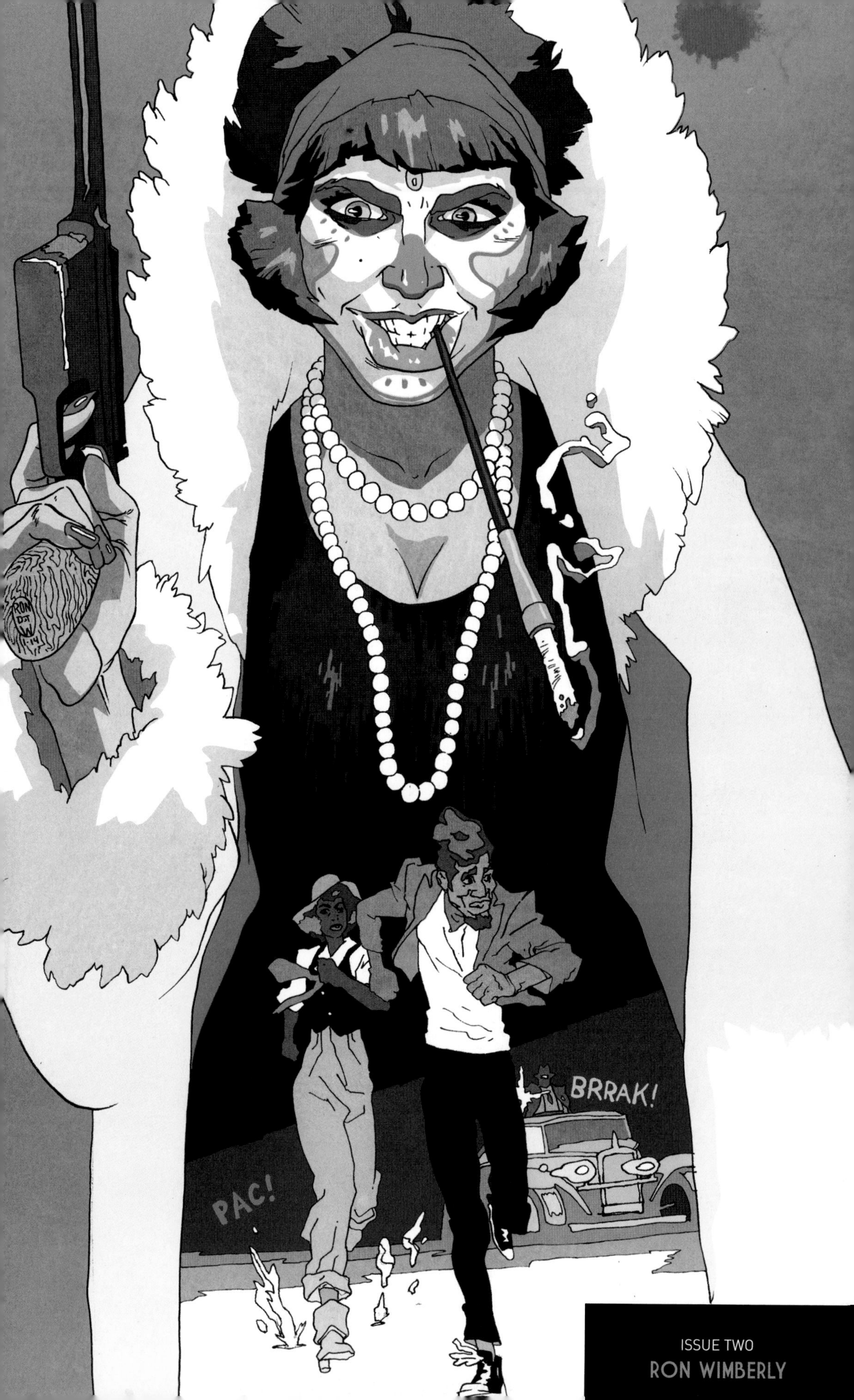
BRRAK!
PAC!

ISSUE TWO
RON WIMBERLY

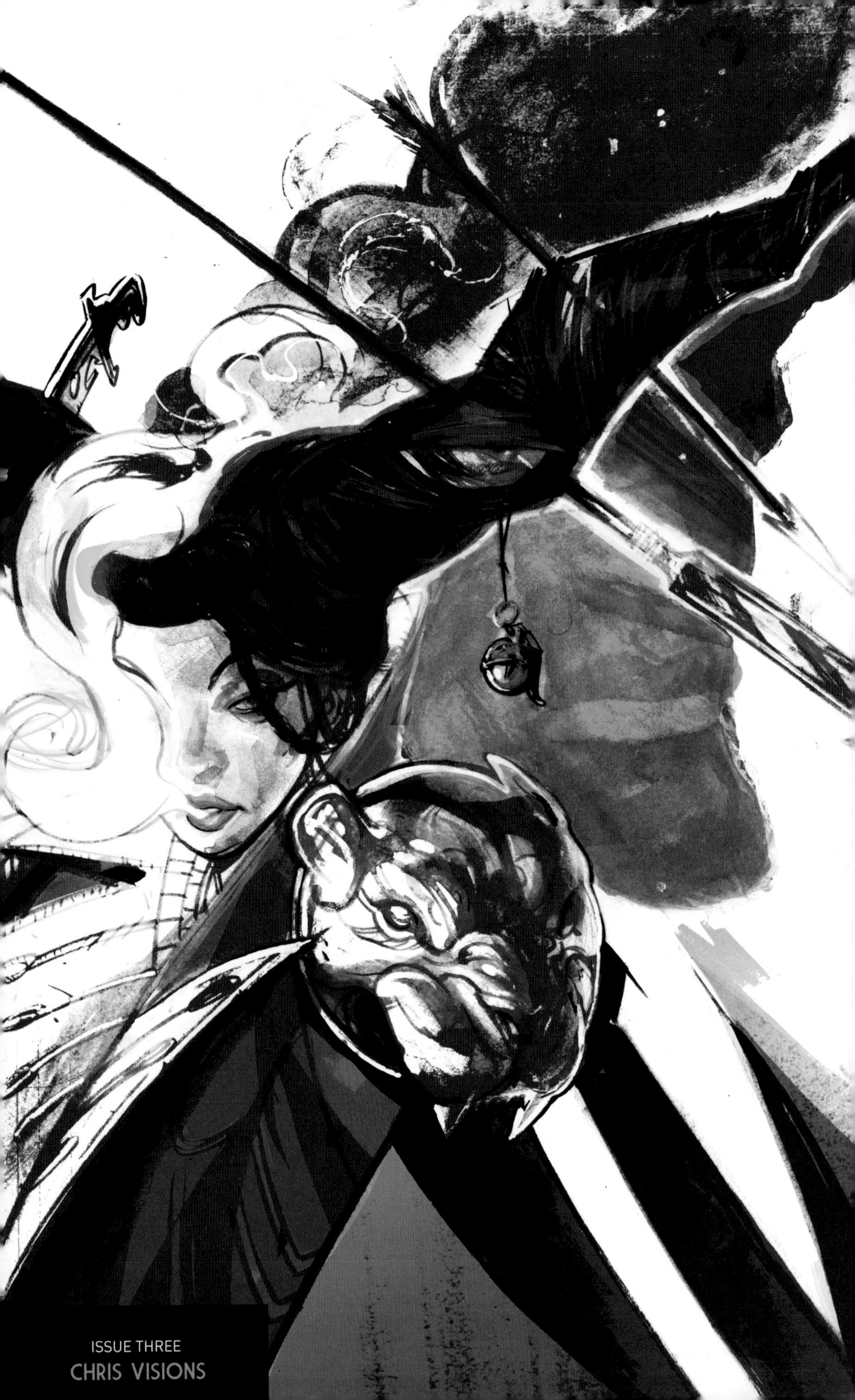

ISSUE THREE

CHRIS VISIONS

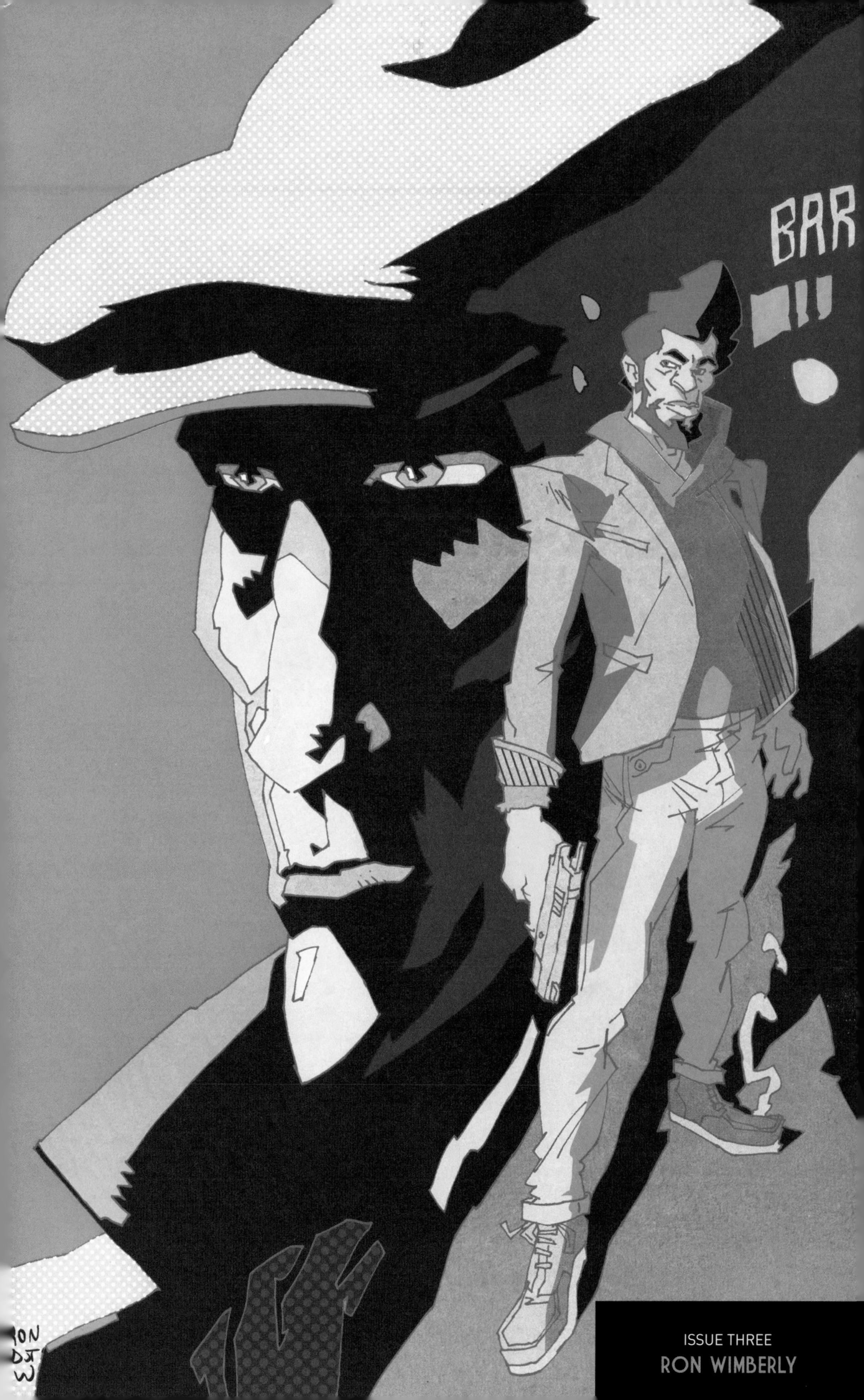
BAR

ISSUE THREE

RON WIMBERLY

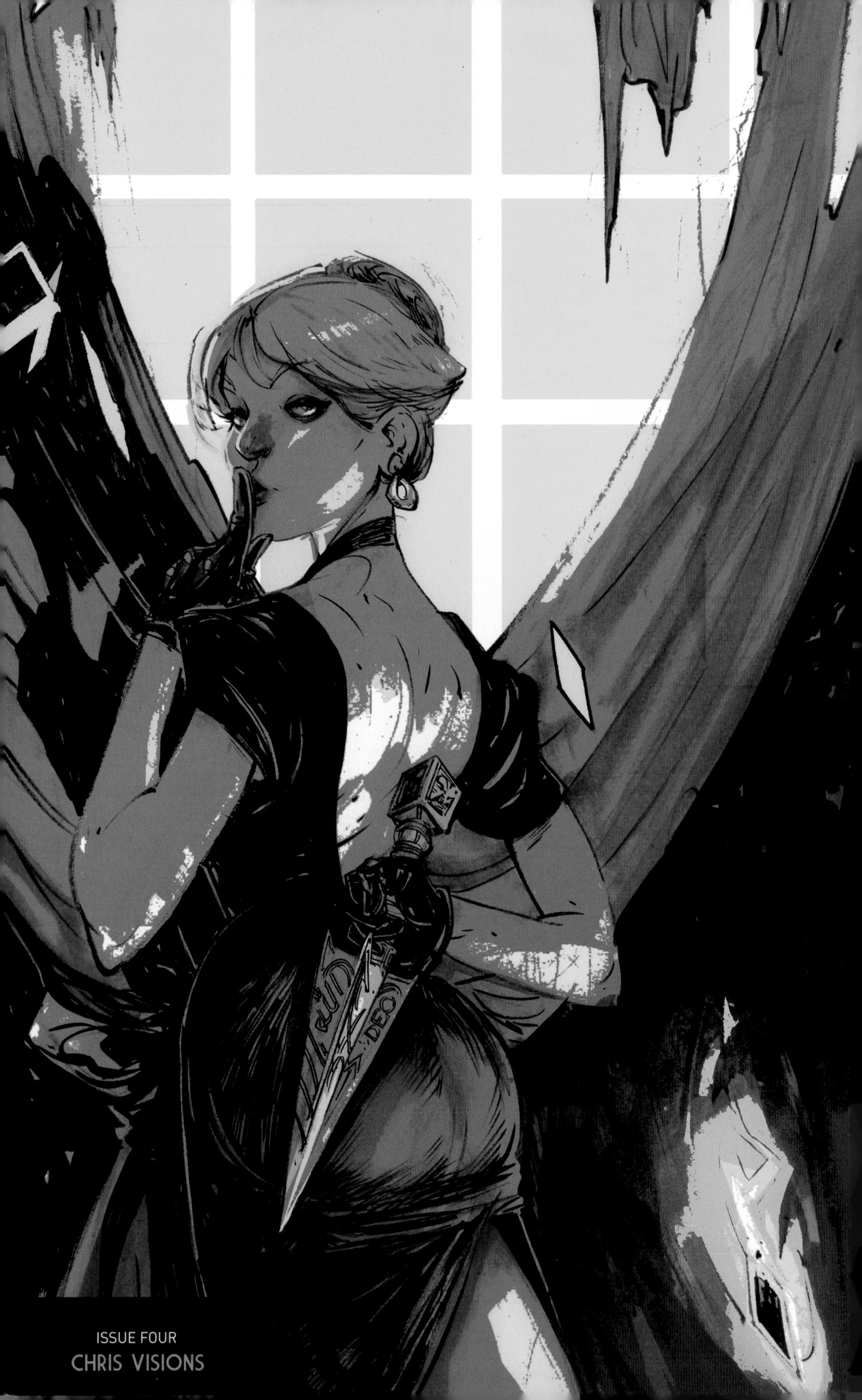

ISSUE FOUR
CHRIS VISIONS

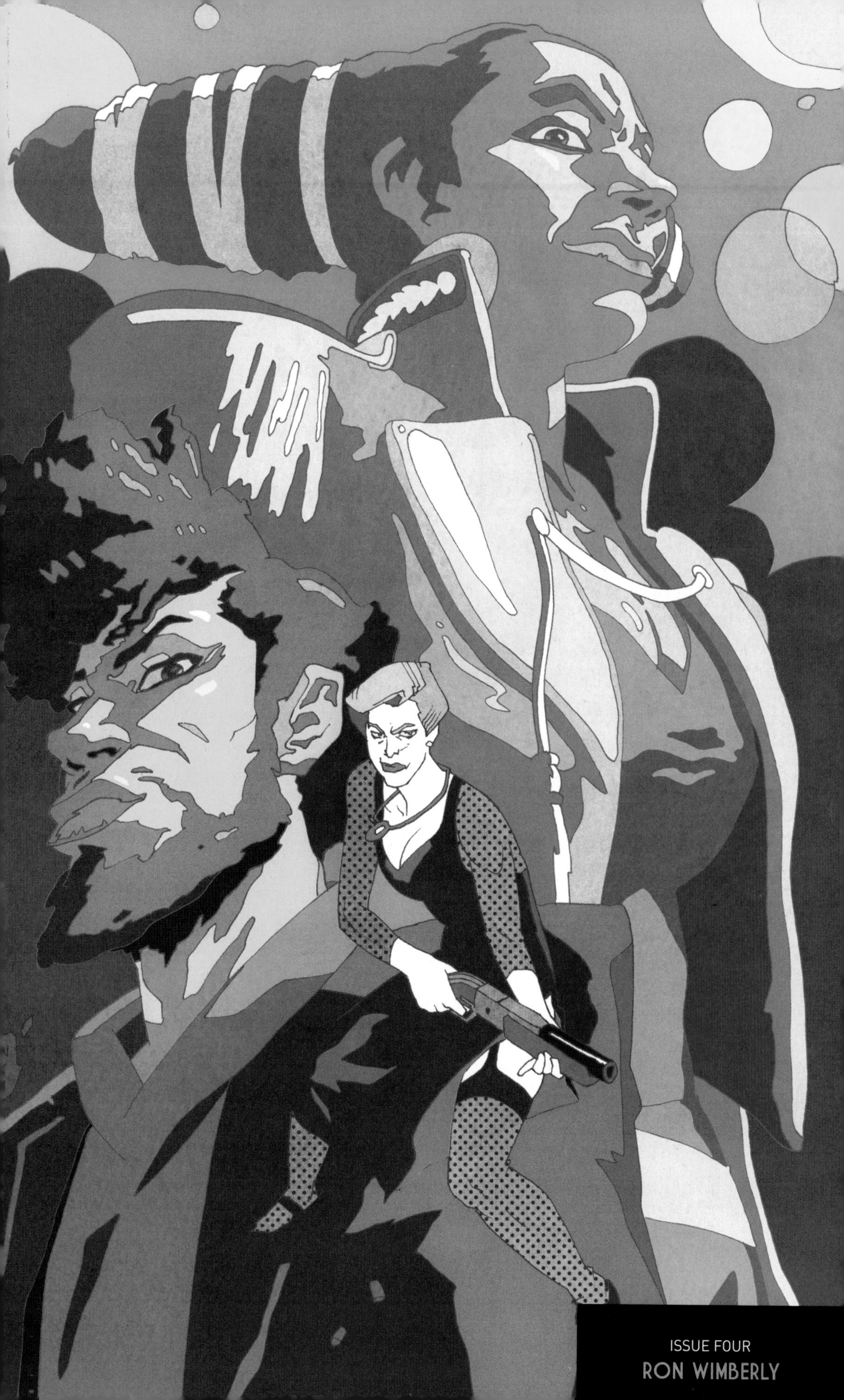

ISSUE FOUR
RON WIMBERLY

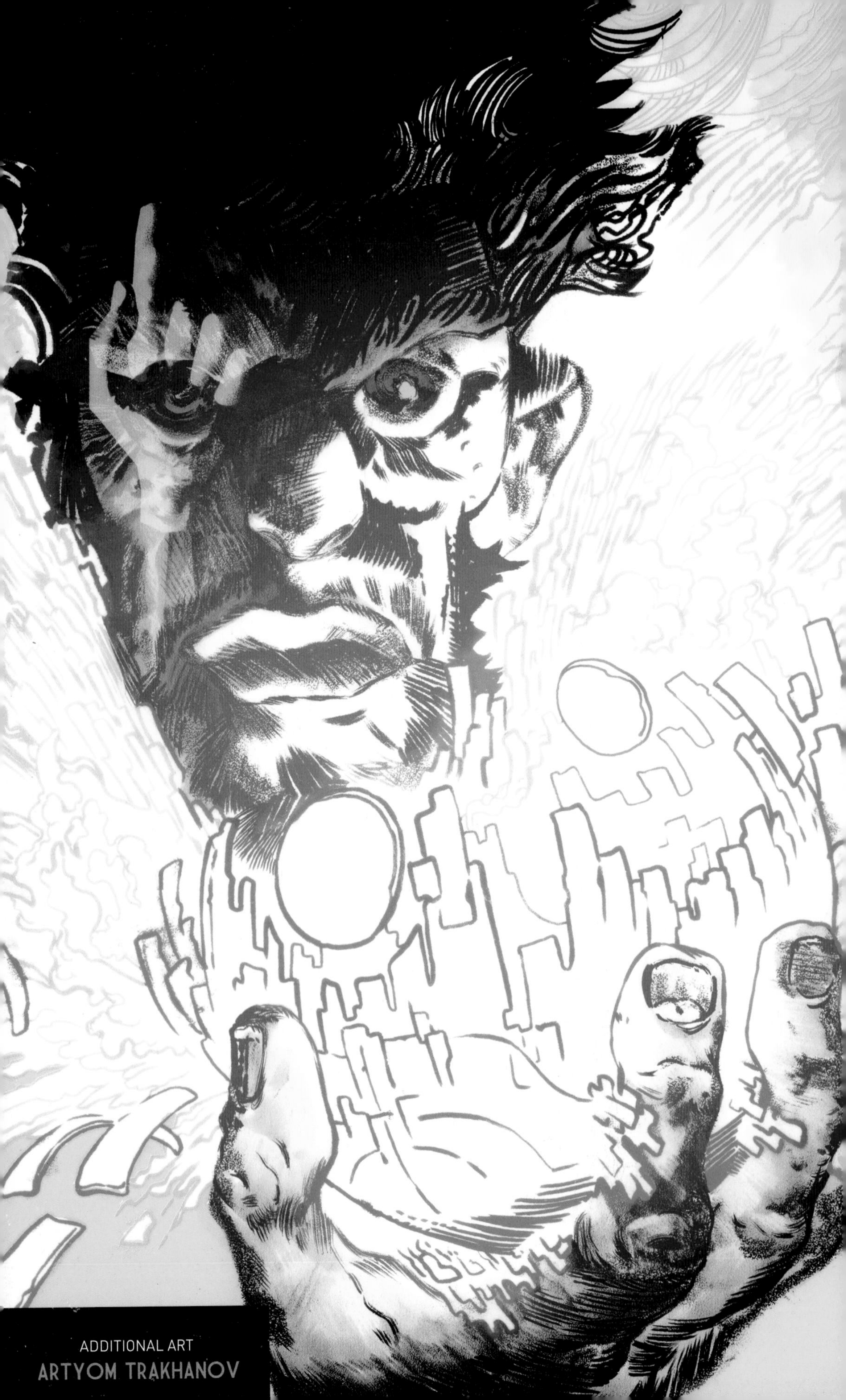

ADDITIONAL ART
ARTYOM TRAKHANOV